STALIN

THE MACMILLAN COMPANY
NEW YORK · BOSTON · CHICAGO · DALLAS
ATLANTA · SAN FRANCISCO

STALIN IN 1932

STALIN

A new world seen through one man

by

HENRI BARBUSSE

Translated by Vyvyan Holland

with 16 illustrations

NEW YORK
THE MACMILLAN COMPANY
1935

This book is the authorised English translation of the French volume 'Staline' by Henri Barbusse

Copyright, 1935, by
THE MACMILLAN COMPANY.

All rights reserved—no part of this book may be reproduced in any form without permission in writing from the publisher, except by a reviewer who wishes to quote brief passages in connection with a review written for inclusion in magazine or newspaper.

Set up and electrotyped.

PRINTED IN THE UNITED STATES OF AMERICA
BY THE STRATFORD PRESS, INC., NEW YORK

FOREWORD

The Red Square, centre of Moscow and of vast European and Asiatic Russia. The Mausoleum, centre of the Red Square. On top of the Mausoleum, in the depths of which Lenin sleeps, as though resurrected, stand five or six people in a row, looking, at a few yards' distance, almost exactly alike.

All around, a great multitude sways to and fro. A ceremony is taking place, kaleidoscopically, through the length and breadth of the Square; an interminable fluttering procession of red canvas and red silk covered with letters of the alphabet and phrases—of clamouring fabric, as it were. Or else a gigantic sports parade which, as it advances, keeps on forming different patterns. Or, again, the swarming of the most enormous army in the world, the soldiers of the Red Army, grouped into huge rectangles.

Here and there details of the ceremony can be seen at close quarters: a glittering palisade of bayonets filing by, or a line of young men and women, or just their faces close together, proud and happy, full of laughter and brightness.

These thoughtful parades which last for hours, and the enthusiasm which is reflected by the crowd massed tier upon tier in the stands erected before the red, crenellated wall of the Kremlin, form a vortex of muttering and roaring centred around a single point. The clamour assumes a human form: "Stalin!" "Long live Comrade Stalin!" One of the men standing on Lenin's monument raises his hand to the peak of his cap or waves his hand at the end of his arm bent into a right angle at the elbow. He wears a long military cloak, but this does not distinguish him in any way from the people with him.

That man is the centre, the heart of everything that radiates from Moscow on the surrounding world. His portrait, either in the form of sculpture or as a drawing, or as a photograph, is to be found everywhere throughout the Soviet continent, like that of Lenin and beside that of Lenin. There is hardly a corner of any factory, military barracks, office or shop window in which it does not appear on a red background, between a list of striking socialist statistics (a sort of anti-religious ikon) and the emblem of the crossed hammer and sickle. Latterly, a poster of enormous dimensions has been put up on the walls, all over Russia and the Soviet Republics, representing the superimposed profiles of two dead men and one living: Karl Marx, Lenin and Stalin. And we may multiply these a thousandfold; for there are not many rooms, whether occupied by working men or by intellectuals, in which Stalin does not figure.

Whether you love or hate this nation which occupies one-sixth of the world's surface, that is the man who is at the head of it.

And in this country, if the cobbles in the streets could talk, they would say: Stalin.

Some hours later comes the luncheon hour. (This is variable in Russia: among the large number of the "responsible people" everything is subservient to the work in hand.) On this day, let us say, it is two o'clock.

The Kremlin is a brightly coloured, fortified enclosure, a sumptuous little city, which rises out of the centre of Moscow in one solid block. Inside the high wall, with its barbarian towers, painted red and green, stands a whole city composed of ancient churches with gilded domes and of old palaces (and even one large palace built in the nineteenth century by a rich landowner of the Romanoff family, which looks like a huge modern hotel).

In this Kremlin which makes one think of an exhibition of churches and palaces, at the foot of one of the latter, stands a little three-storeyed house. This insignificant edifice, which would probably escape your notice if it were not pointed out to you, was formerly part of the outbuildings of one of the palaces, and was inhabited by some servant of the Tsar.

One goes up to the first floor, where white linen curtains hang over three of the windows. These three windows are Stalin's home. In the tiny hall a long military cloak hangs on a peg beneath a cap. In addition to this hall there are three bedrooms and a dining-room. The bedrooms are as simply furnished as those of a respectable second-class hotel. The dining-room is oval in shape; the meal has been sent in from a neighbouring restaurant. In a capitalist country a junior office clerk would turn up his nose at the bedrooms and would complain about the fare. A little boy is playing about the place. The eldest son, Jasheka, sleeps at night in the dining-room, on a divan which is converted into a bed, the younger sleeps in a tiny recess, a sort of alcove opening out of it.

The man has finished his meal and is smoking his pipe by the window, sitting in an arm-chair. He is always dressed in exactly the same way. In uniform? That would be saying too much. It is more a suggestion of a uniform, the outfit of a private soldier still further simplified: top-boots, khaki trousers and a high-necked khaki tunic. No one can ever remember him being dressed in any other way, except, in the summer, in white linen. Each month he earns the few hundred roubles which constitute the meagre maximum salary of officials of the Communist Party (amounting to between £20 and £25 in English money).

Perhaps it is the exotic, slightly Asiatic eyes of the man smoking the pipe which give his rather rough workman's face an ironic expression. Something in his features and in his look make him seem to be perpetually smiling. Or, rather, as though he were just about to laugh. Lenin used to look like that, too. It is not so much that his expression is a little wild as that there seems to be a perpetual twinkle in his eye. It is not so much the wrinkling of the lion's face (although there is something of that too), as the shrewdness and cunning of the peasant. Actually he does smile and laugh very readily. He does not talk much, although he can discourse to you for three hours on some casual question you may put to him, without leaving a single side of it unexamined. He laughs, often uproariously, much more easily than he talks.

He is the most important of all our contemporaries. He is the leader of 170,000,000 human beings distributed over nearly 8,000,000 square miles. He has a large number of associates who are in close touch with him. But these men love him and believe in him, and they form a group which supports him and throws him into relief. He rises high above both Europe and Asia, both now and in the future. He is the most conspicuous man in the world, and yet he is one of the least known.

The biography of Stalin, says Kalinin, is an extremely important part of the Russian's worker's revolutionary movement.

It is an integral part of it. And all those who know anything about it, wherever they may be, will tell you the same thing in the same terms.

FOREWORD

It is a very serious undertaking to try to give a clear idea of a man mixed up to such an extent with the work of a whole continent; of a political fighter through whom one can see whole worlds and epochs. In following him one sets one's foot into the realm of history, one strides along untrodden paths, and one encounters new situations in the sacred annals of humanity. Documents crowd in upon one another and accumulate. There are too many of them, because of all that is contained in this resurrected land. One has to hew one's way, stroke by stroke, through this impassioned, still living and appealing encyclopædia of events.

And this brings us to the heart of what is not only the burning question of the hour, but is also the burning question of all time, namely, what is to be the future of the human race, so martyred hitherto by history, and what is the amount of comfort and the amount of earthly justice to which it may aspire? To sum up, to what have 2,000,000,000 human beings to look forward.

This question has come from the lowest strata of humanity and has been lifted out, adjusted and presented to the world by a few contemporary inventors, who claim that everything can be altered here below by upheavals. And the man with whom we are dealing is their representative.

CONTENTS

		PAGE
	FOREWORD	V
CHAP.		
I.	A REVOLUTIONARY UNDER THE TSAR	1
II.	THE GIANT	29
III.	THE MAILED FIST	61
IV.	THE NATIONAL CONSTELLATION	88
V.	1917–1927. THE FIRST STONES	110
VI.	THE PARASITIC WAR	157
VII.	THE GREAT WATCH-WORDS, 1928–1934	192
VIII.	THE PEASANTRY	217
IX.	WHAT OF TO-MORROW?	242
X.	THE TWO WORLDS	249
XI.	THE MAN AT THE WHEEL	275
	INDEX	285

ILLUSTRATIONS

Stalin in 1932	*Frontispiece*
	FACING PAGE
The House Where Stalin Was Born at Gori in Georgia	2
Stalin as a Boy	8
Koba at the Head of a Demonstration at Batum, 1902	14
Photograph of Stalin Taken in a Group of Political Deportees in the District of Tourouchansk in 1903	20
Koba, 1902–3	26
A Group Taken in Prison	30
From the Police Files, Koba Djougachvili, 1910	42
Lenin and Stalin	54
Enoukidze, Vorochilov, Kaganovich, Kuibishev, Ordjonikidze, Stalin, Molotov, ...	62
Egorov and Stalin	74
Stalin in His Room at the Kremlin	126
Stalin While Watching Beside Lenin's Body, 1924	146
Stalin Addressing a Congress	170
Stalin's Secret Library, Now in Tiflis Museum	206
Enoukidze, Stalin and Maxim Gorky, 1931	232

STALIN

Chapter One

A REVOLUTIONARY UNDER THE TSAR

It was at Gori, a town in Georgia which was really no more than a village, that, over half a century ago, in 1879, a boy named Joseph was born in a hovel whose corners and foundations were made of bricks, with timber walls and a plank roof and with the front door on one side and the cellar door on the other. The surroundings were not very luxurious. Before the house ran an alley paved with rough stones, on the far side of which stood a row of shanties which were a mass of patches and bristled with stovepipes. Through the middle of the alley ran a small stream.

His mother, Catherine, had a beautiful, serious face and black eyes, so black that they seemed to overflow into dark bruises on the skin around them. Recent portraits show us her regular features squarely framed by a black veil, in the old severe manner of Caucasian women of a certain age. His father, Vissarion Djugashvili, was born in the village of Didi-Lilo and was a shoemaker by trade. He worked hard in a boot factory not far from there, at Tiflis, the capital of Georgia. In one of the museums is shown the mean rope-seated stool which gradually wore out beneath his weight. He was a poor man, of very little education; but he was a good man and he sent Joseph, first to the Gori school, a little house shaded by trees with the appearance of a farmhouse, and then to the Seminary at Tiflis. That is to say he did really everything he possibly could do for him.

Then, to use his own words: "I joined the revolutionary

movement at the age of fifteen, when I found myself in sympathy with the secret groups of Russian Marxists existing in Transcaucasia. These groups exercised a strong influence over me and gave me a taste for clandestine literature...."

Joseph Vissarionovitch looked around him. Among human beings the majority accepts constituted authority, keeps its counsel and carries on. This is the herd of which Tacitus speaks when he says that it is thanks to such dumb citizens that "anything can be done." There are others, a tiny minority, who find fault with it and refuse to accept it.

So he looked and listened.

Georgia forms, with Armenia and Azerbaijan, the district of Transcaucasia—south of the Caucasus, between the Black Sea and the Caspian Sea. After a long and very gallant history Georgia (the last bulwark of Christianity against the Turk) lost her independence and, at the beginning of the nineteenth century, was included within the boundaries of the Russian Empire. Central Russia, lording it at St. Petersburg, strove to denationalize the country and to Russianize it, as it was her policy to do with all the incongruous elements of the enormous imperial agglomeration, and according to the traditional procedure of all large countries in dealing with their colonies or with the regions they have annexed. The central power first of all devours and then tries to assimilate by all kinds of artificial means, especially by cruelty and persecution. (So far as Russia is concerned, the Tsar was content to deprive them of all liberty and of as much education as possible.) To govern foreign nationals, like the Georgians, meant to deal severely with them. It has been said that in those days "the Caucasian populations had no right save that of being tried." The only thing they were free to do was to groan—provided that they did

THE HOUSE WHERE STALIN WAS BORN AT GORI IN GEORGIA

so in Russian. As a result of this state of affairs, there grew up, in this colony directly adjoining the ruling territory, a certain nationalist movement which had as its ideal the liberation of Georgia. The question was complicated by the fact that a very large number of different races swarmed, not only in Transcaucasia, but also in Georgia. There were Georgians, Armenians, Turks, Jews, Kurds and some dozens of other races, and all this motley herd of subjects, equally ill-treated by the Russian, lived at daggers drawn among themselves. Had they been able to do so, they would have hurled themselves, not only on their warders from St. Petersburg but, even more violently, upon each other.

Side by side with this old separatist tendency, which was gradually consolidating itself into a fairly strong "Federalist" Party, there was also the Socialist movement.

All the strong currents of collective liberation which had re-echoed through Russia had also re-echoed, after a fairly rapid development, in the Caucasus.

After the disaster of the Crimean War of 1854-56 (wars always stir the people to their very depths), a reaction took place against the despotism which kept Russia in a special and privileged state of barbarism as compared with other great nations. A well-intentioned reformist middle class had its eyes fixed on the light that shone from the West.

Between 1860 and 1869 a certain number of reforms kept these tendencies satisfied; such as the abolition of serfdom, the creation of *zemstvos* (autonomous municipalities) and judicial reform. But, however sensational these reforms were in appearance, it was observed that they did not really alter the situation much. The abolition of serfdom, for instance, had not been decided upon from equitable motives, but, primarily, from purely financial ones, secondly, in the interest of the big landowners, and thirdly, for political reasons, "so that the liberation of the peasants should not come from themselves, from below, as it were" (actual words of the Tsar). Out of this failure, out of this disillusionment, was born the violent movement of the Populists (*narodniki*). With them it was no longer a question of hypnotizing oneself by gazing towards the West but, on the contrary, of returning to specifically Russian traditions such as the *mir* (rural commune) and the *artel* (workmen's association), by which road the Russian people would arrive at Socialism "without having to pass through the torment of Capitalism." The great period of Populism, whose leagues were called "Land and Liberty," "The Liberty of the People," etc., was from 1870 to 1881, during which the Populists, whom the rest of Europe called Nihilists, hurled themselves with bombs and terrorism against the régime of the potentates at the Winter Palace. Then the repression following the murder of Alexander II in 1881 destroyed the Populist organizations and nothing remained but the literary theorists.

In his extreme youth Lenin frequented Populist circles. His elder brother, Alexander, was mixed up with "The Liberty of the People" and was, for this reason, hanged in 1887. Maria Ulianova, Lenin's sister, tells us that, when the Ulianoff family heard the sad news of the execution, Vladimir Ilitch, then aged seventeen, murmured, with a far-away look on his face: "No, we must follow a different path. That is not the one that we must take."

This different path was that of scientific Socialism, the improved successor of the old ideal of political liberty, of the suppression of privileges, of equality and of universal brotherhood, brought to perfection by Karl Marx in the middle of the nineteenth century. One of the fundamental features of the Marxist doctrine, which pruned the older Socialism of its absurdities and disastrous puerilities, was the union of economics with politics, and of Socialism with the workers' movement. The necessity for such unions may appear obvious to us nowadays, but it was not always so and at a moment when everything had to be unravelled and put into words, this formula had taken a good deal of finding.

Socialism had constituted an international network. The First International, founded directly by Marx and Engels, which had "laid the ideological foundations of the proletarian struggle," had been succeeded by the Second International, which "prepared the ground for the far-flung and comprehensive development of the workers' movement." The Marxian Socialists—as opposed to the Revolutionary Socialists, who were much reduced in numbers but still violent—did not believe in terrorism or outrage. These blind surgical methods which, for the most part, went savagely beyond their object and were always going wrong, were no business of theirs. Their business was to *organize* the great tide of those who were being exploited and oppressed, by showing them where their interests lay, by conscious discipline and by the positive soundness of a practical doctrine.

Marxism made fairly rapid progress because of the ruthless and mechanical disruption of Populism and because of the increase in the industrialization of Russia during the last years of the nineteenth century. Lenin threw himself wholeheartedly into it. We see him launching out on a wide and bitter campaign in favour of the Marxist order and the organization of the masses, against the disordered romanticism and the practically reactionary dreams of Populism. An eye-witness tells us of a very secret and "very conspiratorial" meeting which took place in Moscow in 1893, at which everyone's "lips were unsealed." Witnesses tell us that there "this young, slightly bald man, a strange figure and already a person of importance among the Marxists" (Lenin was then only twenty-three) victoriously opposed the famous populist theorist V. P. Vorontsoff.

It was, however, in 1884 that the first programme of the Russian Social-Democrats was launched by the group calling itself "The Liberation of Labour." At that time nearly all the members of this group lived together on one of the Swiss lakes. This group was, to begin with, an almost exclusively intellectual one, like Populism. The great famine of 1891 brought the intellectual pioneers, such as Plekhanoff and Axelrod, into contact with the working classes, and many circles and leagues were formed. An initial congress at Minsk in 1898, united the groups and elected a Central Committee, but the arrest of most of the members of this Congress prevented its resolutions being carried into effect.

Certain splits were already appearing in the midst of the young party, notably on the question of the line of demarcation that should be established, according to some of them, between the economic struggle (devolving on the workers) and the political struggle (devolving upon the whole democracy).

Lenin set out to consolidate this Social-Democratic Party which had only existed strictly since 1898, and to give it proper constitution. By hard work he succeeded in his object, at the height of reaction, at the height of the slavery of the bovine people of all the Russias, at the height of the bestial rule of the Romanoffs, at the height of the fantastic pilfering of the public funds by the gold-laced warders of the people, whether situated at the top or at the bottom of the ladder.

A REVOLUTIONARY UNDER THE TSAR

The period at which Marxism came on the scene to discipline both Russian and extra-Russian revolutionary tendencies and forces almost coincides with the one upon which we had our eyes fixed a little while ago, since it was in 1897 that Joseph Vissarionovitch Djugashvili was leading the Marxist circle at the Tiflis Seminary, transforming the dormitory, as Sandro Mirabishvili says, into a second Seminary.

This Seminary, like all Seminaries, was an official hotbed of traditional obscurantism and asphyxia, being, besides, in the hands of treacherous directors.

He himself says: ". . . . We were subjected to the most humiliating régime and the most despotic methods there. Spying was rife in this establishment. At nine o'clock the bell called us to breakfast. We went into the refectory, and when we returned we discovered that, while we were at table, all our cupboards had been searched and turned upside down."

All the same, in spite of that—because of that—the Seminary was a "nursery of ideas." For, willy-nilly, the establishment sheltered a nucleus of discontent and of protest against these things and against many others of the same sort. Nonconformist and subversive circles were formed there which expressed their ideas in corners (in whispers, naturally). There was a Nationalist circle (when will Georgia be an independent nation?), a Populist circle (down with tyranny!) and a Marxist Internationalist circle. It was into this last that Joseph or, rather, Sosso Djugashvili threw himself by an intense affinity of soul.

"I can still see young Sosso Djugashvili, as I met him at first at Tiflis in 1900," says Enukidze.

What was he like? As a child he was small and slim, with a bold, almost brazen expression, and always held his head proudly erect. Later, when he grew taller, he was rather frail in appearance; his features were very delicate and he had an intellectual head with abundant thick hair, as black as ink. The slimness of youth accentuated the Georgian oval of his face and the somewhat languid eye of his race. At the time of which Enukidze speaks, this young militant presented a mixture, curious enough because it was almost perfect, of the intellectual and the worker. Not very tall, narrow-shouldered, with a long face, a small beard, rather heavy eyes and a thin straight nose, and with his flat cap worn a little to one side on his plentiful black hair—that is what he was like then, this conqueror of multitudes, this upsetter of worlds.

Since then Stalin's face has grown stronger, and especially to-day when his hair, still thick but worn *en brosse*, is greying slightly, one is tempted to believe that his features have become more proletarian and even more military—partly, possibly, because of the suggestion of his dress. But he cannot be said to have changed greatly. At most one can say that the energy and combative power which this face indicated in those days is more apparent now, for if any man has not changed fundamentally, it is he.

One could already recognize in him, from the temperance of his speech, the man whom Ketskoveli described thirty-five years ago as "a good sort." This young man had a strange dislike of florid phraseology. He was the complete opposite of the people who try to get their effects by the sonorousness of their utterances and the aerial designs of their gestures. Brevity, clearness and accuracy were his main characteristics.

Unfortunately for his tranquillity he secretly studied, at the Tiflis Seminary, books on the natural sciences and on sociology. He introduced into this well-ordered house the

STALIN AS A BOY

written poison of positive knowledge. This scandal was discovered by the authorities of the place. The need for genuine self-instruction being incompatible with the pure tradition of the Seminary, young Sosso was expelled on the ground that he displayed a lack of "political balance."

"He went, without a backward glance, straight over to the workers."

In 1898 he joined the Tiflis branch of the Russian Social-Democratic Workers' Party. This, as we have already seen, was the same year as that of the official birth of this Russian section of the Second International.

So we see him launched upon his course. He had lost no time in finding it. He had reached it immediately by the shortest route. This intellectual, the son of a peasant worker, embraced the calling of "professional revolutionary," first among the Tiflis railway workers and later among the tobacco workers and the workers in the boot factories, and, later still, among the workers at the meteorogolical observatory—a little everywhere, in fact: a workman in the workers' cause.

Enukidze, one of the earliest workers in the cause of the Revolution in the Caucasus and nowadays an important leader, saw a great deal of Sosso Djugashvili in those days, and he tells us how successful he was in "talking to the workers." This gift of being accessible to everyone was also a characteristic of Lenin, his senior by ten years, who was working, at that time, in the principal centres of the Russian Socialist movement. Lenin, who foresaw the electrification of half the old world, at a time when the whole of Russia was nothing but a heap of ruins and dust attacked from within and from without, the visionary who could visualize to their fullest extent, dotting all the i's, the most vast temporal schemes that have ever been conceived by the human brain, also knew how to talk to the workers, even individually. With his cap pulled down over his round, bald skull, a twinkle in his eye, his hands in his pockets and the general air of an honest tradesman, dogged and astute, he would loiter about at factory gates. He would approach a worker, speak to him in a friendly way, and attach him to himself for ever. He would make a malcontent of one who was apathetic, and a revolutionary of a malcontent. And the peasant said of him: "Do you know, that red-head is an ordinary man like you and me. He might just have left his plough." Joseph Vissarionovitch was a man of the same sort, and that is why these two silhouettes come together in one's mind's eye out of so many thousands of others.

"Sosso's natural simplicity, his complete indifference to the conditions of personal life, his strength of character and his knowledge, which even at that time was remarkable, gave him authority, called people's attention to him and kept it there. The Tiflis workers called him 'our Sosso.' "

This sort of genius of his for putting himself on a level with his audience is the real reason for the confidence which he inspired in the people and for the part which has been given him to play. Let us make no mistake, however; putting oneself on a level does not mean lowering oneself or humbling oneself or becoming stupidly familiar. Very far from it. Orakhelashvili, who was Sosso's companion at that time, puts the matter in a nutshell: "He was neither pedantic nor vulgar." He looked upon the militant Socialist as an interpreter who said the same things as the wisest theorist, but adapted them to the intelligence and degree of education of his listeners. How did he do this? By imagery and by giving vivid examples.

"We," explains Orakhelashvili, "who formed a group of propagandists with him, were unable to rid ourselves of a certain amount of terminology. We were haunted by thesis, antithesis and synthesis and by other pivots of logic. And all this paraphernalia crept much too much into our speeches to workers and peasants. Not so Stalin's speeches. He approached matters from another side, from the angle of life. For instance, he would take the idea of middle-class Democracy and would show, as clear as daylight, why it was good compared with Tsarism, and why it was not good compared with Socialism. And everyone would understand that Democracy, although it was quite capable of sweeping away the Empire, might itself one day constitute a barrier against Socialism which would have to be broken down...." Again, he was naturally very gay, but only out of working hours. The two things must not be mixed. "One day," goes on Orakhelashvili, "we all met in the house of an important Caucasian comrade. (We always met in someone's house because it was almost impossible to meet anywhere else.) During dinner the young son of the master of the house came and sat on his father's knee, and the father petted him and tried to calm the impatience of the child, who was too young to be interested in the serious discussion. Then Stalin rose, took the child gently by the hand and led him to the door, saying: 'My young friend, you're not on the agenda to-day.'"

"He never abused an opponent," adds the same eye-witness. "We suffered so much from the Mensheviks that when we found ourselves addressing one of them in a speech we could not prevent ourselves from going for him hammer and tongs and lashing him with our tongues. Stalin never liked this form of attack. Violent language was for him a prohibited weapon. At the very most, when he had nonplussed and reduced an opponent to silence by concise argument and the said opponent was speechlessly trying to escape, he would fling after him some current Transcaucasian remark, such as: "You're such a fine fellow, I wonder you are afraid of people as unimportant as us."

The vocation of secret agitator and professional Revolutionary, which attracted him in the wake of so many others, is a terrible vocation. One becomes an outlaw, spied upon by all the machinery of the State, hounded by the police; the quarry of the Tsar and of his countless and well-nourished underlings, all armed to the teeth and huge of fist. One is like an exile whose temporary liberty hangs by a mere thread and who hides himself and watches. One is the tiny Revolutionary, almost alone in the crowd, swamped by the immense forces of Capitalism which have the nations in their grip from pole to pole—not only the 180,000,000 subjects of the Tsar but everyone else in the world—and one is the man who, with a few friends, wants to alter all that. One appears now here, now there, to arouse resentment and to excite people to action, and one's only weapons are one's own convictions and the power of one's words. To follow that calling in which, clearly silhouetted on the horizon, no matter what path one takes, stand prison, Siberia and the gallows, it is not sufficient merely to have a vocation.

One must have iron health at the service of indomitable energy, and an almost limitless capacity for work. One must be in the championship class for doing without sleep and one must be able to throw oneself from one task into another at a moment's notice, to fast and to freeze, to avoid capture and to know how to escape if one is captured. One must prefer to have one's skin seared with a red-hot iron or one's teeth smashed sooner than blurt out a name or an address. One's whole heart must be devoted to the cause; it is impossible for it to harbour any other object, for one is a wanderer on the face of the earth and one never has either leisure or money.

And that is not all. One must have hope so firmly implanted in one that in the darkest moments and when faced by the bitterest defeats one must never cease to believe in victory.

And even that is not enough. *Above everything else* one must have clarity of vision and a perfect knowledge of what one wants. It is in this that Marxism specially arms Revolutionaries and gives these new men such a grasp of circumstances (and allows, and has allowed them such extraordinary foresight!).

Formerly it used to be quite sufficient to be brave in order to succeed in a revolutionary operation, temporarily at least—for to achieve permanence is a much more complicated story. . . . One day, Blasco Ibañez, that amiable but bogus great man, told me with a deep sigh how sad it was that the days were past when, to usurp power, it was enough to go down into the street with a small but very determined group of followers. Nowadays, there are machine-guns—and barricades are no longer made only of cardboard. The profession is spoiled and he was, in consequence, disgusted with it.

Of course there are machine-guns. But it is not merely for that reason that the old revolutionary scenario which, from being realistic, has become romantic, is only fit for the scrap-heap. Nowadays, revolutions are of a quite different nature and are much bigger affairs than those political skirmishes which have so often, hitherto, substituted one lot of people for another in a central palace, without thereby altering anything at all, except a few labels. What the downtrodden classes of the world are wearily waiting for in their own interest is something quite different.

Marxism illuminates the depths and necessities, bound one to the other, of these great logical upheavals of present-day society, and lays down hard and fast rules for their elaboration. Marxism is not, as one might be tempted to think, if one knows nothing about it, a collection of complicated principles or of commandments to be learned by heart, like a grammar or like the Koran. It is a system, and it is quite a simple one. It is the system of complete achievement. It is the concentration of all ideas, the groping of one's way towards a firm basis, a concrete foundation, a framework—cutting across religious or abstract mysticisms, processions of phantoms and other sidetracks leading nowhere. There are no ideas or formulæ suspended in the air, as though they could stay there of their own accord. Karl Marx was the one modern thinker who was great enough to blow the clouds away from the firmament of thought. The Marxist system encourages one to return constantly to first causes and to follow matters to their logical conclusion without ever losing sight of the end in view, and to combine theory as closely as possible with practice: truth, reality, life.

From that point Socialism ceases to be a nebulous or sentimental dream, in which one never comes across anything substantial except to run one's head against it, but it becomes the doctrine which calculates the logical needs of everyone in advance and which everyone ought to work loyally to realize by the simplest methods. It implies a modification of the existing state of affairs. It clears things away and shows them up and allows one to see the present and the future. It is solid wisdom which tends naturally towards the double task of demolition and construction.

KOBA AT THE HEAD OF A DEMONSTRATION AT BATUM, 1902

A REVOLUTIONARY UNDER THE TSAR

The Marxist conception is a scientific one. It becomes confused with the scientific conception. The Revolutionary always remains an apostle and a soldier, but he is, above all, a scholar who goes out into the highways and byways. Moreover, all the scholars in the world practise Marxism without being aware of it, in the same way as Monsieur Jourdain, in Molière's *Bourgeois Gentilhomme*, spoke in prose.

It is by careful and critical judgment of society that the ordinary man becomes a Revolutionary, not by a sudden outburst of hatred, fury or generosity—or rather, not only by that. It is a *calculated* outburst. Social injustice is like a spelling mistake. Every kind of error tends to rectify itself in time but the human mind must hasten this organic rectification, by foresight and by putting things in order. The human mind first. Sentiment—a valuable incentive—must not come until after the intellect, and must obey it. Sentiment must only be the servant of the clearest evidence, for left to itself it may easily become the servant of folly.

It made me smile to hear the German writer Emil Ludwig ask Stalin, as he did two years ago: "Perhaps you were ill-treated by your parents in your childhood, to have become such a Revolutionary?"

The excellent Emil Ludwig still firmly believed in the old adage of the wisdom of nations, which lays it down that, in order to be a Revolutionary, one must be vicious or embittered, and, from one's earliest youth, have been beaten by one's parents. A poor argument, too paltry to be harmful. No doubt individuals and the masses are egged on by misfortune, but Revolutionaries are far beyond any small personal grievances on the road to collective progress. Stalin replied patiently to Ludwig: "Not at all. My parents did not maltreat me. The reason that I became a

Revolutionary is simply because I thought the Marxists were right."

"Politics based on principles are the only honest ones," said Stalin, repeating Lenin. That is the declaration of basic principle, the major precept which, as Stalin again says, "enables one to storm impregnable positions." And the great incentive, for those who are trying to bring about social progress, is faith in the masses. This faith in the great mass of the workers is the watch-word, the battle-cry which Stalin has uttered most often in the course of his career. "The most unseemly malady which can attack a leader," he tells us, "is fear of the masses." The leader needs them more than they need him. He learns more from them than they learn from him. As soon as a leader begins to make his plans without taking the masses into his confidence, he is damned, as regards both victory and the cause.

So this practical agitator, armed roughly with realism, and with a hatred of catch-phrases and abstractions, began to fight.

Let us note here the influence of Kurnatovski, Lenin's companion in arms and a pioneer of his ideas in Transcaucasia. He was the liaison agent between J. V. Djugashvili and Leninism. Marxism, according to Adoratski's striking formula, "enables us to take advantage of the circumstances of any particular moment," and Leninism was Marxism already largely adapted to the situation created by the period and surroundings.

Our man assumed all sorts of different names: David, Koba, Nijeradze, Tschijikof, Ivanovitch, Stalin, and his methodical agitating took all sorts of forms.

At the very beginning, he declared his position, his fundamental policy, in the struggle, within the Party itself, between the old and the young members. The older members were in favour of the distribution, in small doses, of "pure propaganda" to selected workers who should be charged with spreading the gospel. The younger members were for direct contact, for "the street." It is hardly necessary to add that Stalin supported the latter tendency, and made it triumph.

Strikes. In 1900–01 there were several big strikes in which this agitator, who set out to make his presence felt, took a very important part. This, and especially the huge demonstration which took place in May, 1901, resulted in the dispersal of the Social-Democratic committee of Tiflis and the illegalizing of everything, so to speak.

He was penniless. Comrade Ninua and a few others gave him food, in about 1900 at Tiflis, where he held discussions each evening in the eight circles which he directed.

One of the most important supplemental parts of the agitator's work consisted in hiding himself. At Tiflis is shown a house which contained one of the "illegal hiding-places" of the man whose career we are following. With its slim little columns, its covered balcony and its narrow ogival double doors, the house is like a great many other houses in Tiflis, which was the first condition it had to fulfil in view of the use to which it was being put.

He would appear suddenly at meetings, and would sit down without a word and listen until the time came for him to speak. He was always accompanied by two or three comrades, one of whom would keep watch by the door. He would not speak for long. If he took a train journey, he would take endless trouble to throw people off his track.

". . . And he was at that secret meeting which was held near the wings of a theatre, so that when the police surrounded the building, they had only to break down a door and mix with the audience with a look of absorbed attention on their faces."

". . . He walked into the huge Popoff library. He asked for a book of Belinski's, which he began to read attentively, all the time keeping an eye on the manœuvres of one of the assistants, to whom he handed, unseen and unrecognized by anyone, two false passports. They were to secure the escape of two comrades whom the police intended to arrest a little later—a little too late. This Popoff was a Monarchist librarian, which was the reason that the comrades could easily meet there: Sturona, Rykoff, Todria, Enukidze."

He had a wonderful intuition. By this shrewd intuition of his he prevented the Baku workers, counting on the sympathy of a certain regiment (this was a trap), from trying to free the demonstrators who had been thrown into prison as a sequel to a brush with the Black Hundred[*] carrying the portrait of the "Adored One."

But if the Revolutionary was losing more and more ground in his native land, he acquired a solid support on the international basis in the shape of the paper which Lenin succeeded in establishing abroad, *Iskra (The Spark)*, a centre of doctrine and, as it were, of public conspiracy, and whose first number, printed in Munich in January, 1901, ended its first leading article with the assertion: "We must capture the enemy fortress, and we will succeed in doing so if we unite all the forces of the awakening proletariat."

However, he did not always hide himself. There were moments—carefully chosen—when he came out into the open. For instance, on the occasion when, thanks to him— May-day was celebrated for the first time in the Caucasus

[*] An ultra-conservative tsarist organization which operated through direct action and terror. (Translator.)

(1901). Or else when, advancing at the head of a crowd of Tiflis railway strikers who were threatened by the officer of police with being shot if they did not disperse, he replied in their name: "You do not frighten us. We will disperse when our demands have been satisfied." (The charge which followed did not overcome the strikers.)

He went to Batum, Adjaristan, in southern Georgia, and established a committee there. This, as Lacoba says, "constitutes a fresh page in the great Biography." From his headquarters in the marshy suburb of Chaoba, Sosso created discontent among the workers at the Mantascheff and Rothschild works.

He was chased away by the police and fled to Gorodok. His movements were complicated by the presence of the secret printing-press which he carried with him and which was his loud-speaker (in a whisper).

After the 1st of March demonstration, at the head of which he placed himself like a target and on which occasion there were 14 killed, 40 wounded and 450 arrests, the printing-press and its moving spirit had to move again.

In the neighbourhood there was a cemetery (that of Su-Uk-Su) whose grave-digger was a friend of his. Secret meetings were held in this cemetery (when they were over, the cigarette ends had to be carefully concealed among the jumble of Moslem tombs!).

One day the printing-press was brought there in haste. The grave-digger took charge of it and of a large jar containing the type. He was carrying his load towards the neighbouring maize-field when he had suddenly to lie flat on his face because a party of police came by, followed by a party of Cossacks, actually looking for the press.

So that another place had to be found to house the press

and its manager. They hit upon the house of a certain Khashim.

Khashim was an old man who had suddenly, in the depths of his simple Moslem peasant's heart, begun to understand and to revere Sosso. One day he had said to him: "I am the most insignificant and the most persecuted of men, and I have never spoken to the chief, but I *recognize* you." Later on, when he had heard him speak a little more, he said to him: "I see quite well what you are; you are an *afirkatza* (an Abkhasian hero); you seem to have been born of thunder and lightning; you are supple and you have a great heart and a great soul."

The old peasant and his son moved the press to their home, and Sosso lived there too. And women with long Moslem veils who seemed, at close quarters, rather heavily built, appeared in the village. These were the printers who had to take precautions before entering the improvised workshop.

From that time onward, Khashim could be seen leaving his home each morning, with his turban and his white beard, carrying a basket full of vegetables and fruit. But beneath the fruit would be a pile of tracts and proclamations. He would go up to factory gates selling the fruit and the vegetables. If he knew the purchasers or liked the look of them, he would wrap his wares up in the tracts.

However, the continuous bustle that went on in the workroom, and the noise of the printing-machine, led the neighbouring peasants to believe that Sosso, Khashim's guest, was making counterfeit money.

They were not quite certain what to think of this profession, which evidently demanded a great deal of technique, but was very questionable. They came to see Sosso one evening and said to him: "You're making counterfeit

PHOTOGRAPH OF STALIN TAKEN IN A GROUP OF
POLITICAL DEPORTEES IN THE DISTRICT OF
TOUROUCHANSK IN 1903

money and, after all, perhaps it isn't such a bad business for us, because, poor as we are, we don't think we run any risk of suffering from it. When are you putting your money into circulation?"

"I'm not making counterfeit money," replied Sosso. "I'm printing tracts telling of your misery."

"So much the better!" exclaimed the peasants. "Because we could not have helped you to imitate roubles, since we don't know how to. But this is our business. We understand, we're grateful to you, and we'll help you."

... And, disregarding chronological order for a moment, let us make a short excursion into the future. The same place, the same garden of Khashim's, but in 1917. The old peasant, after the Revolution was over, returned home and examined his garden. He had buried the secret printing-press there, many months before, when he had to leave home hurriedly. The house had been occupied by soldiers who, in the course of their rummagings, had unearthed the printing-apparatus and had scattered it all over the garden. Khashim found all the pieces and when he had put them carefully together, he said to his son: "Look, it is with that that the Revolution was made."

... And now let us return to April, 1902. One day Sosso was talking to Kandelaki, smoking a cigarette; he was, at the time, a very dark young man, very slim, wearing a neckcloth with red squares on it. He wore a black beard like a romantic art-student, with his coal-black hair "which seemed to be blown back by the wind," "his small moustache, long face and intrepid gaiety." Now the *Okhrana* (the Police Service) was again taking an interest in him, and at that very moment police were filling the basement of Darachvilidze's house where he was, and were also surrounding it. Sosso was caught in a trap. He merely said: "It's nothing," and went on smoking. The sound of heavy boots and the clanking of arms mounted the stairs. The police came in and the inevitable happened. Sosso was arrested, imprisoned at Batum and then transferred to Kutaïs (where he organized a successful strike of prisoners).

After this he was deported to the province of Irkutsk, in Siberia. Tsarism, which had been unable and unwilling to govern Siberia economically, had ruled it politically by endowing it with a chain of concentration camps or convict settlements, in which its prisoners were shut up, and submerged in the vastness of the country.

But one day a man appeared at Batum dressed as a soldier. It was Koba, who had unceremoniously left the custody of the police and returned from Central Asia at his own expense.

This meant the loss of a great deal of time—not, however, so much as one might think, because the revolutionary remains a revolutionary even in prison.

Simon Vereshtchak, a Revolutionary Socialist and a fierce political enemy of his ("nothing about Stalin pleases him," Damian Biedny tells us, "neither his nose nor the colour of his hair, nor his voice—nothing at all!"), informs us that in 1903 he was in the same prison as Stalin, in Baku —a prison, made to hold four hundred prisoners, into which fifteen hundred were crowded. "One day a new face appeared in the cell containing the Bolsheviks. Someone said: 'It's Koba.'" What did Koba do in prison? He educated people. "Educational circles were formed, and the Marxist Koba stood out prominently among the professors. Marxism was his subject and he was undefeatable on it. . . ." And Vereshtchak describes this young man, "wearing a blue, open-necked, satinet blouse, no belt or hat, a cloak thrown over his shoulder, and always carrying a book in his hand," arranging big organized debates. (Koba always preferred these to individual discussions.) At one of these debates, on the peasant problem, Serge Ordjonekidze exchanged first arguments and then blows with one of the chief speakers, the Revolutionary Socialist Kartsevadze, and finally Ordjonekidze was half killed by the Revolutionary Socialists. Later, when Vereshtchak met Stalin in prison, what struck him most was the impressive faith which this Bolshevik prisoner had in the ultimate triumph of Bolshevism.

A little later, when he occupied cell No. 3 in the Bailoff prison, Koba again organized courses of study. Imprisonment only succeeded in altering his activities in a relative way.

Constant overwork and terrible hardships began to sow disease among the militants. Koba began to observe the first signs of tuberculosis in himself. It was the *Okhrana* that cured him—in such circumstances, however, that he had nothing for which to be grateful to it. He was in Siberia, in the open steppes, when suddenly that terrible icy blizzard known as the *Purga* or *Buran* started to blow. The only means people have of sheltering from it is to lie down and dig themselves into the snow. But Koba kept his course which was along a frozen river. It took him hours to walk the couple of miles that separated him from the nearest hut. When at last he crossed the threshold, people took him for a ghost: he was nothing but an icicle from head to foot. They thawed him out, and he collapsed and slept for eighteen consecutive hours. As a result of his adventure, his tuberculosis disappeared for ever. Siberia is like that: if it does not kill consumptives, it cures them permanently. There is no middle course: the cold either carries off the man or the malady (rather haphazardly).

He was in prison, in 1903, when he heard a great piece of news. At the Second Congress of the Russian Social-Democratic Party, a split began to appear, on Lenin's initiative, between the Bolsheviks and the Mensheviks. The Bolsheviks were the extremists, the wagers of uncompromising class warfare, the iron militants. The Mensheviks were the reformers, the adapters, the arrangers, the technicians of compromise and combination. The Mensheviks were irritated with the Bolsheviks, who appeared to them to increase their demands whenever they felt inclined to do so. (What an idea! The vanquished crying for the moon!)

The split grew wider. There came a definite parting of the ways. Even though the question was not as serious—at the height of Tsarist power and persecution, at the height of the prosperity of capitalist evil-doing and ruin—as it became later, Stalin did not hesitate. He chose Bolshevism, and decided for Lenin.

A moment always arrives at which a man of action must make a decision of this sort which is destined to affect the whole future course of his life. One is reminded of the old Greek myth, impressive because of its antiquity, of Hercules being compelled to choose, at the beginning of his divine and sportive career, between Vice and Virtue. But were there not, in this case, reasons for and against? Reform is very tempting. It has an atmosphere of wisdom and prudence, and seems to avoid the shedding of blood. But far-seeing people, who understand the great principles of logic and social arithmetic and, in an ever-increasing degree, historical experience, know that on the path of opportunist resignation and reformist vassalage lie first mirages,

A REVOLUTIONARY UNDER THE TSAR

then snares and finally betrayal—and that it is the path of destruction and of massacre. People may say that it is only a question of degree. But no, it is a crucial question, a question of life and death, because minimalism (which is also called the "least evil") is really conservatism.

So Kobi (which was another of his names) made his first escape. And from that moment, detachments of police here, there and everywhere tracked him down periodically, found him, recaptured him and then tried to find him again. This occurred six times, neither more nor less. After his sixth escape, Kobi carried on a campaign against the Georgian Mensheviks. "From 1904 to 1905," writes Ordjonekidze, "Kobi was, for the Mensheviks, the most hated of the Caucasian Bolsheviks, whose recognized leader he became."

One day an Olibadze workman addressed him:

"Anyway, damn it, Comrade Sosso, the Mensheviks have got a majority in the Party, after all!"

And this workman remembers quite well to-day that Sosso answered him:

"Majority? *Not as regards quality*. Only wait a few years and you will see who was right and who was wrong."

The militant members of the Party who were in the Caucasus at that time, still remember the outcry made by the Menshevik authorities, like Noah Ramishvili or Seide Devdariani, when they got wind of the fact that Koba, "a professional Bolshevik," was coming to debate with them, or, in other words, "to disorganize their peaceful existence."

What Bubnoff wrote recently is very accurate and very illuminating: "The Russian Bolsheviks were very lucky in the fact that for fifteen years they were able to carry on a systematic and intensive fight against all deviations in any direction, long before the Revolution." It meant so much groping which had not to be gone through later, and revolutionary progress benefited by the fact that the Party had already tried out its strength, and had been able early to establish and verify the reasonable point of view, the true point of view, in the study of theory and especially in tactical organization.

We are quite aware of the fact that Napoleon said that "if one is in the wrong, one must persist, and one will end by being in the right." The phrase is amusing and has a certain picturesque and even artistic and literary turn about it. But (I beg the artist's pardon), it is utterly false. Nothing can subsist which is not in harmony with reality and the march of events. To proclaim the contrary is to propagate one of those encyclopædic errors on which capitalist morality battens; it will eventually die of indigestion caused by them (as, for instance, Versailles did in the old days).

Thus it was that, at the same time that they were fighting the Anarchists and the Revolutionary-Socialists (who are much the same as Anarchists) and the Nationalists who could see no further than their national noses, they had also to fight, and did indeed fight, against the Mensheviks at Tiflis, at Batum, at Chiaturi, at Kutaïs and at Baku. In 1905, among his other activities, Stalin edited the illegal Bolshevik newspaper *The Struggle of the Proletariat*, and wrote a work in the Georgian language entitled *Some Remarks on the Differences in the Party*. "Oh! How stolidly the author stands upon his feet!" was the remark made by Theophil Chichua at Donidze, after a public reading of the work; Chichua remembers the remarks to this day.

Under the influence of Stalin the workers' movement developed. Their methods changed. They no longer went in for revolutionary propaganda by stages and through the intermediary of a few very carefully chosen workers.

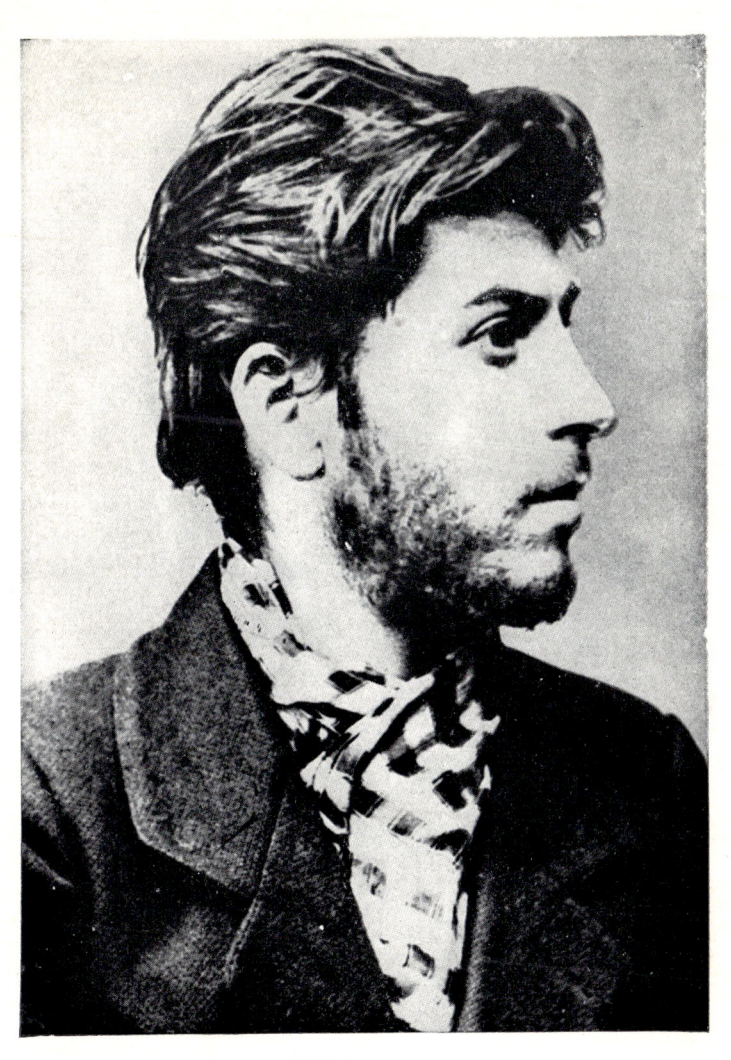

KOBA, 1902-3

Their infectious faith in the masses strongly impelled the militants to go to work in a more direct and more palpable manner, both with individual men and in street oratory. Under the new leadership the system of active offensive triumphed, consisting of public demonstrations, improved meetings and the bold distribution of tracts and leaflets.

Years went by in indomitable and patient labour.

"Comrade Koba had neither home nor family; he lived and thought exclusively for the Revolution," says Vazek. And he never missed an opportunity for a demonstration. Vazek relates how, at the burial of the apprentice Khanlar, killed by order of the management of the factory in which he worked at Baku, an orchestra played a funeral march in front of the mosque. The Chief of Police forbade it to play. "Then Comrade Koba organized two choirs among the workers, one of which marched in front of the coffin, while the other marched behind it." These choirs sang revolutionary dirges in full view and hearing of the police. The police succeeded in silencing them too. Then Koba made the workers whistle—long, mournful whistles. This fresh choir swelled without anything being able to stop it and the mourning demonstration became very impressive.

The reports which the secret agents of the *Okhrana* made to the Most Noble the Chief of Police of Tiflis on "a Social-Democratic revolutionary organization which comes within the terms of Article 250," declared that this organization consisted of "those who are called the Workers' Advance-Guard," and of intellectuals such as Iossip Djugashvili. This latter, said one of these reports, strove "to revive the morale of disheartened workers, by means of agitation and the dissemination of illegal literature"; he "recommended the union of all nations," and urged the common people to maintain a secret fund destined for "the struggle against Capitalism and Autocracy."

Elsewhere, the Chief of the Baku section of the *Okhrana* informed His Honour the Archbishop of Detectives that "the peasant Iossip Djugashvili" was the leading spirit in a meeting having as its object the founding of a secret printing-press. Elsewhere, again, an agent informed his revered superior that the self-styled Kaisom Nijeradze, who was at that moment in gaol, was none other than the peasant Djugashvili and that, in addition, this individual had the effrontery "not to recognize his guilt."

Daniloff tells us of one of these interrogations, conducted by one of the chiefs of that police force which was charged, above all, as were then and are still all the police forces of the world—with one exception which proves the rule—to keep the people on the move with truncheons. This satrap, "clad in turquoise blue, a cigar in his mouth and diffusing an aroma of opoponax, gave free rein to his talents as a psychologist." This is what he said afterwards in his report on the person interrogated: "Djugashvili, Iossip Vissarionovitch . . . stoutish . . . deep voice . . . small birthmark on left ear . . . shape of head normal . . . gives one the impression of an ordinary man." As one can see, nothing escaped this keen observer. A complete report on Stalin: "Small birthmark on left ear!"

Chapter Two

THE GIANT

So THERE was, somewhere in Russia (and also travelling to and fro from time to time in Europe), a great guide, a giant brother of all the Revolutionaries—and we have already caught a glimpse of him. Lenin had to fight, not only against the public authorities, but also against a large proportion of the men of his own Party. He insisted—and this was his great conception and his great work, which embraced everything else—on an out-and-out Revolutionary Party, pure, sharply defined and homogeneous, unsusceptible of any sort of compromise. He used to say that this Party could only fulfil its mission of changing the face of the world on this express condition, and that it was the first and most important question. And it is in this sense that he remodelled Socialism within Socialism.

We have already seen that Stalin, kept informed of how matters were progressing, by his comrades whilst he was in prison, identified himself completely with the position adopted by Lenin at the Second Congress of the Party. At this assembly, Vladimir Ilitch had doggedly and firmly emphasized the difference which was appearing, from the tactical point of view, between the Mensheviks and the Bolsheviks, and he deliberately widened the breach between the two tendencies—which was, on the part of this lover of unity, a terribly grave step to take. But his reasons for doing so were no less grave. Unity between two tendencies which differ too much from each other can never be more than apparent and fictitious. It can only exist on paper. It is a misleading form of union. Stalin approved. Moreover, this move was in accordance with his own temperament and his own mentality, and one might say that he had already chosen before choosing. There was never, at any time, any difference of opinion between Lenin and Stalin.

On the other hand, they both had bitter opponents in the Party itself, especially Trotsky, an obstinate and verbose Menshevik, who considered that the inflexibility of the Bolsheviks afflicted the Party with sterility. Trotsky considered that Lenin broke up the working classes and divided them against themselves.

Lenin, agitator and world statesman, and almost superhuman in the infallibility with which, in every circumstance, he was completely successful in combining revolutionary theory and practice, never swerved from Marxism. Leninism is synonymous with Marxism. It is a new chapter in Marxism, it is not an amendment, an adaptation of Marxism to a given situation. Stalin wrote: "Leninism is the Marxism of the era of Imperialism and of the proletarian Revolution." "A laconic and clean-cut definition," writes Manuilsky. Leninism is the proper response of Marxism to the times. Lenin never made any alterations in the great basic socialist creed as it was set out in the 1847 *Manifesto*. Lenin and Marx are two colossal concentric personalities, moving in the compass established by the older of the two. Lenin's creative genius applied itself to transforming socialist doctrine into Revolution (and then into revolutionary government).

All realist theory is supple, since it adjusts itself to life. But it is supple at its extremity, not at its foundations; on the side of circumstances, not on that of principles (which

A GROUP TAKEN IN PRISON

Stalin is the fourth from left (No. 4) in the upper row

are, indeed, originally an imaginary synthesis of realities). The rigorous upholding of these principles, and their defence against the slightest attempt at modification, was one of Stalin's most exacting and unremitting tasks.

Let it be thoroughly understood that Bolshevism, in spite of its intense progressive force, does not compel us to choose, always and everywhere, a cut and dried solution. There are certain circumstances in which, by applying such mechanical methods to excess, one would risk over-reaching one's objectives and imperilling the results achieved and, in short, setting back the work of Revolution instead of advancing it.

Conclusion: no submission to a perpetual pre-established Liberalism. "To forge ahead" means nothing. Doctrine, which is in the hands of those who have to apply it, must conform to constantly changing circumstances, and successful achievement is therefore a matter of continual adjustment and of continual creation.

In order to make this clearer, I will give a typical example to illustrate this organic suppleness of the connexion, this cardan-shaft as it were, between Marxist theory and Marxist practice. Lenin was obsessed by the idea that it was essential for the peasants to be allied to the workers in the social struggle, in order that a proletarian Revolution might implant itself into an agricultural country like Russia; but although, in 1894, he had impressed on the peasants the fundamental objectives of Socialism on the agrarian plan (namely, confiscation and nationalization of large estates), he did not go nearly so far as this when he addressed them, six years later, at the beginning of the nineteenth century. In the interval, the idea of the Revolution had matured (it was to take place in 1905) and the peasant problem, of which Lenin had made a profound and masterly study, and in which the Social-Democrats took no interest (a major and unpardonable error, a vital mistake in policy, according to Lenin), became one of the greatest urgency so far as the co-operation—or neutrality—of 25,000,000 rural families in the revolutionary movement was concerned.

In 1900, Lenin drew up a new agrarian programme in which he only took into account the fact that the Russian peasant class, very backward historically, and even backward when compared with the rest of Russia, was even more the victim of the feudal system than of the capitalist system; for the feudal system still prevailed in the country districts, in spite of the sinister farce of the abolition of serfdom (and was even strengthened by the ruinous and restrictive measures of that demagogic gesture of Alexander II).

So Lenin's 1900 peasant programme confined itself to demanding the abolition of those feudal laws and customs under which the peasantry were still labouring—the situation having become aggravated as a result of the feudal reaction under Alexander III—and the restitution of all the sums extorted from the peasants who had been forced to buy their land at a scandalously inflated valuation.

So here Lenin, driven by immediate tactical necessity, employed immediate arguments capable of impressing the peasantry as directly and as widely as possible, to obtain the maximum amount of combination and the maximum possibility of eventual co-operation between the peasants and the workers in the first act of the revolutionary drama, namely the seizure of power. In those days he considered, so far as the rural districts were concerned, only the first act, and not the last which was the organization of the new society, which would be dealt with after.

THE GIANT

So much for Marxism. The whole principle of it is to look far enough ahead, to foresee and to act in time, not to lose sight of all the various conditions which may arise and which often seem to clash with one another; in short, to possess that sense of essentials which enables a fact to be dominated as if it were a human being, and which is the characteristic of all those who create something new, whether they be scientists, artists or people bent upon altering the structure of society.

This example of an important reservation touching the most important revolutionary objectives, on the eve of a rising which might only too easily become merely a middle-class revolution, gives us an insight into the genius for initiative which one must have merely in order to be a "disciple of Marx," like Lenin, or a disciple of Lenin, like Stalin.

The meeting between Lenin and Stalin, in Stalin's own words:

"I first made Lenin's acquaintance in 1903. I did not meet him then, but we corresponded. I have retained an unforgettable memory of that first epistolary meeting. I was an exile in Siberia at the time. In studying Lenin's revolutionary activities from the end of the last century, and particularly after the appearance of *Iskra* (*The Spark*), in 1901, I had arrived at the conviction that in Lenin we possessed no ordinary man. To my mind he was not just a mere Party leader, but a real creator, for he alone understood the nature and the urgent needs of our Party. When I compared the other leaders with Lenin, they always seemed to be a head shorter than he. Beside them, Lenin was not a person of the same order of things, but a commander of a superior type, a mountain eagle, a fearless fighter leading the Party forward through the hitherto unexplored paths of the Russian revolutionary movement. This impression anchored itself so firmly in the depths of my mind that I felt compelled to write about him to a close friend of mine who happened to be away from Russia at the time, and to ask him for his opinion of him. Some time later I received an enthusiastic reply from my friend, addressed to Siberia, and at the same time I received a simple but profound letter from Lenin. I understood that my friend had shown him my letter. Lenin's letter was relatively short, but it criticized incisively and intrepidly the practical work of our Party, and disclosed with remarkable clarity and precision the whole future plan of action of the Party."

This letter, which Stalin considered it to be his duty to burn "from conspiratorial habit," and which he never forgave himself for having destroyed, this little letter succeeded in enlightening this militant Revolutionary of twenty-four years of age, both on the duties of a Revolutionary and on the man who was the most complete, brilliant and authoritative incarnation of those duties. It was at that date that Stalin considers that he really made Lenin's acquaintance. But:

"I met him for the first time in December 1905, at the Bolshevik Conference of Tammerfors (in Finland). I was expecting to see, in the eagle of our Party, a great man, not great only in the political sense, but physically great also, for in my imagination I pictured Lenin as a giant, fascinating and symbolical. What was my surprise then, to see before me a man of less than middle height, in no way distinguishable from ordinary human beings!

"A great man is supposed to arrive late at meetings, so

THE GIANT

that the assembly may anxiously await his arrival. The appearance of a great man is always heralded by remarks such as: 'Sh! . . . Silence! . . . Here he comes!' But I found that Lenin had arrived long before the others, and I saw him in a corner engaged in the most ordinary conversation with one of the least important of the delegates. He was quite clearly not behaving according to the accepted rules.

"This simplicity and modesty of Lenin's, which struck me the moment I met him, his desire to pass unnoticed, or at any rate not to emphasize his superiority, was one of his strongest points as the new chief of the new masses, the great simple and profound masses of humanity. . . ."

". . . It was thus that, in the North and in the Russian antipodes of Georgia, the young Revolutionary, whose field of activity had already spread beyond the Caucasus, found himself for the first time in contact with the man whom one of his disciples, Lebedeva, has defined and portrayed in this single phrase: 'He was simple, accessible to all, and so great.'"

All this took place on the eve of the Russian Revolution of 1905. The repulses of the Russo-Japanese War forced it to break out before its time, rather accidentally. It was a first revolution, the one which failed and was crushed, but was not without its uses, the prologue which left behind it, in the midst of the most appalling persecution, some great lessons.

Stalin explained afterwards that the result of the 1905 Revolution would no doubt have been quite different if the Russian Mensheviks, who possessed an important organization among the workers' class and who might have been able, at that period, to take control of the whole situation, had not abandoned the conduct of this revolution to the middle classes, in virtue of what Lenin and the Bolsheviks described as the Menshevik "schema," a vague summary theory, according to which, the Russian Revolution being necessarily a middle-class one, the proletariat had only to play the part of the "opposition of the extreme Left" in the general combination. All these reservations being announced and all this casuistry propounded at a moment when what was needed was to throw oneself wholeheartedly into the adventure and to put life into theory with watchwords that were capable of inflaming the workers, caused the failure of the great rising of 1905 (or was, at least, one of the causes of its failure), even though the "legitimate" Marxists took a great deal of literary pains to endeavour to make the workers carry through a middle-class revolution.

Some Latin poet has said that a thing well begun is half done. As against this, one may assert, with no less justice, that a thing which is only half done is not done at all. A succession of great proletarian adventures through the ages has shown us that whenever and in so far as the proletariat does not take everything into its own hands, it takes nothing.

There was a terrible back-wash of reprisals. Persecution broke out everywhere, and spread, and kept on spreading. It is sufficient to record that between 1905 and 1909 the number of political prisoners in Russia rose from 85,000 to 200,000 annually. The police persecution proper was aggravated by the blood-thirsty marauds of the Black Companies, who were an off-shoot of the Union of the Russian People (an ultra-tsarist organization), and were composed of bands of White fanatics wearing black masks, of *agents provocateurs* and bandits.

THE GIANT

At the same time as the methodical and savage suppression of the 1905 Revolution was taking place, a parody of Democracy was imposed upon reactionary Russia—from the top. A semblance of a Constitution, a pretence of a Parliament, a shadow of Liberalism. Contemporary history has given us a great many of these huge public caricatures (indeed, it still gives them to us).

The Tsar, ignorant and stupid, the slave of the Tsarina (who loathed the liberty of other people and longed to purify Holy Russia of it completely), the plaything of the Church and of fortune-tellers, was ferocious in his lucid moments.

"No one is to be acquitted," and "above all, do not ask me for mercy," declared, after 1905, the crowned jailer and executioner of the Russians, who was, in addition, the person responsible for the war against Japan over a Manchurian business venture in which he had financial interests.

Surrounding the Tsar, and under him, were the State Ministers whose main business was to keep the workers in a state of sordid ignorance, to ill-treat the lower classes, to stifle proletarian aspirations, to keep the peasants in an even more squalid condition than they were in before the abolition of serfdom, to overlook the indecent assaults of the thaumaturgists who were the intimate spiritual advisers of the great ladies of the Kremlin, to take no notice of the fantastic prevarications of officials of every sort and description, of the crimes of assassins drunk with tsarism who formed the Black Companies, and to arrange pogroms (one of the most flourishing industries in Russia).

There existed vague, extremely emaciated, Constitutional Parties, which the so-called democracy of their programmes inoculated against Socialism, and which were Red only in the eyes of the Whites—such Parties as the Octobrists and the Constitutional-Democrats. They were waiting, with a great deal of patience and respect, for a middle-class revolution to hand over the control of the State to them.*

After the 1905 rising and its failure, the organization of the Bolshevik Socialists proceeded imperturbably. They alone never lost their heads because they never lost their faith. "They kept before their eyes the coming rise of the masses."

In 1906 a congress was held at Stockholm, to which Stalin, under the name of Ivanovitch, was delegated by the Bolshevik elements of the Tiflis organization. At this congress, Lenin declared war against the Mensheviks. There was a brilliant phalanx of them there! Plekhanoff, Axelrod, Martoff. Lenin destroyed their arguments one by one with his implacable, aggressive and overwhelming lucidity.

Lenin did not at all conform to the accepted idea of an orator. He was just a man speaking. Except at certain periods (notably the days of October) when it was important that the direct and immediate impulses of the people should be aroused, and when it was necessary at all costs to make an impression on the mighty surging tide

* We may merely note, as regards the Constitutional-Democratic Party, which never had time to play the slightest part in affairs, crushed flat as it was between the reaction and the October Revolution, that its leaders, sworn enemies of the Bolsheviks, had declared, long before the War, that in the event of a Constitution of a Western nature replacing the tsarist power, this new Government would not recognize the debts contracted by the Imperial Government after 1905, "the money borrowed by the Tsar to use against his people." In 1906, when the Russian Government was at the height of its terrorist activities, its coffers were empty. They were replenished by France. This act of the Minister Rouvier allowed the work of suppression to be savagely revived. Even the most moderate Russian elements have admitted the truth of this.

of humanity, Lenin made hardly any gestures at all when he spoke. At congresses, people commented on his quietness and even on the "dryness" of his delivery. He merely endeavoured to *persuade* his listeners, to convey his convictions from within, not from without, by the weight of their contents, as it were, and not by the gesticulations and acrobatics of the container. The oratorical gestures which are sometimes seen in representations of him are not quite correct, and he may be said never to have moved so much as in his statues.

The simple and efficient method of delivery which Lenin employed was also that which Stalin had instinctively adopted and which he was destined never to abandon (he has even accentuated it).

For neither did Stalin aspire to make a pedestal of the platform and to be a "big noise" on the Mussolini or Hitler model, nor to imitate the performances of advocates like Alexandroff who know so well how to act on the retinas, the ear-drums and the lachrymatory glands of their audiences, or the contagious bleating of Gandhi. He was and has remained even more sparing of words than Lenin. Serafima Gopner, who played a prominent part in the Revolution, tells us how much she was impressed by the speech which Stalin made in 1917 on the activities of the Petrograd Soviet (of which he was the only Bolshevik member). It was "a very short speech in which he said everything there was to say." The whole situation was completely reviewed, and it would have been impossible to have cut out or to have changed a single word. In the same way, Orakhelashvili declares that "Stalin's speeches do not contain a single drop of water."

But although he speaks (between his teeth) in rather a muffled voice, without any pantomime and solely to express his thoughts, Stalin, like Lenin, holds one's attention and convinces one by the very substance of his speeches, which clearly retain all their weight and power, all their architectural logic, when one reads them afterwards in print. The speech, so full of perspective and prophecy, which Stalin delivered at the end of 1933 on "The Balance Sheet of the Five-Year Plan," is a literary masterpiece.

However, at the Stockholm Congress, the Mensheviks were in the majority. Most of the members of the Congress were not so much listeners as avowed adversaries. The Bolsheviks were defeated. What then . . . ?

"... For the first time I saw Lenin in the rôle of defeat. But he was not downcast. He thought of the future victory. The Bolsheviks were a little discouraged. Lenin roused them: 'Don't whimper, comrades,' he told them; 'we are bound to triumph because we are in the right.' Contempt for whining intellectuals, faith in our own powers, faith in victory, were what Lenin inspired us with then. One felt that the defeat of the Bolsheviks was only momentary and that they would unquestionably triumph in the end."

In the following year, Stalin went to Berlin and remained there for some time conferring with Lenin.

In 1907 another Congress of the Party took place in London. This time the Bolsheviks triumphed. Then:

"... For the first time I saw Lenin in the rôle of victory. But he was not like those leaders whom victory intoxicates. Victory only made him more vigilant and circumspect. He told us, the delegates grouped around him: 'In the first place, we must not cry, "Victory." Secondly we must destroy the enemy, for he is only beaten, not exterminated.' And he sternly rebuked those delegates who light-heartedly declared that 'henceforward we have done with the Mensheviks.'"

THE GIANT

One should not boast until one has reached one's goal, and when one has reached it there is no need to boast.

"Not to whimper over defeat. . . ." "Not to cry 'Victory.'" These great words, uttered by Lenin and echoed far and wide by Stalin, who employed them on many an important occasion, are applicable to the vast development of contemporary Socialism, to the final struggle for an entirely new civilization. But do they not evoke the rugged calm of the most serious moralists of antiquity, the highest pinnacles—without foundations, alas!—of Greek and Roman stoicism, and do they not recall the austere and oracular utterances of an Epictetus or a Marcus Aurelius?

Towards the end of 1907, on his return from the London Congress, Stalin installed himself at Baku, where he edited the *Baku Proletarian* (he had already edited the newspaper *Dro* [*The Times*] at Tiflis in the course of 1907). In two months, he brought the majority of the Social-Democratic organizations of Baku into the Bolshevik ranks.

And in that year, too, he launched with Lenin a violent campaign against the Otzovists, members of the extreme Left who contended that the revolutionary members of the Duma ought to be withdrawn by the Party. Lenin and Stalin declared this to be a mistake. However rotten this young organization might be to begin with, the good elements in it should remain there as long as possible, in order to be able to make new contacts and to get new outlets for propaganda. (This proves that, in spite of their inflexible policy, the Bolsheviks knew quite well that they should never go beyond the limits of practical common sense, and that, in any case, they admitted the employment of legal methods.) He went abroad again to see Lenin. He was arrested once more by the *Okhrana* and escaped again.

Then he launched a campaign—also with Lenin—against those who favoured "The Edification of the Divine Principle," and against its founder, Bogdanoff, and its eminent defenders, Lunacharsky and Gorki, who wanted to make a religion of Socialism so as to make it more popular. They declared that there was nothing either serious or sound in giving a mystical and artificial basis to evidences which could be so clearly assimilated through the channels of common sense and crying personal interest!

And in the years that followed, it was the same. Painfully, heroically, but surely the great cause of these persevering rectifiers gained adherents within the Party. In 1910 Stalin was arrested.

From 1909 to 1911 was a hard period for the Revolutionary Party scattered over the Empire. A period of arrests, discouragement, almost of panic. The Russian Social-Democratic Party, dislocated by the uninterrupted onslaught of the counter-revolutionary agents, began to lose faith. The intellectuals began to abandon it, and a good many of the workers also. More and more, not only among the Mensheviks, but also among the Bolsheviks, they began to consider means of attempting to bring themselves back within the law. The tendency towards the "liquidation" of secret activities went as far as envisaging a legal, almost official, Liberal Party. Measures of this sort were suicidal. It was a case of "losing one's object for living, in order to live," if one may be allowed to resuscitate the magnificent platonic aphorism. Lenin resisted this weakening masterfully and passionately, and Stalin with him. During this period of epidemic they had to contend against the whole world. But in the end Lenin triumphed "because he was right."

In 1911, interrupting his imprisonment by his own meth-

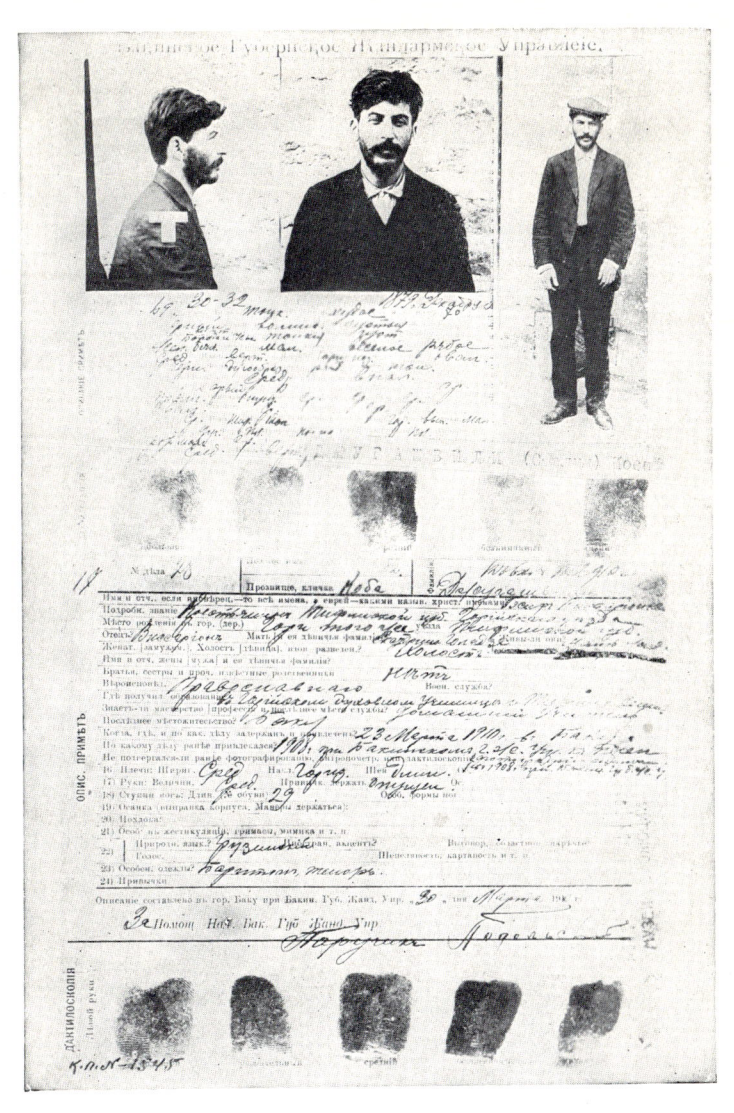

FROM THE POLICE FILES, KOBA DJOUGACHVILI, 1910

ods, Stalin established himself in St. Petersburg. He was recaptured; his exile to Vologda was curtailed by a fresh flight towards the scene of action. He returned to St. Petersburg and there displayed intense activity, turning incessantly this way and that in clandestine and semi-clandestine clashes with the Mensheviks (especially Trotsky), and the Anarcho-Syndicalists.

He was everywhere at once. Stalin inspected the Party organizations in various parts of Russia, edited the newspaper *Zvezda* (*The Star*) and was one of the founders of *Pravda* (*The Truth*). He was arrested and again sent into exile and again returned, to the discomfiture of his guards and of the police. In the autumn he went abroad to confer with Lenin. He appeared and spoke at the Bolshevik Conference of Cracovia (at the end of 1912).

It was at this period that Russian diplomacy was plotting with French diplomacy in the field of foreign policy and was exchanging official notes with France which, since published, place—in the naked light of history—the greater part of the responsibility for the World War on the Franco-Russian alliance (Constantinople and the Straits, Alsace-Lorraine [revenge and iron], Isvolsky, Poincaré). And "that scoundrel Isvolsky," as Jaurès called him, that scoundrel Isvolsky (who knew men as well as Jaurès did) made the Press and the pressmen hastily change their opinions, especially the *Temps* and Monsieur Tardieu, by almost magical methods of persuasion.

At this time, too, there was a new "revolutionary impulse," which clearly foreshadowed to a large number of people the huge upheaval in which the ignominious tsarist régime was to collapse. The disgraceful shooting affair of Lena, in Siberia, where the troops fired on a delegation of strikers and on the crowd and killed five hundred people

(1912), caused tremendous indignation, and one heard a precursory mutter on that occasion.

The real Revolutionaries, at their battle stations, made a supreme effort towards creating a homogeneous Party that should be powerful and efficaciously revolutionary, and should bring to humanity the real benefits of a thorough political and social change, instead of a defeated Menshevism which was already thoroughly mutilating itself. They concentrated upon keeping to the straight path among all the criss-crossings and side-turnings—between the "liquidators," who tried to persuade the Party to rid itself of revolutionary methods and to sink into legality; between those who, going to opposite extremes, flew into a panic when the question of exploiting certain possibilities of legality was discussed and those who, "covering themselves with the toga of conciliation," preached union at all costs and wanted to make diametrically opposed tendencies march side by side, in utter disregard of common sense (which was Trotsky's position).

Lenin and Stalin endeavoured to make use, simultaneously and to the greatest possible extent, of all the resources of illegality and all those of legality. They rejected an illusive union, as being a pitfall that would retard matters, but they strove for true unity, for the conquering integrity of the Party.

It is only too easy for us, now that we can survey past history like a map spread out before us, to say that they were right. But, let us repeat, those who were being submerged and swept away in the whirlpool of that period had to possess very great genius for realism to dominate the period in the way posterity is able to do, and to see all the issues and *clearly to visualize the future*. In a case of this sort, clear-sightedness is creation.

Lenin put the greatest value on Stalin's writings. In 1911 he expressed himself as follows: "Kobi's articles deserve the closest attention. It is difficult to imagine a better refutation of the opinions and hopes of our pacifiers and our conciliators."

Lenin added: "Trotsky and his like are worse than all the liquidators who express their thoughts openly—for Messrs. Trotsky and Co. deceive the workers, conceal the malady and make its discovery and cure impossible. All those who support the Trotsky group are supporting the policy of lies and deception towards the workers, the policy which consists in masking the policy of liquidation." For a long time Stalin had no longer had any private life. Without a passport and in disguise, he had to change his lodging every day. But nothing could stop the work he was doing to consolidate the Bolshevik Party in its illegality. "He had to establish a General Staff, to form a Central Committee of management, capable of organizing and guiding the masses in the incipient revolutionary impulse." (V. Schweitzer.)

Another preoccupation of Stalin's was the socialist policy with regard to nationalities. This is a highly important question upon which the realization of Soviet ideals have largely depended. He had found means in 1912 to write a series of studies, later collected into a book, bearing decisively upon this subject, entitled "Marxism and the Question of Nationalities," in which reference will be made further on.

The *Pravda* was suppressed. Stalin and Molotoff brought it out again under the bold pseudonym *For the Truth*. This, too, was suppressed and reappeared as *The Path of Truth*.

Later, he was arrested again, and in July, 1913, he was

taken to the Tulukhansk district of Siberia—the "terrible Vissarionovitch," who had already outwitted the guards of Vologda, of Narym and other places, and who possessed the gift of slipping through the fingers of the police. This time they locked him up securely. He was taken to a village called Kuleika, twenty miles from the Arctic Circle. It consisted of two or three houses and enjoyed about the same number of months without snow. "He had to live like a Robinson Crusoe," Chumiatsky tells us, "in the frozen tundra." He made himself fishing and hunting implements, from nets and snares to harpoons and axes to cut holes in the ice. He spent all day hunting and fishing, chopping wood with which to warm himself, and cooking. All day long . . . and yet, on the rough table in his hut, under the inquisitorial and stupid eye of the special guard detailed to ensure the exile remaining where he was, pages and pages dealing with all the great problems began to pile up.

He was to remain in Siberia until 1917. On the horizon, on the dark side loomed the World War, on the bright side the second Russian Revolution.

And that ends the first period of the career which we are studying. If one asks a good judge, someone like Kaganovitch, for instance, to sum up the characteristics of that period of Stalin's life, he answers (with how much contained enthusiasm in his voice!): "He was a typical Bolshevik of the old school!" And he adds: "The most remarkable and most characteristic feature of all Stalin's political activities is that he never drifted apart from Lenin and never swerved to the Right or to the Left." Bela Kun who, after having triumphantly led the Hungarian Bolshevik Revolution, was compelled to yield when confronted with circumstances represented principally by the defection of Hungarian Social-Democracy and the armed forces of

European Imperialism—Bela Kun, who had worked in close collaboration with Stalin both before and after Lenin's death, expresses himself in the same terms as do also Piatinski, Manuilsky, Knorin and Jdanoff. And Ordjonekidze says: "During those reactionary years when the Bolshevik organization in Russia was being created and built up, Stalin was Lenin's faithful disciple, whilst Trotsky was carrying on a bitter struggle against Lenin and his Party." Trotsky called Lenin "the seceder," accused the Bolsheviks of employing improper methods and asked, in threatening tones, by what right their official organ called itself *Pravda* (*The Truth*).

The general massacre was decreed by the masters then in power. The Russian people marched to it for the British Empire over the seas, the English people for the armament manufacturers, the French people for Constantinople, and all of them for their enemies.

The events of August, 1914, justified the Bolsheviks in the sense that International Social-Democracy decided by a majority in favour of national defence and the sacred union of the Proletariat with the Capitalists and the National Imperialists. It was an alliance of victims and executioners for the benefit of the executioners. Liebknecht described it as "the union of wolves and sheep." One cannot be nationalist and internationalist at the same time without being dishonest, and this surrender marked the moral decline of the Second International.

Lenin and Zinovieff were in Galicia when war broke out. They retired to Switzerland, founded the *Social-Democrat*, the organ of the Russian Bolshevik Party, and edited a series of articles which were published together under the title *Against the Current*. The Bolshevik minority, tossed about like a raft on a stormy sea, and battered by the chauvinism let loose over Europe, kept steadfastly on, buffeted by wind and wave towards the shores of sound logic and true morality. The men who set themselves against the current of the world were but a handful of earnest men—not many for the whole of humanity. But these apostles of a deep-rooted doctrine were destined to wear down and to destroy adverse conditions, because "they were right." At the right moment, history will take a hand in the game and will say what it thinks of those who wanted this dogma and those who did not want it.

In its very first number, published on November 1st, 1914, the *Social-Democrat* tarred with the same brush Renaudel, Sudekum, Haase, Kautsky and Plekhanoff. The vital importance of the uncompromisingness of Bolshevism was proclaimed in it. Was it sectarianism? Or fanatics each trying to go one better than the other? No, quite the contrary: it was terrific common sense. Actually, Plekhanoff, Kautsky and Jules Guesde have abandoned the proletarian cause and had crept over to the middle-class camp (nationalism is the avenue through which all socialist failures pass).

It was the challenging and unyielding attitude which a few militant apostles defended with their own lives, that saved the Russian Revolution. Everything goes to prove this. Without them it would have been irretrievably lost, like the German and Austrian Revolutions. And it is a fact that the only way in which one can prevent war in this world is by putting the whole of society back into its proper place; there is no other way. There is no more noble moral law than the one which enjoins us to desire the means when we desire the end.

Lenin, irreproachable super-moralist, rose against the moralists of the idea—the destructive idea—of Motherland,

THE GIANT

when this idea of Motherland consists purely and simply of deifying geography. (It is not the same thing when it humanizes progress throughout an entire nation.) He also said: "The Second International is dead, destroyed by opportunism. Down with opportunism and up with the Third International, freed not only of turncoats but also of opportunists!"

This was written on November 1st, 1914. It was not until four and a half years later that the Third International was to spring fully armed from Lenin's brain.

Whilst from 1914 onwards the Bolsheviks struggled in Petrograd against governmental reaction, against the Mensheviks and other enemies, and the members of the Bolshevik groups in the Duma were being sent to Siberia, Lenin was struggling in Europe. In 1915, at the Idealist Conference of Zimmerwald, he carried a motion on the Imperialist character of the war and the socialist bankruptcy of 1914. In 1916, at Kienthal, he confirmed this attitude of his in the middle of the Social-Democratic "confusionism" of the Assembly. Social-Democracy suffered a strong reaction (in the physical sense also) against Kienthal, and became more and more openly the party of patching everything up and of goodness knows what else, and so, of course, of counter-revolution. The fact remains that the "Socialist" Renaudel managed to get a decision in France to the effect that those who took part in the Zimmerwald and Kienthal Conferences should be deprived of all rights of delegation in future.

In February, 1917, occurred the Russian middle-class Revolution, the abdication of the Tsar, the Government of Prince Lvoff and the rise of Kerensky.

Lenin returned from Switzerland via Germany. France

had refused to let him through by another route. (One knows the story of the "sealed wagon" and all the rest of that lying legend.) He arrived at Petrograd on April 3rd, 1917. Stalin arrived at the same time, from the opposite direction. He was elected a member of the Central Committee after the Pan-Russian Bolshevik Conference, at which the two old divergent currents appeared again, and at which Stalin defended the line taken up by Lenin against the opportunism of Kameneff and others. The Political Bureau of the Central Committee of the Party was formed: Stalin was elected to that too.

The situation was a serious one for those who wanted to pursue an undeviating course, for those who truthfully and genuinely wanted to change the future for the better, precisely because the dislocation of the tsarist machine had resulted in a brilliant and theatrical realization of revolutionary aspirations.

Was the Revolution going to stop there? Was there any possibility of its being betrayed by the band of obscure, faint-hearted people who had been put into the Kremlin by the wretched, frenzied populace? There was the greatest danger of this happening in exactly the same way as it had always happened hitherto (except in the case of the ephemeral Paris Commune of 1871) whenever, in any part of the inhabited globe, an attempt at a popular rising had been made.

A large number of people did not wish to push things further than the overthrow of the historic muck-heap surmounted by a hedged-in crown, further than by replacing the hereditary dictatorship of Peter the Great's descendants by a middle-class government professing to be democratic, to which would be returned in rotation two or three Parties all equally democratic in word and anti-democratic in deed;

with a President instead of an Emperor, an armchair instead of a throne. No difference except the erasure of a few coats of arms, slight alterations in the flag and the postage-stamps, and, at the beginnings of almanacks and directories, a change in the personnel charged with keeping the people in subjection. And the dictatorship of the proletariat and, in consequence, social justice sinking head first into this republican mixture. And the system of endemic warfare and the exploitation of man by man remaining intact. A fresh lie, in fact, a fresh political crime against the people.

Stalin specified very explicitly: "The essential task of middle-class revolution may be summed up in the seizure of power and in making it conform to the *existing* middle-class system of economics, whereas the essential task of proletarian revolution consists, after the seizure of power, in constructing a *fresh* socialist system of economics.

In other words, middle-class revolution is conservative. A half-revolution is really a counter-revolution. And that is why the situation was really such a pathetic one for the men who had prepared "the great evening" with their lives and with their blood, and whose clear duty it was thenceforward to extinguish the harm done by the middle-class revolution by a second revolution.

Lenin, that man (in Stalin's words) whom difficulties changed into a bundle of energy, undertook this high-minded and highly important task. He brought into existence what one might call *duality of power:* a Socialist State within the State. Side by side with the official Government, he created another Government, fully constituted, having its form in the Petrograd Soviet, functioning and consolidating itself, quite ready to become the only one.

And the mass of workers openly began to prefer this Government to the official Government beside it.

Stalin whole-heartedly supported Lenin. At the Sixth (illegal) Congress of the Party, in August, 1917, Stalin reported upon the political situation. He strongly opposed the addition to the ninth point of the Resolution on the political situation, of an amendment, inspired by Trotsky and proposed by Preobrajensky, making the construction of the Socialist State dependent on the outbreak of proletarian revolution in the West (this question of "establishing Socialism in one country only" is one of those around which the Opposition and the majority of the Party have fought one another most bitterly—even until quite recent years). Stalin wanted to put his whole faith in a Russian proletarian revolution: "Why should not Russia give an example to the world?" Lenin and Stalin knew perfectly well what they believed. Preobrajensky's amendment was not adopted. If it had been, things would not have been as they are to-day.

"Just before October," Kalinin tells us, "Stalin was one of the few people with whom Lenin decided to rise, without the knowledge of Zinovieff or of Kameneff, who were at that time members of the Central Committee."

Zinovieff and Kameneff did not take part in the rising. "At that moment," says Stalin, "they openly declared that in organizing the rising, we were rushing to our own destruction, that we should wait for the Constituent Assembly, that the conditions necessary for Socialism were not yet ripe and would not be so for some time . . . Zinovieff and Kameneff joined the rising out of fear: Lenin drove them to it with a stick. . . . They were obliged to drag themselves into the rising. . . . Trotsky joined it willingly enough, but with a reservation which already, at that time, brought him nearer to Zinovieff and Kameneff. . . . He declared that if the Revolution did not break out and was not successful in Western Europe, revolutionary Russia would not be able to hold out against conservative Europe, and that to doubt this Trotskyist opinion was to give proof of national narrow-mindedness.

"But," adds Stalin, "apart from these three, Lenin and the Party went forward without reservations."

Zinovieff and Kameneff carried hostility and lack of discipline to the point of publicly attacking, in a newspaper article, the decision to rise—which, naturally, was a secret. This betrayal allowed Kerensky to take armed defensive measures. Lenin treated Zinovieff and Kameneff as "strike-breakers," and spoke of excluding them from the Party. As a result, they both left the Central Committee.

During October, the Central Committee appointed Stalin a member of the Assembly of Five (for the political management of the Revolution) and of the Assembly of Seven (for the organization of the Revolution).

The proletarian Revolution took place on October 25th. Lenin gave the deciding impetus to that admirable historic storm and one can see his strong hand in it from the very beginning. On October 24th, the eve of the great day, he wrote to the Central Committee that the moment had come and that they must act: "Temporization in insurrection is really equivalent to death. . . . Everything hangs by a hair. . . . It is all a question of people, masses and arms. . . . The power should not, in any circumstances, or in any degree, be left to Kerensky and his associates, longer than to-morrow. . . . The matter must definitely be decided this evening and to-night. . . ."

A clearness of vision penetrating far into the future was necessary for anyone to let the Revolution loose at that moment. It meant, in fact, venturing upon direct intervention just when the workers, peasants and soldiers, at the end of their patience, were clamouring violently for peace; it meant risking everything at the moment when the General Staff and the middle classes were preparing for a military dictatorship, and when Kerensky was about to declare the Bolshevik Party to be an illegal one. It was "a leap in the dark." Yet, because of that, we must not read into it a chance throw of the dice or a despairing effort. Into the dark? Not for anyone who, like Lenin, could see daylight through the chaotic upheaval of the world, and who knew that "he was right."

When, in future years, humanity celebrates the various stages of its liberation, the date which it will commemorate with the greatest solemnity and enthusiasm will be October 25th, 1917, the date of the ruthless passage from the comedy revolution to the real Revolution. And humanity will pay homage to the men who were responsible for this.

The October Revolution, the super-Revolution, was successful. It decreed, following upon immediate peace (the first practical condition, the first sweeping up to be done in the general confusion), that all power should be vested in the Soviets, that is to say the dictatorship of the proletariat, sovereignty coming from the earth in all directions, the rights of man. It decreed the destruction of middle-class power from top to bottom, not merely in order to substitute for it permanently that of the hitherto oppressed and exploited classes, but so that the whole social order of things might be reorganized by the sole means of intervention capable of reaching such an objective (the intervention of the proletariat); and so as to construct a real fellowship of labour, a society that should be entirely co-operative, without classes, without oppression or ex-

LENIN AND STALIN

ploitation, an indivisible assemblage which should be logically open to all. The capitalist front, which until then had completely encircled the world, had been penetrated on a large sector, equivalent to one-sixth of the Earth's surface.

Unblemished Socialism, which had stood its ground and preserved its revolutionary integrity, blazed forth from the Kremlin, and suddenly the other Socialism, the Socialism of half-measures, of subterfuges and of dreams, which blissfully recommended gradual and piecemeal progress, all of whose acquisitions middle-class power would gradually have absorbed and assimilated so as to reinforce itself thereby against the masses—was relegated into the past, with all the old superstitions and obsolete ideas.

The account of this episode which John Reed gives in *Ten Days that Shook the World* conjures up reality, and is at the same time a terrible caricature because it is so like the truth. Some social-democratic magnates of the Duma, with their long sacerdotal beards, feeling as bewildered as alchemists suddenly torn from their laboratories, went into the streets of Petrograd to try to control the excesses of the Revolution; their passage was barred by a sentinel, and one of them said: "I am a deputy of the Duma, my friend." "I know nothing about that. We've swept all that away," replied the private soldier who barred the way to the socialist pontiff dethroned, in his turn, after the Tsar. These poor pontiffs, who had been unable to foresee their own downfall, found themselves, overnight, in the position of Rip van Winkle returning home after sleeping for a hundred years. But it was not so much that they had slept as that the great mass of the people had awoken. This was an entirely new phase in the history of mankind. Nothing of the sort had ever happened before since the beginning of the world.

Then began the era of overwhelming difficulties and indescribable obstacles.

But "Lenin was really a genius of revolutionary explosions," Stalin tells us, going on to say: "At awkward corners he foresaw the direction in which the classes would move and the unavoidable paths that the Revolution would take, as though he could read them in the palm of his hand."

It was necessary to reconstruct everything, but in the first place the position that had been captured had to be maintained—against the Whites, against the Mensheviks, certain of whose unhealthy tendencies filtered their way through into the very heart of the Party, against those whom Stalin called "the hysterics," that is to say the Revolutionary-Socialists and the Anarchists (Spiridovna threatening Lenin with a revolver at a meeting; Lenin remaining quite impassive, apparently almost amused—Anarchists who have only one battle-cry, as comprehensive as space itself: "Neither God nor Master," who persist in multiplying 1 by 1, and who will one day declare war on the order of letters in the alphabet!), against the Great Powers and their spies, against ruin, famine, economic destruction and financial collapse.

The problem of the Imperialist War had to be solved and that of the various nationalities, of whom many, still trembling with hatred for the tsarist yoke, and intoxicated at seeing their prison doors flung open, began to rise on their own account and threatened to upset everything.

Peace, then, had to be concluded with Germany and Austria. Right at the outset a catastrophe occurred which was tragically decisive. This, too, gave a dizzy feeling of a "leap into the dark." Stalin played a part in it. The Council of People's Commissars, anxious to enter into conversations with the Germans with a view to bringing about an armistice and suspending military operations, gave instructions to this effect to the Commander-in-Chief, Dukhonin.

". . . I remember the day on which Lenin, Krylenko (the future Commander-in-Chief) and I went to the General Staff Headquarters in Petrograd to speak to Dukhonin over a special wire. It was a terrible moment. . . . Dukhonin and the Headquarters Staff refused categorically to carry out the orders of the Council People's Commissars. The Army Commanders were completely in the hands of the Headquarters Staff. And what of the soldiers? No one knew what the army would say, subjected as it was to organizations which were utterly opposed to the power of the Soviets. We knew that a Junker rising was brewing in Petrograd, and that Kerensky was marching to attack the capital. . . . I remember how, after a moment's silence before the telephone, Lenin's face suddenly lit up in the most extraordinary way. One could see that he had already come to a decision. 'We will go to the wireless station,' he said. 'It will serve our purpose well. We will relieve General Dukhonin of his duties by special order, and in his place we will appoint comrade Krylenko to be Commander-in-Chief; and we will appeal to the soldiers, over the heads of their leaders, to arrest their generals, to cease all military operations, to fraternize with the Austro-German troops, and to take the cause of peace into their own hands.'"

And that is what actually occurred.

Negotiations took place at Brest-Litovsk for peace between Germany and Russia. The middle classes of the victorious countries abuse the Treaty of Brest-Litovsk which resulted from these negotiations, and the Larousse encyclopædic dictionary which, biassed, chauvinistic and reactionary, is a more or less official and diplomatic work, qualifies it as a "shameful treaty."

That is a judgment which must be fundamentally revised. When one studies the matter closely, one observes that, contrary to the contention of the officials of the Larousse dictionary, the whole shame was on this occasion with the victorious countries, particularly France and England. The separate Russo-German peace only betrayed those who were traitors to their proclamations and to their public promises.

Jacques Sadoul, in a series of important letters written to Albert Thomas from Moscow in 1918, in the course of the negotiations, has clearly exposed the inside of this impressive business. The theme of the Allies, as published vociferously all through the war, was that they would conclude a peace without annexations and without reprisals—a democratic peace, in fact. With what virtuous ardour all the governmental mouthpieces kept assuring everyone throughout the whole four years of the war, that except for Alsace-Lorraine (for which an exception was clearly claimed from the very beginning) the allied war aims included neither the seizure of territory nor measures of revenge! We all grew tired of hearing, both at the front and behind the lines, these solemn undertakings to conclude a "democratic peace" without any idea of profit—only to be exhorted, at the end, to "fight to a finish."

So that all these protestations were nothing but demagogism and imposture; the Allies always definitely intended to seize and divide up an enormous booty between them, as was shewn some months later. There were even treaties to this effect, signed long before, in existence at the very time that the pundits of so-called civilization were swearing the contrary to the masses with their hands on their hearts. The split that occurred at Brest-Litovsk between Russia and the victorious Powers was caused by the fact that when called upon by the Bolsheviks in November, 1917, to offer Germany a democratic peace and to declare their war aims openly, they refused to do so, and for very good reason. Socialist Russia would not lend itself to the perjury which, by violating the universal yearning for peace and by prolonging the carnage, was, as we can see nowadays, to make new wars loom upon the horizon and to cause the development of Fascism in Germany. This did not prevent the Great Powers, personified, unfortunately, by Lloyd-Georges, Poincarés, Clemenceaus, etc., from adopting the most bitter attitude towards Russia because of her pacific initiative—an attitude which was only modified, at any rate outwardly, when they wanted to trade with the enormous Russian market. The future, which is always patient, will put the actions of these honest shepherds of the people into their right perspective.

It was Trotsky, who had rallied to Bolshevism and was an important member of the Government, who carried out the negotiations on the spot. Lenin directed them from the seat of government, with the help of Stalin. To a telegraphic demand for instructions which Trotsky sent him on a private wire, Lenin replied by the following telegram, dated February the 15th, 1918: "Reply to Trotsky. I must first consult Stalin before replying to his question." A little later, on February the 18th, Lenin telegraphed to Trotsky: "Stalin has just arrived. We will examine the situation together and send you a joint reply as soon as possible. Lenin."

Too little is known of the decisive part played by Stalin at the time of the Treaty of Brest. A large section of the Left of the Party—those who had been most energetic in seizing power—were against the signature of the Treaty; Trotsky was also against it, with his formula of "neither peace nor war" because he believed that the war would not really end except with the world Revolution. Lenin and Stalin alone were for its immediate conclusion. Lenin hesitated to use his personal authority. Stalin decided him to do so. This little conversation of theirs must have weighed heavily on the destinies of the Revolution.

Indeed, at that time, "Lenin never let a day pass without seeing Stalin," writes S. Piestoffski. "That is no doubt why our office at Smolny was next door to Lenin's office. All day long Lenin would either speak to Stalin on the telephone or would come into our office and take him away with him. In this way Stalin spent the greater part of the day with Lenin. I witnessed a very interesting scene one day when I went to see Lenin. A large-scale map of Russia was hanging on the wall. Before it were two chairs on which Lenin and Stalin stood and followed a line to the north with their fingers."

And at night, when Smolny became a little quieter, Stalin would spend hours at a time telephoning on private lines.

Chapter Three

THE MAILED FIST

THERE was another problem to be faced by the new Government, one of the most appalling urgency, namely that of the Civil War, with all her enemies in arms—some of them powerfully equipped by the Great Powers of Europe—encircling Russia, pressing on her frontiers and having, indeed, crossed them at numerous points.

"There were times, especially in October, 1919, at which the new Republic seemed to be on the point of succumbing. But neither the White Armies, nor Poland's entry into the war, nor the peasant risings, nor famine could overcome its indomitable will-power, and, galvanized by Lenin, its ragged battalions triumphed over fourteen nations." These words appeared in a report by Monsieur Mallet, a reactionary journalist who had the capitalist cause at heart and was, in every respect, very much biased.

At this point I want to reveal the personal part played by Stalin during this period.

Wherever on the Civil War front the danger was greatest, there Stalin was sent.

"Between 1918 and 1920, Stalin was the only man whom the Central Committee kept sending from one front to another, to the point at which the Revolution was in the greatest peril." (Kalinin.)

"Wherever the Red Army faltered, whenever the counter-revolutionary forces were piling success on success, when at any moment the excitement and confusion and discouragement might turn into panic, at that point Stalin would arrive. He would not sleep a wink, but would take complete charge and would organize, smash and drive until the turning-point was reached and the situation was in hand." (Kaganovitch.)

So that, in his own words: "I was turned into a specialist for cleaning out the Augean stables of the War Department." *

This is one of the most astonishing periods of Stalin's career, and one of which the least is known. The way in which he behaved, and the success which he obtained on the battle-fronts during two years, would have been sufficient to make a professional soldier famous and a popular hero.

Here are a few glimpses which Vorochiloff and Kaganovitch give us into the "military work" during this turbulent time of the man whom Kaganovitch calls: "One of the most famous organizers of the victories of the Civil War."

In the course of two years, Stalin found himself on the Tsaritzin front with Vorochiloff and Minin, on the Third Corps front at Perm with Djerjinsky, on the Petrograd front (against Yudenitch's first advance), on the western front at Smolensk (the Polish counter-offensive), on the southern front (against Denikin), again on the Polish front in the west, in the region of Jitomir, and again on the southern front (against Wrangel).

It is impossible to imagine a more terrible situation than the one in which the October Revolutionaries found themselves in 1918, in a country which was nothing but a battlefield littered with ruins and corpses, and on which

* An allusion to the disorders in the services directed by Trotsky.

Above—ENOUKIDZE, VOROCHILOV, KAGANOVICH, KUIBISHEV
Below—ORDJONIKIDZE, STALIN, MOLOTOV, ...

fighting still continued for one supreme war aim: the political régime.

At Moscow, the Revolutionary-Socialist rising was brewing. To the west, Muravieff was abandoning the cause. In the Ural district the Czech counter-Revolution was developing and consolidating. To the extreme south, the English were advancing on Baku. "Everything was blazing in a circle of fire." Stalin arrived at Tsaritzin. A continuous stream of telegrams passed between Lenin and him. Stalin had not come to Tsaritzin as an army inspector, but in order to organize the food supply through Southern Russia. The situation at Tsaritzin was vitally important. The revolt of the Don region and the loss of Tsaritzin also meant the loss—the disastrous loss—of the whole wheat area of Northern Caucasia.

From the moment of his arrival: "I am bullying and swearing at all those who need it. Rest assured, Comrade Lenin, that no one is being spared, neither myself nor anyone else—and that whatever happens we will send you wheat. If our military specialists (who are blockheads) had not been idle or asleep, our line would never have been pierced, and if we manage to re-establish it, that will not be thanks to them but in spite of them."

For Stalin found the whole region in a state of "incredible disorder." The Soviet organizations—Syndicalist and Communist—and also the military organizations had become completely dislocated and were all at sixes and sevens. On all sides they were confronted by the tremendous spread of the Cossack counter-Revolution which had received powerful reinforcements from the German Army of Occupation in the Ukraine. The White troops had seized, one by one, the districts around Tsaritzin, putting a complete stop to the "corn collection" awaited by

Moscow and Petrograd and, moreover, seriously threatening Tsaritzin itself.

At the first superficial glance, Stalin realized that he must take over the military command, which was weak and wavering. On July 11th he telegraphed to Lenin: "Matters are complicated by the fact that the Headquarters Staff of Northern Caucasia is absolutely incapable of fighting the counter-Revolution. . . . Considering themselves to be employees of General Headquarters, and to be charged solely with preparing plans of campaign, they hold themselves quite aloof, like onlookers, and take no interest whatever in the operations. . . ."

Stalin was not the sort of man to be content merely with finding things out. Where action was necessary, he acted: "I do not think I am justified in looking on at such indifference when Kalinin's front (in Northern Caucasia) has its supplies cut off and when the whole of Northern Russia is cut off from its wheat-fields. I will rectify this weakness and many other local weaknesses too. I am taking and will take the proper measures, even to the extent of removing the regimental and staff officers who are ruining the cause—in spite of any formal difficulties which I will over-ride if necessary. For this, naturally, I take full responsibility on myself with the superior authorities."

Moscow replied telling him to set the whole Red organization on its feet: "Re-establish order, form the detachments of troops into a regular Army, appoint a proper command, get rid of all insubordinates." This order came from the Revolutionary War Council, mentioning that "this telegram is sent with Lenin's approval."

When this summary order, these two lines of writing in which was compressed a colossal task, arrived at Tsaritzin, the situation had grown much worse. The remains of the Red Army of the Ukraine were pouring in, helter-skelter, retiring before the advance of the German Army over the Don steppes.

It seemed impossible that order could be established in such a situation. But the indomitable will-power of one man set itself to do so. Out of the earth itself he made a Revolutionary War Council rise which there and then set to work to reorganize the regular Army. Army Corps were swiftly created and divided up into divisions, brigades, regiments. All counter-revolutionary elements were removed from the staff, from the supply system and from the military formations behind the line—as well as from all the Soviet and Communist organizations there. There were plenty of staunch Bolsheviks of the old kind to give them a firm foundation and set them on their feet. And that is what happened. Everything was put into order again, and at the very edge of the counter-revolutionary canker of the Don there arose a strong and clear-headed Red Staff, presenting an unbroken front to the brigands on both sides of the line.

But that was not all. The whole town was contaminated with White elements. Revolutionary-Socialists, Terrorists and ultra-Monarchists, all met together there. (This constant, inevitable collaboration of so-called pure Revolutionaries with the worst enemies of the Revolution—they attacked it together as fiercely as they could—calls for no comment.)

Tsaritzin served as a shelter for masses of middle-class refugees, who flaunted themselves in the company of White officers, who scarcely troubled to conceal their identity, who monopolized the side-walks and filled the streets and the public gardens round the orchestras. Tsaritzin was a centre of open conspiracy.

But it suddenly ceased to be so. The local Revolutionary War Council, directed by Stalin, created a special *Cheka* charged with examining all these people closely. And at the moment when Civil War was redoubling its fury on all sides, and on all sides the alien enemies of the Revolution were endeavouring to stifle it by every means they could devise, not a day passed without the most dangerous plots being discovered.

A certain Nossovitch—who, from being Chief of the Military Direction of operations, went over to Krasnoff's Army, gives a full account of this situation in a White newspaper entitled *The Surge of the Don* (in the issue for February the 3rd, 1919). He is obliged to render justice to Stalin who, even though his mission of chief provisioner was gravely compromised by the succession of events in the neighbourhood, "was not the sort of man to abandon anything he had begun," and he shows him taking the whole military and civil administration into his own hands at the same time, and thwarting one by one all the attempts and all the machinations of the avowed enemies of the Revolution.

For instance: "At that time," says Nossovitch, "the local counter-revolutionary organization was greatly reinforced and, with money that had come from Moscow, was preparing for active intervention, with the object of helping the Don Cossacks to free Tsaritzin. . . . 'Unfortunately,' the heads of this organization, to wit a certain engineer named Alexieff and his two sons, had very little knowledge of the exact situation, and thanks to a false step the organization was discovered. Alexieff and his two sons, together with a considerable number of officers, were shot. . . ."

Lenin greatly feared an attack from the Revolutionary-

Socialists of the Left at Tsaritzin and telegraphed his fears to Stalin who replied: "So far as the Hysterics are concerned you may rest at ease; we are being firm. With enemies, we will behave as enemies."

These stern measures, which were necessary when dealing with an adversary who delivered armed attacks upon them in the midst of a foreign campaign, and whose only tactics consisted of murder, had a salutary effect on the morale of Red regiments at the front. The military and political leaders and the rank and file of the Army began to feel that they were being led by a strong man with one great, definite ideal, a man who was ruthless towards those who wanted to put the former slaves back into their old state, to try to entrap this newly formed people which had broken its chains and, in the shadow of their white flags and even in that of their red flags, to stab these freed liberators to death.

Stalin took the responsibility, but he wanted the authority too, as all those who use it to good purpose want it. The renegade Nossovitch again bears witness to another interesting event: "When Trotsky, alarmed at the destruction of the existing military commands which had been so painstakingly created, sent a telegram saying that it was necessary for the Headquarters Staff and the Commissars to be re-established in their offices and given an opportunity of doing their work, Stalin took the telegram and, with a firm hand, scrawled upon it the words: 'No attention to be paid to this.'" Thus no attention was paid to the telegram and the whole of the Artillery command and a part of the Headquarters Staff remained where they had been put, on a ship at Tsaritzin.

Moreover, in order to ensure that his orders were carried out, and to consolidate the Bolshevik régime, Stalin personally visited the whole front (a front which measured nearly four hundred miles). This man, who had never served in the army, possessed such a comprehensive sense of organization that he was able to understand and to solve all the most intricate and difficult technical problems (especially as the situation became more critical daily and rapidly complicated all these problems still further).

"I remember, as though it had happened to-day," said Kaganovitch, "that at the beginning of 1918 Krasnoff's Cossack troops attacked Tsaritzin, trying by an encircling movement to throw the Red troops back on the Volga. For several days these Red troops, which were under the orders of a Communist Division largely formed of Donetz workers, repelled the attack of the perfectly organized Cossacks with incredible vigour. Those were indeed terrible days. You should have seen Stalin at that time. Calm and, as always, wrapped in his thoughts, literally never sleeping at all, he divided his tireless labours between the firing-line and Army Headquarters. The situation at the front was almost desperate. Krasnoff's Armies, led by Fitz Khalauroff, Mamontoff and others, were pressing our exhausted troops hard and causing us immense losses. The enemy front, horseshoe-shaped, with its flanks resting on the Volga, was daily closing in more and more. There was no way out for us. But Stalin did not trouble about this. He had one idea only: they must win. This indomitable will of Stalin's transmitted itself to his immediate assistants and, in spite of being in a situation from which there was practically no escape, no one for a moment had any doubts about victory.

"And we triumphed. The routed enemy army was thrown well to the other side of the Don."

The same gloomy situation and the same epic achievements took place on the eastern front at Perm.

At the end of 1918 this front found itself terribly threatened, and almost lost.

The Third Army had fallen back and had been compelled to surrender Perm. Harassed and pressed by the enemy, who were advancing in a half-circle, this Third Army was, by the end of November, completely demoralized. The story of the previous six months, filled with perpetual fighting, was a heart-breaking one; with no reserves, in utter ignorance of what was happening in the back areas, with abominable rations (the 29th Division went for five days without receiving a single mouthful of bread), thirty-five degrees of frost,* the roads absolutely impassable, an excessively long front—more than 250 miles of it—and a backboneless Staff, "the Third Army was in no condition to resist enemy attacks."

In addition to this, the officers, ex-servants of the Tsar, went in for wholesale betrayal and whole regiments, disgusted by a command of incompetent carousers, surrendered to the enemy.

A rout followed: a retreat of nearly two hundred miles in twenty days, and a loss of 18,000 men, dozens of guns and hundreds of machine-guns. The enemy was drawing closer and was threatening Viatka and the whole of the eastern front.

Lenin telegraphed to the Revolutionary War Council of the Republic as follows: "We have received from the neighbourhood of Perm a series of reports from the Party informing us of the drunkenness and catastrophic condi-

* Centigrade. This is equivalent to 31° below zero Fahrenheit. (Translator.)

tion of the Third Army. I am thinking of sending Stalin there."

The Central Committee sent Stalin and Djerjinsky. Stalin temporarily shelved the main object of the mission, which was to "enquire into the loss of Perm," and substituted for it the question of the steps to be taken to restore the situation. This situation was much more serious than anyone had thought, as he explained to the President of the Council for National Defence (Lenin) in a telegram in which he asked, in order to meet the peril, for immediate reinforcements. A week later he enumerated the various causes for the surrender of Perm and, with Djerjinsky, proposed a series of measures for raising the fighting efficiency of the Third Army and for providing for the future. With his extraordinary rapidity of decision he applied these numerous measures of military and political organization—and in the same month (January 1919), the enemy advance was checked, the eastern front took the offensive, and its right wing seized Uralsk.

And a drama of the same sort occurred during the spring of 1919 in the Seventh Army, before Yudenitch's White Army, to whom Kolchak had issued orders "to seize Petrograd," and to draw into his sector the Revolutionary troops of the eastern front.

Yudenitch, backed by Esthonian and Finnish White Guards and supported by the British Fleet, suddenly took up the offensive and actually seriously threatened Petrograd, as will be remembered.

Moreover, they had confederates in the city itself; a plot was discovered at Petrograd. The threads of this plot were held by the military technicians who served on the

Staff of the western front in the Seventh Army and at the naval base of Kronstadt.

Whilst Yudenitch was advancing on Petrograd, Bulak-Bulakhovitch was meeting with a series of successes in the direction of Pskoff. Betrayals and desertions became more and more frequent. The garrisons of the Krasnaya Gorka and the Seraya Loshad forts openly sympathized with the enemies of the Soviets. The distance between the White Armies and Petrograd was lessening and the Reds were giving way. Abroad, the workers watched the news closely and held despairing public meetings, with rage and agony in their hearts. (You remember them, you comrades in France!)

The Central Committee sent Stalin off and in three weeks he re-established the victorious revolutionary resistance. At the end of twenty days all signs of hesitation and confusion had disappeared from the Army and from the Staff. The workers and Communists in Petrograd were mobilized and the desertion to the enemy ceased. The enemies and traitors were seized and destroyed.

And Stalin even directed operations which were purely military. He telegraphed to Lenin: "Immediately after Krasnaya Gorka, Seraya Loshad has been dealt with. . . . All the forts and citadels are being rapidly restored to order. Naval specialists assure me that the capture of Krasnaya Gorka has upset the whole theory of naval science. I can only deplore what they call science. The swift capture of Gorka is explained by violent intervention on my part and by that of civilians in general in the operations—intervention going so far as cancelling orders issued on land and at sea and insisting upon our own orders being carried out in their stead. I feel it my duty to inform you that in future I shall continue to act thus, in spite of my respect for science."

And the whole conclusion of this lightning campaign is contained in another telegram despatched, six days later, to the same person:

"The metamorphosis of our troops has begun. During the entire week there has not been a single case of either individual or collective desertion. Deserters have returned in thousands. The passing over of enemy troops into our camps has become much more frequent. During one week four hundred men joined our ranks, nearly all with their arms. Yesterday we launched our offensive. We have not yet received the promised reinforcements, and yet we have managed to advance. It was impossible for us to remain on our old line, as it was too close to Petrograd. At the moment our offensive has been successful and the enemy is in flight. To-day we are occupying the line Kernovo, Voronino, Slepivo, Kaskovo. We have captured prisoners, guns, machine-guns and ammunition. The enemy ships have not shown themselves. They are obviously afraid of Krasnaya Gorka, which is now completely in our hands."

And now the southern front.

"Everyone," writes Manuilsky, "remembers autumn 1919. It was the deciding, critical moment of the whole Civil War."

Manuilsky traces the essential features of the situation, the main one of which was Denikin's penetration of the entire southern line. Provisioned by the Allies, supported and helped by the British and French General Staffs, Denikin's White Army advanced upon Orel. The whole vast southern front was falling back in slow waves. Behind the line the situation was no less disastrous. Difficulties of supply grew momentarily greater and greater, and presented almost insoluble problems. Industry, three-quarters of which was destroyed, lacked raw materials, fuel and manpower, and was coming to a standstill. Throughout the whole country and even at Moscow, the activities of the counter-revolutionaries were increasing. Danger threatened Tula as much as Moscow.

What was to be done in this headlong rush towards disaster? The Central Committee sent Stalin to the southern front as a member of the Revolutionary War Council.

"To-day," writes Manuilsky, "there is no longer any need to conceal the fact that Stalin, before leaving, insisted on the Central Committee complying with three conditions. First, Trotsky was not to meddle with the southern front and was to remain where he was. Secondly, a number of Army leaders whom Stalin considered to be incapable of restoring the situation in the Army were to be recalled immediately. And thirdly, other leaders, chosen by Stalin and capable of carrying out this task, should immediately be sent to the southern front. These conditions were accepted in their entirety."

But the colossal war machine consisting of the southern front extended from the Volga as far west as the Polish-Ukrainian frontier, and massed hundreds of thousands of soldiers on the borders of the nation. In order to be able to handle and to move an apparatus of this kind, it was essential to have a definite plan of operations and it was necessary that the "tasks to be carried out at the front should be clearly defined." Only then would it become possible, by proposing a definite objective to the troops, to re-organize the forces, to steady them and to distribute them intelligently to the right tactical sectors and at the right moment.

Stalin discovered nothing but confusion and deadlock

at the front. An atmosphere of mingled storm and despair. The Red Army of the Republic was beaten along the main line of defence: Kursk-Orel-Tula. The eastern flank was uselessly marking time.

What was to be done? There was a plan of operations upon which the Superior War Committee had decided in the previous September. This plan consisted of launching the main attack by the left wing, from Tsaritzin to Novorossisk across the Don steppes.

The first thing that struck Stalin was that this plan had remained unchanged since September. "The attack is to be launched by Korin's group, and its task is to annihilate the enemy on the Don and the Kuban."

Stalin examined this plan carefully and critically—and decided that it was no good. Or, rather, that it was no longer any good. It had been quite good two months before, but the circumstances had altered. Something else must be found. Stalin saw what was wanted and sent Lenin fresh suggestions. Let us read his letter, a historic document which throws a light on the situation in the vast southern sector and, at the same time, on the undaunted clear-sightedness of the man who wrote it:

Two months ago, the Higher Committee agreed in principle that the main attack should be directed from west to east through the Donetz basin. This operation was not carried out because of the situation created by the retreat of the troops from the south during the summer, that is to say because of the automatic re-distribution of the troops on the south-eastern front which caused a considerable loss of time of which Denikin took advantage. But now the situation, and with it the re-distribution of the forces, is completely altered. The Eighth Army (one

EGOROV AND STALIN

of the principal forces of the old southern front) has advanced and has the Donetz basin before it. The Budienny Cavalry Army (another important force) has also advanced. A new force has also been added, namely the Lettish Division which, in a month's time, when it has been re-organized, will again threaten Denikin. . . . What is there to compel the Higher Committee to keep to the old plan? It can obviously only be the spirit of obstinacy, so short-sighted and so dangerous for the Republic, which is fostered in the Higher Committee by the "Ace of Strategists." *

Some time ago the Higher Committee gave Korin directions to advance on Novorossisk across the Don steppes, by a route which might perhaps be practicable for our airmen, but over which it would be impossible to take our infantry and our artillery. It is childishly easy to show that this senseless advance in the midst of hostile country, on an impossible line, would in all probability be utterly disastrous. It is easy to show that such an advance upon Cossack villages could only have the effect, as it did not so very long ago, of grouping the Cossacks round Denikin for the defence of their villages against us, and of enabling Denikin to pose as the saviour of the Don; that is to say, it could only succeed in strengthening Denikin's hand. For this reason the old plan must be changed at once, without a moment's delay, and must be replaced by that of a central attack on Rostoff through Kharkoff and the Donetz basin. So that, in the first place we would not find ourselves in the midst of hostile country but, on the contrary, in friendly surroundings, which would facilitate our advance. Secondly, we would occupy an important railway line (that of Donetz) and the principal line of commu-

* An allusion to Trotsky.

nication of Denikin's Army, the Voroneje-Rostoff line. Thirdly, we would split Denikin's Army into two portions of which one, the "Volunteers," can be dealt with by Makhno, whilst we would be threatening the rear of the Cossack Army. Fourthly, we might succeed in estranging the Cossacks from Denikin, for, if our advance were successful, Denikin would try to make the Cossacks fall back to the west, which the majority of them would refuse to do. And fifthly, we would obtain coal, whereas Denikin would not be able to get any. No time must be lost in adopting this plan of campaign. . . . To sum up: the old plan, which, owing to recent events, is now out of date, must in no case be put into operation, as it would endanger the Republic and would certainly improve Denikin's position. A new plan must be substituted for it. Not only are conditions and circumstances ripe for this, but they urgently call for such a change. . . . Otherwise, my work at the southern front becomes meaningless, criminal and useless, which gives me the right, or, rather, compels me to go no matter where, even to the devil, but not to remain here. Yours, Stalin.

The Central Committee did not hesitate to adopt Stalin's plan. Lenin with his own hand wrote to the General Staff of the southern front giving them their change of orders. The main attack was launched towards Kharkoff, in the Donetz-Rostoff basin. One knows what happened. Denikin's armies were pushed into the Black Sea. The Ukraine and Northern Caucasia were delivered from the White Guards, and the Revolution won the Civil War.

Stalin's successes seem, because of their rapidity and completeness, to be little short of magical. What is rare, indeed quite exceptional, is to find such a perfect mixture of all the elements which go to make up successful achievement—both in theory and in practice—in the same man. To be really successful one must have the clear-sightedness to see and the courage to declare that the longest way round is often the shortest way home, and one must also have the power to direct the march of events accordingly.

Another result of Stalin's transfer to the southern front was the creation of the Cavalry Army, which played so important a part in finally mopping up the Whites. By his pertinacity he succeeded in getting ideas adopted in this respect which were not shared by the whole of the Revolutionary Military Committee, starting with the southern front. To him also is due a certain modification in military tactics, namely the part played by shock troops. Once the main point of attack was decided upon, the best troops were immediately concentrated upon it, with a view to gaining a rapid initial success. At the same time as he was developing his strategy of direct action, Stalin did not lose sight of military organization and of the necessity of subordinating everything to the harmony of military organization as a whole. In 1919 he had written, in agreement with Djerjinsky: "An Army cannot act as an independent, self-sufficient and completely autonomous entity; in its actions it depends entirely upon the Armies on its flanks, and above all upon the Revolutionary Military Committee of the Republic. The most aggressive Army, under no matter what conditions, may be defeated as a result of bad leadership from the centre and by absence of contact with the neighbouring Armies. On each front, a strict system of centralization of the activities of the various Armies must be established as regards carrying out definite and carefully considered strategic orders. Capriciousness or lack of proper care in the issuing of orders, without considering their effect carefully and from every angle, manifested by their being suddenly changed or by their vagueness (as is sometimes the case with the Revolutionary Council of the Republic) makes it impossible to command armies successfully."

We must not forget, in this chapter about the war, that, at the Eighth Congress of the Party, Stalin defended the idea of "another army," of a regular Army formed in a spirit of discipline and enrolled by political sections.

Meanwhile the Civil War flared up again owing to the activities of Wrangel, lavished with money, soldiers and munitions by France and England, who insisted at all costs on fulfilling their mission of aiding and abetting the White Russians in their attempt to restore the régime of the knout and of slavery.

Wrangel announced far and wide that he was about to embark upon a Polish campaign, and he left the Crimea and seriously threatened the only recently freed Donetz basin and through it the whole of the South.

The first thought of the Central Committee was once more to have recourse to Stalin and on August 3rd, 1920, it passed the following resolution:

"In view of Wrangel's success and the alarm over the Kuban, the tremendous and altogether exceptional importance of the Wrangel front must be recognized and it must be considered as an independent front. Stalin must be charged with forming the Revolutionary Military Council; all available forces must be concentrated on that front; Egoroff or Frunze must be put in command at the front, as arranged by the Higher Council in consultation with Stalin." Stalin was told by Lenin: "The Political Bureau has divided up the various fronts so that you may be able to devote yourself exclusively to that of Wrangel."

Stalin organized the new front. He then had to leave the work temporarily owing to illness, but was back when the Polish campaign began, as a member of the Revolutionary Military Committee of the south-west front. The rout of the Polish army, the liberation of Kieff and of the Ukraine, and the deep thrust into Galicia were, in large measure, the result of his direction of affairs. It was he who conceived the idea of the famous raid of the First Cavalry Army.

The Red troops were enabled to launch a general offensive after the collapse of the Polish front, the almost complete annihilation of the Third Polish Army below Kieff, the Berdicheff and Jitomir attacks, and the move of the First Cavalry Army upon Kovno. But the defeat of the Red troops near Warsaw by the European Polish forces checked the advance of the Cavalry, which was preparing to attack Lvoff, and had arrived within eleven miles of it.

Stalin was twice decorated with the Order of the Red Flag and elected a member of the War Council of the Republic (on which he sat from 1920 till 1923), following on the masterly way in which he had invariably managed to restore the situation in all the most keenly contested and stormy sections of the Civil War front.

We say "Civil War," but the term is inaccurate. The Russian Revolution was counter-attacked not only by the Whites, but also by the Great Powers. The Red Army had before it the rank and file and the Staffs of the Tsarist, French and English Armies, and also those of the Japanese, American, Rumanian, Greek—and others.

The great Imperial Powers were not content with giving

the most open assistance, in money, in men and in staff officers to the chiefs of the White hordes (officially recognized, one after the other, by the French Government). But, at that period when the Great War was over, when peace had been made and, contrary to every kind of right of nations, the French and English troops, in succession to the German troops, coming both by land and by sea, occupied, trampled upon and plundered Russia, massacred its inhabitants, shot its leaders and scrupulously destroyed its industrial regions. The German Army had seized the Baltic Provinces and Finland from Russia. The Allies robbed her of Poland and, after adding to it, made an independent State of it, not from any love of Poland, but so as to create a buffer State between Russia and the rest of Europe; and they also stole Bessarabia from her to pay Rumania, in utter disregard of the wishes of the Bessarabians. This was done—let us repeat—at a time when neither England nor France were in any way in a state of war with Russia. This military invasion was a general counter-revolutionary enterprise. It was not undertaken merely as revenge for Russia having concluded a separate peace. (Let us not forget that the first signatories of the Treaty of Brest-Litovsk were not the Bolsheviks, but the Ukrainian Nationalists who were protected by both the Germans and the Allies, and it is unnecessary to lay stress once more upon the fact that the position taken up by Soviet Russia at Brest was that of equity and of the rights of humanity as against the treacherous policy of imperialist greed, the fatal results of which are apparent to-day.) "Free" England and "revolutionary" France could not stomach an anti-capitalist revolution, and considered that they had to do their utmost, by no matter what means,

THE MAILED FIST

to annihilate this nightmare of popular government in Europe.*

The Allied intervention which tried to confiscate from Russia the countries to whom the October Revolution had given a new social form was essentially counter-revolutionary: the proof of this is glaringly obvious from the mere fact that the German troops of the Baltikum (under von der Goltz and Rosenberg) fought in collaboration with the Allies.

Then the whole of the rest of Russia was freed from the counter-Revolution.

The qualities which Stalin displayed in these moving circumstances were no revelation to those who knew him. He merely applied in a new sphere of activity his strength and personal resources, namely lightning-like promptness and sureness of action, thorough grasp of the outstanding points of any particular situation, a thorough understanding of the real causes and inevitable consequences of any particular set of circumstances and of the proper place occupied by such circumstances in the general scheme of things, a horror of disorder and confusion, and dogged perseverance in preparing, creating and co-ordinating all the conditions necessary for the success of a project once it had been thoroughly examined and it had been decided

* Monsieur René Pinon, a Conservative author, constitutes himself the mouthpiece of the French Government with reference to the monstrous scandal of the despatch of a French naval squadron with a division of infantry to the Black Sea in 1919, a gross interference by armed force, without any declaration of war, in the affairs of a foreign people. Monsieur Pinon assures us that "this intervention did not, properly speaking, constitute an interference with the internal affairs of a foreign State," and that it must be regarded from another point of view—namely "that of delivering a country and at the same time the whole world from a danger to social and general order. . . ." It would be difficult to conceive a more blatant example of reactionary Jesuitism.

to embark upon it. All this is true Marxism, transferred to the field of battle.

This leader, who had fathomed the secrets of success and had brought them to such a pitch of perfection, was very severe, even ruthless, towards incompetence, and inexorable in dealing with treachery or sabotage. But a whole series of cases may be quoted in which he warmly intervened in favour of men who seemed to him to have been accused without sufficient proof, for instance Parkhomenko, who was condemned to death and whom he set free.

In those periods in which one sees the fate of nations tossed hither and thither, in which each man stakes his all on one throw, in which responsibility, whether one seeks it or not, fastens itself on to one, the question naturally arises of the value of human life and of the extent to which it may be destroyed for the good of a cause.

The question has to be put in the light of Socialism. If one found oneself faced with a capitalist régime, or with imperialist authority, there would be no reason to put it. It is only too evident that the principle of imperialist Capitalism is based on contempt for human life, on enforced trade, on commerce militarized by customs tariffs, on the system of supremacy and of war (either individual or collective), raised into an institution. The colonizing system is a penitentiary system giving large returns. Colonizing countries rob weaker nations of their freedom, confiscate their land, and turn the native into either an enemy or a domestic animal; he is overtaxed, decimated and condemned to hard labour; if he tries to regain his liberty he is executed. Look at the Belgian Congo, Morocco, French West Africa, India, Indo-China, Java. And, moreover, they foment wars which make appreciable gaps in the ranks of humanity, for the benefit of a national-international group represented by a few individuals.

But the socialist system is the one which, in contradistinction to the capitalist system, serves the interest of humanity. By the logical and fair organization of human beings, it aims at improving the lot of mankind as far as possible. One might say that it is the "humane" system in its highest degree.

So the question of respect for human life arises especially with the Bolsheviks—the effective socialists of our age—in the strictest and most serious way, and it is a question which they are constantly considering.

It is precisely out of respect for human life that they say that they must make it impossible for certain types of men to do harm (to "punish" is not the right word here; it would be necessary for God to exist and that he should specially intervene, for one to have the right to evoke the supernatural idea of expiation).

Actually, and obviously, it is one's duty to strike down a fellow-creature to save a thousand, to save a hundred thousand, to save the future, and to build a better world in which man will no longer be the slave or the victim of man.

Victor Hugo, in his great epic novel, *Les Misérables*, expresses himself on the subject of the French Revolution with his customary grandiloquence, but also with a breadth of vision which is very much to the point, as follows: "From its cruellest blows there resulted a caress for the human race." Although this lyrical declaration has become debatable insofar as concerns the great curtailed Revolution of 1789, which made the middle classes masters of the nineteenth century, it is not debatable for the complete

Revolution which the men of October carried out with such terrible sincerity.

One says, complacently: "All revolutions are bloody, so I do not want any revolution, because I am too sensitive." Those preservers of the existing social order who express themselves thus are, unless they are merely playing a part, pitiably short-sighted. The countries which are not Soviet ones are actually in the very midst of a régime of blood. We hear, on all sides, of outrages and massacres. One has only to look around one to see them. But most people cannot see so far. They are incapable of noticing the sufferings of others. And, above all, they do not consider revolution from the point of view of what it brings to man, but from that of the discomforts and worries which it brings to themselves.

Menjinski, the head of the O.G.P.U., who died recently, once explained to me at length how absurd it was in principle to tax the political Party which directs the Soviet Union with cruelty or indifference to human life, since its ultimate aim is to bring everyone in the world together and to work for universal peace. And, in fact, he pointed out to me that the revolutionary police, brothers of the great mass of workers, are constantly on the look out for any opportunity for "setting right" or "curing" not only common law prisoners (on this side of prison organization the Bolsheviks have carried patience and indulgence to an almost paradoxical point), but also political prisoners. Communists start from the double principle that transgressors of the common law are people who do not understand their own interests and are ruining their own lives, and that the best thing to do is to impress this upon them, and that the enemies of the proletarian Revolution, the forerunner of universal Revolution, are equally (if they

THE MAILED FIST

are sincere) people who are mistaken, and that the best thing is to prove it to them. Hence the constant effort to turn every kind of prison into a place of education.

The problem of repression, therefore, is reduced to a question of the necessary minimum, having due regard to general progress. It is just as wrong to fall short of this minimum as to go beyond it. The man who spares people who are working against the cause of humanity is a malefactor. The duty of true kindness is to think of the future.

If the Russian Revolution had, to the intense satisfaction of a few sanctimonious idealists, adopted the system of automatic forgiveness and of not defending itself with the same weapons with which it was attacked, it would not have survived for long. It would have been stabbed in the back by France, England and Poland, who would immediately have brought the Tsar and the Whites back to Petrograd, as they tried to do by every other means in their power. The reason the work of the Revolution subsists and is already brightening the future of humanity is because it fought without faltering and without mercy that appalling network of treachery, and all the plots—all stabs in the back—woven by White Guards, imperialist spies, diplomats and detectives, wreckers, Revolutionary-Socialists, Anarchists and Nationalist Mensheviks, the degenerate Oppositionists, all more or less subsidized from abroad—all that rabble furiously attacking the country which had given the subversive example of rising in order to make the liberty of the worker and human dignity secure.

Stalin, replying some time ago (towards the end of 1931) in an interview relating to "the severe and implacable attitude of the Soviet Government in its struggle against its enemies," said as follows:

"When the Bolsheviks came into power, they began by

showing leniency towards their enemies. The Mensheviks continued to exist lawfully and to bring out their newspaper. So did the Revolutionary-Socialists. Even the Cadets (Constitutional-Democrats) continued the publication of their newspaper. When General Krasnoff organized his counter-revolutionary march on Petrograd and fell into our hands we might, according to the rules of war, at least have kept him prisoner. More than that, we ought to have shot him. But we freed him on parole. What was the result of this? We soon found that this leniency only undermined the stability of the power of the Soviets, and that we had made a mistake in giving proof of our forbearance towards the enemies of the working classes. If we had continued to be so forbearing we should have committed a crime against the working classes and we should have betrayed their interests. This soon became an obvious fact. We quickly discovered that the more indulgent we showed ourselves towards our enemies the stronger was the resistance they put up against us. In a short time the Revolutionary-Socialists, Gotz and others, and the Mensheviks of the Right, organized the rising of the pupils of the Military School at Petrograd, which resulted in the death of a great number of our Revolutionary sailors. The same Krasnoff, whom we had freed on parole, organized the White Cossacks. He joined Mamontoff and for two years carried on an armed struggle against the power of the Soviets. . . . It is easy to see that we had made a mistake in being too gentle."

And I will add to this what Stalin said to me personally, seven years ago, with regard to the famous "Red Terror." He was speaking of the death penalty. "We are naturally all in favour of the suppression of the death penalty. Indeed we believe that there is no need for us to retain it in the interior administration of the Soviet Union. We would have abolished the death penalty long ago had it not been for the outer world, the great Imperialist Powers, which have compelled us to retain it in order to perserve our existence."

By these words Stalin referred to the accumulation of the most treacherous secret attacks to which the U.S.S.R. had been subjected by the "great foreign policy" of the middle-class Empire who have always and everywhere identified themselves as closely as possible with the worst enemies of the Revolution.*

* To-day—at the end of 1934—French diplomacy is opening its arms wide to Russia, and sympathy with the Soviets is the fashion with us, for reasons of European equilibrium. These superficial gestures of higher capitalist politics should deceive no one. . . . Nevertheless, this state of affairs enables a far greater amount of truth to be inculcated into the minds of the French public concerning the Russian Revolution and its consequences, and that is, at any rate, a permanent result to have achieved.

Chapter Four

THE NATIONAL CONSTELLATION

AFTER the "October days" Stalin was elected People's Commissar for Nationalities, the functions of which office he was to fulfil until 1923.

The problem of nationalities, or "Homogeneousness in heterogeneousness," was one of the greatest problems that had to be faced.

About ten years ago, in very solemn circumstances, Stalin observed that although the main basis of the Soviet Republic was the alliance of the workers and the peasants, the subsidiary basis of the Republic was the alliance of all the different nationalities existing in Russia: Russians, Ukrainians, Bashkirs, White Russians, Georgians, Azerbaijanians, Armenians, Daghestans, Tartars, Kirghiz, Usbeks, Tajiks, Turkomans.

After the abolition of the old Russian régimes—the tsarist and the middle-class régimes, which had lasted for three centuries and six months respectively—Stalin seemed to everyone, and especially to those at the head of affairs—Lenin and the Central Committee—to be one of the theorists and workers most qualified to deal with this question of nationalities. And to-day he is looked upon as the man who understands it most thoroughly in the whole Union.

It was a vital question, the question of the framework of the new State, in particular, and of the whole geographic framework of Socialism, in general. It seemed to identify itself with the outline of the Russian map and of that of

THE NATIONAL CONSTELLATION

the whole criss-crossed and crowded map of the world.

We in the West sometimes used the word "Russians" to describe the citizens of the nation which extends from Poland to Alaska over three thousand miles of the Earth's circumference. But this is only, nowadays, a summary, abbreviated and, so to speak, symbolic way of expressing oneself. For Russia is only one of the countries forming the U.S.S.R.; not a province, but a country, a republic. Apart from Russia there are, over the eight million square miles of the Union, a dozen nations and a hundred little countries whose various racial agglomerations are collected under the existing Federation, after having been taken pell-mell into the patrimony of the Russian family installed beneath the painted domes of the Kremlin. Russia, properly speaking, is only the most important of these nations, and it is a Russian town which is the administrative centre of this territory which extends half-way round the world: one must have an administrative centre for purposes of organization. But a Georgian is a Georgian. A Ukrainian is a Ukrainian. They are no more Russians than you or I are.

Under the Tsars these regions and these peoples annexed by violence were kept, also by violence, in the bosom of the nation; and in those days the nation meant—and what a brutal meaning it was—Russia. Russification meant denationalization and painting everything, both structural and mental, in Russian colours; frontiers obliterated by military heels, and native languages shouted down by Russian. As we have seen, incidentally, in the case of Georgia, the business of the central power at St. Petersburg and at Moscow, and of the holy gilt-edged man who, from the supreme palace, shook his clenched fist over "all the Russias," was to bring about a complete change in any foreign populations they colonized. And the result was a series of virulent laws intended to destroy all racial characteristics—even to the very blood of the people.

At the present time these races are under an entirely different régime, resulting logically from socialist principles. And of these principles, which, quite apart from the constitution of the Workers' and Peasants' State, govern a question which is at the very basis of world civilization and place this question ideologically on the international plan by effectively solving it on an enlarged national plan—of these principles Stalin was and still is the recognized interpreter. It is one of the most fascinating of all his "specialties," and the other Soviet specialists in the matter recognize that "they learned what they know about it by reading his articles which appeared during the years preceding the war, in the review *Prosveshtchenie* (*Enlightenment*)."

However, instinctive antagonism towards the Russian, the dislike of dictation by Russia (even on the socialist system) marked, as we have observed, the first phase in the history of revolutionary propaganda in the heart of this queer continent of which the Russian Empire consisted. From the first formation of the Party, national and nationalist currents could be seen creating antagonism among the workers and general distrust began to appear against the Russian proletariat.

As early as 1905 the Polish and Lithuanian workers, who were then Russian subjects, possessed their own Social-Democratic Parties distinct from and quite unconnected with the Russian Social-Democratic Labour Party. It was the same with a great many Jewish workers (e.g., the Jewish Workers' League).

It was only at the Fourth Social-Democratic Congress at Stockholm in 1906 that the Lithuanian and Polish parties and the Jewish League joined up with the Russian Party.

However, the severity of the imperial repressions which followed the 1905 Revolution quite naturally provoked such a revival of the old tendencies toward national and "little-national," as it were, separatism, that the general diffusion of this racial resistance automatically resulted in the various national proletariats again drifting apart from the Russian proletariat.

The fundamental principles of the programme and of the tactics of the Party on the question of nationalities, as formulated in 1913 by Lenin's and Stalin's articles, were presented, in the form of a Resolution, at a conference of the Party in August 1913.

The following were the main points of this Resolution: The right of the nations to do what they wished with themselves, even to the length of separation from tsarist Russia. For those who wished to participate in a federation, a union of national governments, there should be territorial autonomy, abolition of a single official language (Russian), the right to speak their local languages (even where their speakers were in the minority), and the removal of the burden of the national (Russian) yoke in all its forms.

Thus Lenin and Stalin, in drawing up this Marxist formula of nationalities, so deliberately and terribly far-reaching in itself, since it contemplated the possibility of the territorial dislocation of the old Empire, bound up the national question with the revolutionary question, without any subterfuge or obscurity. They opened out—as far as was possible—the possibilities of the preservation of the unity of each racial group in the collection of nations called Russia (racial autonomy being not only a moral factor to be respected in itself, but an important factor in the development of the vitality and initiative of a nation), without losing sight of the unity of this collection of nations, which is in itself a problem of considerable practical interest.

Besides, this unity of the whole was solidly reinforced by that of the unique and homogeneous Socialist network, both political and industrial.

This Leninist and Stalinian doctrine, which closely links theory to practice and organically combines ideas with action (Marxism as an applied science needs inventors, struggling with the reality which is constantly urging them into the future), was strongly opposed to the Austro-Marxist doctrine described as "national cultural autonomy" which had its supporters in Social-Democracy. The Austrian opportunists recommended, substantially, the formation of integral national blocks to which Socialism would have to conform, resulting in a sort of socialist separatism. In the scheme of these idealist surveyors it was Socialism that was to be nationalized, instead of Nationalism being socialized. Socialism was to be cut up into distinct slices over the whole surface of the Empire of Nicholas II. This imaginary improvement was a stupid one and Lenin and Stalin resisted it strongly. It involved dangerously over-stepping the mark and upsetting the balance between desirable autonomy and serviceable unity to admit the principles of national division and respect for frontiers into the new and specific domain of Socialism. It offended against the powerful architectural common sense of Marxism.

In the midst of all this came the first rising of February and the overthrow of the throne. It was Stalin who, in April 1917, reported on the national question at the Conference of the Bolshevik Party. "It was not sufficient to proclaim the formal equality of peoples. That would have had no more practical results than had the Proclamation of Equality by the French Revolution" (Manuilsky). They

THE NATIONAL CONSTELLATION

had to go further and deeper than that. Stalin proposed the adoption of the conception recommended during the tsarist régime. The theory was accepted, not without a struggle; a fairly powerful opposition came from Piatakoff, and a certain number of delegates, against the clause establishing the right of nations to independence, even to the length of separation; the possible consequences of this clause frightened them.*

Particular attention must be paid to and stress laid upon the extent to which the adoption of this doctrine of nationalities, so courageous in its magnanimity and its socialist equity, served the interests of the revolutionary struggle. It allowed the Bolshevik Party to appear to the mass of workers and peasants as it really was, namely the only party that was fighting in a consistent way against the old tsarist national oppression which Kerensky, backed by the Mensheviks, was carrying on.

This dogma of racial liberation, this unfettering, combining with that of social liberation, with the slogans of peace, land and the control of production by labour, and welding together national aspirations and Socialism, had the effect of giving considerable impetus to the preparations for the October Revolution. The attitude taken up by the Bolsheviks with regard to the problems of nationalities brought them the sympathy of everyone, without bringing about the national secessions that some people expected. And there, once again, far-seeing wisdom, in its intrepid thor-

---

* Miliukoff, in a juridic study on the Soviet Union, said that the possibility of all the various States withdrawing from it took away from it its juridic personality, and consequently prevented it from "entering into any international agreement." This has not been apparent. What, on the contrary, has been apparent is the enormous moral influence which this absence of coercion has given the Communist Party over the nations adhering to the U.S.S.R.

oughness, completely triumphed. "If Kolchak and Denikin were beaten," wrote Stalin, "it is because we have had the sympathy of oppressed nations."

After October, after the second sweep of the East European broom and the elimination of democratic Tsarism which middle-class domination constituted, Stalin naturally became the authorized director of the policy of the Party on the question of nationalities.

"The Declaration of the Peoples of Russia" was one of the first legislative Acts of the Soviet Government. Conceived and drawn up by Stalin, it enacted:

The equality and sovereignty of all the peoples of Russia. The right to do what they wished with themselves, even to the extent of separation and the formation of independent States. The suppression of all national (Russian) and religious (Greek Orthodox) restrictions and privileges. The free development of national minorities and of racial groups finding themselves in the territory of the former Russian Empire.

This meant, for the nations accepting the Federation: general union of an exclusively administrative nature, and maximum of national expansion. The countries formed among themselves a society of mutual independence.

Another document of capital importance, which appeared in 1917, signed by Lenin and by Stalin, was addressed to all the Moslem workers within the frontiers of the former European-Asiatic Empire of the Tsars. They comprised the most backward and the most oppressed of all the populations called "Russian." The Soviet Government announced that one of its first tasks would be to raise these populations, scattered in their millions in Turkestan, Siberia, Caucasia and the Volga provinces, up to the level of the others.

Let us consider this majestic solution, so human and so morally just, of the most intricate and most tragic of contemporary problems, with the idea that it could be applied just as easily to the regions of a country as to the countries in a continent and throughout the whole world. A tragic problem, indeed, because the question of the relationships of nations between themselves—the question of peace and of war—has been the bloody, vicious circle of the whole of modern times. National feelings and peace are, in strict principle, antagonistic to one another. The word "nation" means "spreading"; the word "spreading" means "appetite"; and "appetite" means "devouring." There is no case in which this devouring has not been carried out as far as is materially possible. In addition, the policy of individual profit and of the social preservation of Capitalism systematically aggravates and fosters the latent catastrophe. The defective result of historic centralizations is the creation of a block (between two disputed frontiers) of a handful of exploiters and of masses of the exploited, a block directed against the masses of neighbouring countries—whereas common sense dictates an entirely different grouping of human beings by affinity of interests. It is indisputable that throughout the world destructive Capitalism is nowadays incrusted on the outlines of national frontiers and that, against deliverance by means of general agreement, the greatest opposition comes especially from the nationalist spirit which gradually impregnates mankind and crams each differently named fragment of the terrestrial jigsaw with exclusive and explosive ambitions. Again, the essential propaganda of Capitalism (which has become even more violent and more formidable at the present juncture of the social struggle to which economic crises and a certain penetration of ideas have brought the present generations) consists in cultivating and exciting to a frenzy the patriotism of crowds, the aggressive partitioning off of "countries," the strict division of the face of the Earth into compartments, because the very existence of the said Capitalism depends upon this unhealthy state of mind, this unbalanced state of affairs.

But the men of October, who succeeded in bringing about their Revolution in the midst of an extremely diversified juxtaposition of races and of countries *—and one into which, moreover, long traditions of oppression had in many cases inculcated an exaggerated idea of nationalism, these men, for the first time in history, put forward a reasonable and serious solution of this age-old antagonism all over the planet, a logical formula which combined the two irreducible essentials, national individuality and practical federation, and placed patriotism not *against* but *in* Socialism.

The secret of this great formula is the selection and exact classification of the two fundamental aspirations of individual liberty and reciprocal union; that is, to assign to each of them, without confusion or infringement, their field of expansion and their means of expansion, in such manner that they are enabled to develop side by side and not at the expense of each other.

Racial characteristics, collective moral and intellectual individuality, national culture, national spirit; everything which expresses itself in tradition and in folk-lore, in artistic and mental production and also in family sentiment and filial pride; everything which is performed by the maternal language (that flexible machine which actuates and develops the heart and soul of peoples)—all these things, not only preserved but enriched and that, not only from the

* These countries differed from each other much more than those which formed the United States of America, and there were far greater contrasts between these races than there are between the Russian, the Frenchman and the German.

THE NATIONAL CONSTELLATION 97

national point of view, but even (and in this one comes even closer to reality) from the regional point of view. At first glance it might appear that too much importance was attached to racial minorities: but in the twentieth century we have seen Moscow scholars inventing alphabets in order to collect and put upon record thousand-year-old traditions in the heart of little minorities a great distance away, so as to enable them to rouse themselves, to take a fresh lease of life, and to expand in their own way. "It is going too far; it is mere folly," say the small-minded, short-sighted wise-acres. But the greater, far-seeing wisdom does not agree with them.

As to national religious tradition, which is hardly ever of national origin but which, in the majority of cases, is a foreign importation (God comes from some other country, like the Russian Tsar and Imperial officials), it is left where it was. It is simply subjected to the moral system of common law, as it were, to which mistaken ideas are exposed in every society which tries to instruct and enlighten itself.

Collective individualities, thus liberated and given autonomy over the whole of a particular friendly and national sector, are also attached to one another by certain other bonds. What are these bonds? Bonds of an administrative, practical, physical order, assuring to the whole of the combining parties a degree of welfare and of power from which each one of them benefits directly. The same administration for the Army, for finance, and for foreign policy. The gathering into a common fund of the whole of the wealth and the natural resources of the Union. Such a combination guarantees to each one of them great benefits of a purely material and tangible nature. For such an organization permits of all sorts of co-operative achievements; economic schemes, works for the general good, carefully considered leadership, more wealth and a wider distribution of production: hence great increase in general and individual prosperity, in mathematical proportion to the extension of collective activity. Let us add: a strong military power *ipso facto* available to each of the States of the Union, even the weakest.

In other words: the nations become independent in the ways in which it is to their spiritual welfare to be independent, and united in the fields in which it is to their interest to be united. Thus replacing, all along the line, by real advantages, the harsh and at the same time fragile bonds formerly imposed by the violence of the Tsars, who pompously and fallaciously styled themselves: "Assemblers of the Russian Lands."

Between the Muscovite and the Tatar, *between these two foreigners*, there are real differences; these differences are given free rein and are cultivated and developed. A national code is made out of them. *But between the two human beings* many things are the same: common necessities, identical and equal rights to life and to peace. From these a general code is drawn up. That is the angle from which the Soviet creators of the future regard the map of the countries included in their racial frontiers (positive, or ideal frontiers). First of all, there is the indispensable minimum of combination in order that the security and prosperity of collective existence should be assured; afterwards there is the maximum possible of national development.

In the face of a world in which peace between nations is literally an absurd formula, each one of the seventy-five or so contemporary nations having but one aim (which some of them do and some do not admit), namely, to live

THE NATIONAL CONSTELLATION

to the detriment of one another—in face of that, the Soviet combination, making use of the new ideal to perfect the old ideal by disarming it and putting the new ideal in its place, has surpassed all its aspirations. To say nothing of the supplementary enthusiasm with which it instilled the continent so governed (and with which, even, it instilled the world), the result of the gradual harmonization of huge tracts of country and masses of people, tending clearly and purely to that of the whole of the inhabited Earth.

What can one object to in this conception—even if, abandoning for a moment one's own continent, one considers it from afar, from as far away as one can without losing sight of the Earth and of the present age (because, further off than that one reaches the dead and shapeless ideal of ikons, of magic lanterns and of books of gibberish)? There can be no profound or solid objections. It can only offend—among the big countries—those sinister megalomaniacs who say: "My race ought to rule all other races here below," and whose nationalism strives to take an infectious form of expansionism. It can only offend—among the smaller countries—the mad fanatics who intoxicate themselves with the word "autonomy" and prefer to everything, even to any kind of progress, complete isolation, incompatible with the ruthless exigencies of universal community of interest, and which compels them to vegetate laboriously and with ever-decreasing dignity, whilst waiting to slip into the maw of some great imperialist monster.

Because, for all weak or backward nations (representing the majority of the Russian group) the system is amazingly more advantageous and intelligent, from whatever point of view one looks at it, than the system of simple and pure independence. Federated nations work towards a common end and are scientifically at peace with one another. As foreigners, however, instead of co-operation there is competition, which changes, by force of circumstances, into antagonism and enmity—with all the burdens, all the slaveries, all the perils and all the smotherings of conscience which go with it. The Soviet nations are at once small and great. If they were to leave the Union they would become small without any compensating factor.

All this is not, or, rather, is no longer, pure abstract theory, as it was at one time. The recent history of the Soviet countries illustrates the principle of this great collective discrimination between the material and spiritual by specific living examples which are brilliantly illuminating: so many weak countries which, in the bosom of the Union, have passed through the first Stages of progress and well-being with fairy-like rapidity thanks to the enormous help of the central administration, that is of the Federation. So many races who were formerly sworn enemies, hereditary enemies, now living in a state of complete reciprocal peace. To arrive at the point at which "the frontiers between states are no longer of any but administrative importance" (Manuilsky's report to the Fifth World Congress is really to impose the law of Peace). It is an amazing result to those who understand the old internal struggles and who compare them to the present state of logical fraternization. It is impossible to observe all these phenomena without emotion if one only remains objective.

But, to return to the beginning of this extraordinary panorama of transformation scenes, it should here be observed that the new policy of nationalities was of immense help for the pacification of the vast territory freed from the Tsars of the knout and the Tsars of finance. It made possible the "liquidation," as they call it in Russia, of the

THE NATIONAL CONSTELLATION

counter-revolutionary governments in the Ukraine, Turkestan and Transcaucasia, and it must be repeated here that it was only the intervention of the German Armies that enabled the counter-revolution to reinforce itself on the frontiers and brought about the fall of Soviet power in the Ukraine, in White Russia, in Finland and in the Baltic provinces. (The situation was only restored in the case of the Ukraine and of White Russia.)

This same policy regarding race and minorities enabled the death-blows to be administered which finished off Kolchak and Denikin—and after the new State had spewed out the Whites, this policy enabled it to mobilize groups of populations into new republics. This policy so clearly served the interests of the masses of these populations that, as soon as they could be made to understand it, they joined the Soviets. As soon, also, as they were understood and were approached in the right way—and it was here that the competence and influence of the man who addressed them placed a determining rôle.

In 1922 the Union of Socialist Soviet Republics was created. The name of Stalin is indissolubly bound up with that great historic event. The Constitution of the U.S.S.R. is, fundamentally, the marvellous set of rules drawn up by the revolutionary minority under Tsarism. It may be summed up as follows. It establishes, or, rather, it proposes: "A close economic and military union, at the same time as the widest possible independence, complete liberty of development of all national culture, systematic destruction of all survivals of national inequality, and powerful aid from the stronger nations for the weaker." (N. Popoff.)

Let us cast three more rapid glances towards the south, the east and the west.

In that Transcaucasia in which Stalin had begun, in

secret, to fire the soul of the masses, this region of "enemy brothers" in which all the elements of the population were at one another's throats, the Soviet policy of nationalities has brought about an almost miraculous state of affairs, namely the complete disappearance, not only of racial quarrels, but of racial hatreds which had been fermenting there for centuries—and that in spite of the Mensheviks, the Dachnaks * and the Mussavatists *—pseudo-socialists who were for a short time in power in the three Transcaucasian countries and took advantage of the fact to re-kindle domestic strife and to sow ruin, whilst all the time appealing for help abroad. In Georgia itself, in Armenia and in Azerbaijan the truth of the following axiom is quite apparent: "For a small country there is no sort of formula which can give it such great assurance of liberty as the Soviet formula."

This question inspired an Abkhasian peasant whose simple, honest soul had been illuminated by Socialism, with an amusing image, of legendary dimensions: "If an elephant sees some children playing in the open and, wishing to protect them from a storm, lies down upon them, he smothers them all, even though he does keep the storm away from them. But the handful of Abkhasians that we are is really protected from the storm by the Soviet elephant, because Stalin holds his legs up."

The Ukraine. The question of the Ukraine was one of paramount importance. The Ukraine, which had so long been coerced by tsarist despotism, which inoculated it by force with Russianism as with a disease, became, after October, a tumultuous theatre of civil warfare; the struggle

* Members, respectively, of the Armenian and Azerbaijanian Parties which were socialist in theory, and were affiliated to the Second International. (Translator's note.)

THE NATIONAL CONSTELLATION 103

of the Ukrainian workers and peasants against the Rada,*
the struggle of the Donetz workers against the hordes of
Kalidin, the German occupation of the Ukraine, the overthrow of the Directorate, which was pseudo-democratic,
and of the power of the Hetman Peliura which did not
even embarrass itself with democratic camouflage, the intervention of the Entente (the Black Sea Squadron), the
invasion of the Ukraine by Denikin, the struggle against
the White Poles, the struggle against Wrangel. In the
Ukraine the way in which the policy was followed and
its tactics carried out had a decisive bearing on the final
result.

Stalin, who was sent there, as will be remembered, in
1918, did not occupy himself only with military affairs,
but also with economic and political affairs. In March,
1920, he was a representative of the Central Committee at
the Fourth Conference of the Party in the Ukraine and
in 1923 he took part in the Fourth National Conference,
after the Twelfth Congress of the Party. Stalin has called
particular attention to "the enormous importance of a
correct national policy in the Ukraine, from the point of
view of the interior, and also from the international point
of view." However, at the present time the designs which
were directed against the Ukraine are again directed against
it. Poland (originally conspiring with France and later with
Fascist Germany), and the Germany of Hitler on its own
account, make no attempt to conceal their covetousness
and weave anti-Bolshevik intrigues and watch. A sort of
permanent secret war seems to be waged against that republic which has loyally and thoroughly adhered to the
Union.

On the opposite side to that of European barbarism, in

* Popular Assembly of Cossacks. (Translator.)

Central Asia, the question of the introduction of Soviets brought into prominence the Far Eastern question and also that of imperialist and capitalist colonization in general. As for the socialist influence, that is to say that of the Communist International and of Soviet power, in the colonial question, Stalin has written: "Tsarist Russia was the focus of imperialist contradictions. It was on the frontier separating the East from the West, and connected two social orders which are peculiar both to highly developed capitalist countries and to colonial countries. It was the mainstay of Western Imperialism which joined the financial capital of the West to the colonies of the East. For these reasons, the Revolution in Russia connects the proletarian revolutions of the most highly developed capitalist countries to the colonial revolutions. That is why its experience, the experience of the Communist Party of the Soviet Union, is of world-wide value."

However, when the Soviets first came into power, there was a somewhat special "Asiatic" conception of the problem of nationalities. It was manifested by strong "colonizing tendencies," that is to say the subjection of the distant country, and a preponderance of the Russian element in its administration and in the development of its Soviet assimilation. Russian workers and Russian propagandists went into Asia, directed everything and settled everything themselves, the native population being "neglected by Socialism," according to Stalin's own expression.

This did not agree with one of the principles of Leninist Marxism, which was a particularly dear one to Stalin, namely the untrammelled, direct and conscious participation of all in the common work. So Stalin fought bitterly against these eruptions of Muscovite exclusivism mingled with socialist organization, and against putting into practice methods which were very nearly "protectorate" or colonial methods in dealing with Soviet natives, as being a system which was erroneous in theory and foolish in practice.

He applied himself to making these populations undertake their own reconstruction and to restoring the development of their own progress to them at the same time as their nationalities, and he changed their passive Socialism into active Socialism. This was achieved by means of great economic undertakings by which the spacious regions, hitherto lost in the vagueness of Siberia, benefited.

It was in this spirit that he proposed to deal with the district of Turkestan (which from that moment took a considerable economic turn for the better), and to mark out new and carefully considered national boundaries for Central Asia. Several republics were created: Usbekistan, Turkmenistan, Tajekistan and the Kirghiz Republic.

All this Soviet East, which is nowadays so much threatened by foreign imperialism—(defiant Japan, modernized from the wrong end of the ladder and armed to the teeth, snuffling in the advance guard, and all those who are behind it)—all this East is strongly defended by the just, positive and high socialist ideal which has taken possession of the people.

And this brings us straight to the Chinese problem. In this gigantic territory, which is as great as that of Europe, the multitude which beats the record for all multitudes since the dawn of time, has also had its pseudo-revolution. This revolution, also, at the start, merely sawed off the feet of an illusive throne, and, after the death of Sun-Yat-Sen, delivered China to a clique of people whose double aim was to prevent it from gaining complete freedom and to make particularly fabulous fortunes out of it. The victim, both yesterday and to-day, of foreign brigandage, this unfortunate country is also the victim of internal brigandage. The Kuomingtang,* and the generals richest in soldiers who hold the Kuomingtang by a halter, have one great aversion, the Communist. Indeed, they exterminate Communists as well as Liberals, and the Chinese Government has those writers who talk of justice, buried alive. And the Japanese and the Great Western Powers have the same aversion. Now there is a large Chinese Communist Party which, in opposition to the governmental and military *omnium gatherum* which has its clutches on China and is attached to some of the Great Powers—is striving to free that great country from its lamentable condition. It has succeeded in a vast region which it has begun to transform, in the socialist sense, and it has crushed and dispersed with its army of 1,000,000 men the five great offensives that have been launched against it by official and foreign bandits. At the present day, about one-quarter of China, with 100,000,000 inhabitants, is "Red," and the great object of this new China is to recover the whole of ancient China. At the present moment a sixth campaign is developing, led in person by Chang Kai Chek, with the German General von Seekt by his side, at the head of an army of 600,000 men, with 150 aeroplanes and 200 guns. This army is proceeding to encircle Soviet China—or, rather, is attempting to encircle it—with the help of a great system of fortresses which it is building as it advances. This sixth offensive against liberated China has hitherto cost parasitic White China 1,000,000,000 Chinese dollars and 100,000 men. The White Chinese have, it is said, captured Chuiking, the capital of Soviet China. But in the meantime

* The Chinese Democratic Party that came into power after the Chinese Revolution and is still in power. (Translator's note.)

the tactics of the Red Army have been skilfully altered: its offensive campaign has been launched: abandoning part of its old positions, it is pursuing, in other regions, a triumphant advance which largely compensates by new conquests for its momentary territorial losses. The situation to-day seems to be very favourable for it, so much so that it seems certain that it will succeed not only in ridding itself of the White invasion but also in making contact with the Japanese forces and in fulfilling its great objective: "The holy war of national revolutionary defence of the Chinese people against Japanese imperialism." All the free-thinkers in the world must hope for it to come and that by it the martyrdom of a continent may come to an end. It is impossible nowadays for anyone with an unprejudiced and practical mind to interpret the formula: "China for the Chinese," other than as: "Soviet China."

Stalin has paid particular attention to the Chinese Communist Party and the heroic efforts of the Chinese Soviets. He personally undertook the stiffening of the line of the Chinese Party at the Chinese Commission of the Komintern in 1926. His intervention, which has become famous in the annals of the Communist International, contended against the errors and faults resulting from diffidence with regard to the Workers' and Peasants' Revolution, and a certain tendency to consider the Chinese Revolution as having to remain a middle-class democratic revolution. Well, "all the measures which he recommended have been ultimately justified by events."

This policy of nationalities, and the powerful way in which it spreads far and wide from its centre of origin, has not only a therapeutic action in colonial and semi-colonial countries (in which national freedom is the first step towards social freedom and to which Socialism brings both at once). It influences, and will go on influencing, directly or indirectly, a whole series of European States containing sacrificed minorities: heterogeneous nations made up of a central district and its colonies, formed or artificially enlarged by the war of 1914; Jugoslavia, which is not a federation, but a grouping, brought about by political means, of Slovenia, Croatia, Montenegro and a slice of Macedonia, under the dictatorship of Serbia; or, again, Czechoslovakia, a queer extract from the baroque jumble of Austro-Hungary; or, again, Poland, which contains only fifty per cent. of Poles; or Rumania, on to which the childish and barbarous surgeons of Versailles have recklessly grafted Hungarian Transsylvania, Russian Bessarabia and the Dobrudja; or even, arising from a much earlier piece of jiggery-pokery, England and its marriage to Ireland (which is in process of being dissolved), or the Walloon-Flemish agglomeration called Belgium.

In all these countries racial Leninism is a leaven of order and of revolution and, deep down, in their teeming masses, millions of eyes are fixed on these new enlightened laws of territorial nationalization.

In colonial or semi-colonial countries, among the oppressed minorities, the Soviet principle, with the double emancipation it produces, must inevitably transform vast numbers of people, which are now capitalist reserves, into vast reserves of Socialism.

But let us make no mistake; this light shines for the whole world without any exception. In the eastern half of Europe and the northern half of Asia it is the national application of an international formula. This formula is crystal clear and it is quite ready to be put into operation.

The Soviet constellation is henceforth an integral part of a world constellation of countries and of races.

On the day upon which Europe shall have been completely sovietized, it will contain a France, a Germany, an Italy, a Poland, etc. . . . which will develop in accordance with their intellectual and moral traditions, exactly as they do to-day, and even more than they do to-day—but between them there will be only administrative frontiers that will be permanently non-offensive.

It is thus, then, to our eyes, to us who are not accustomed to see new work undertaken upon such a colossal scale, that the Soviet solution to the insoluble problem of nationalities appears. There it is, in theory and in practice. There are the basic elements of socialist construction "in space," principles so simple and so just, so scientific and so ethical at the same time, which converge simultaneously upon so many ideals. Even if Socialism did not exist, it would have to be invented in order to unravel the tangle in which things are at present; it would have to be invented, firm in its framework and yet flexible in its movements.

We see it here in action, for the setting in order of existing humanity whose aspect is one of envy, hatred and quarrelling, and in order to put a successful end to the age-old and disconnected gropings of huge crowds spread over the land, towards a better form of society. Across the barbaric confusion of our transition period, of our Middle Ages, are written the watchwords, henceforth indelible, of the pioneers, of the men who have had the glory of discovering the world such as it really is.

Chapter Five

1917–1927. THE FIRST STONES

THUS, as the result of "an original combination of historical conditions, the first country to have entered the paths of Socialism was Russia, a country economically and culturally backward, in spite of its exceptionally powerful revolutionary leaders." To have leaped in one bound over the cardboard republics and all the small samples of different capitalist formulæ in force in the democratic monarchies and in the monarchic democracies, was marvellous, in theory. But, what was happening in practice?

As soon as they acquired the power, they had to make use of it, and that without wasting a single moment. The vast state machinery had passed from the hands of a wicked and abnormally swollen puppet and, after a short tottering stay in the gloomy limbo of the Provisional Government, into the hands of practical extremists and ardent thinkers, and it had, at all costs, to continue to run over the largest country in the world, between the Destiny that was no more and the Destiny that had not yet come into being.

There were three great problems to be faced: the war against the foreigner, civil war and social and economic disorganization in the interior. Of these, it cannot be said that the first—the war against the foreigner—was settled, even after Brest-Litovsk, even after the Armistice, since, if the majority of the former enemies had publicly abandoned the strife, the Civil War which was to succeed the Revolution for two years was strongly streaked with foreign intervention.

What was there to be done? Everything. To live from day to day and to build up, stone by stone. And all at once. At one and the same time to organize the Revolution, to repel the counter-revolutionary hordes on every frontier and every horizon, and to transform the former Russian Empire, an agricultural and ignorant country (80 per cent. peasants, 70 per cent. illiterate), a ruined, pillaged, bloodstained ex-empire, into a great nation, politically socialist (alone of its kind among all others), and with an economic system improved to the same level as, or to an even greater one than other nations.

Let us hark back, once more, to those days, days of achievement and days of recommencement. What was the balance-sheet like, what the inventory? What were the remnants of Russia like, in November 1917, from the hour in which, at the Smolny Institute, Lenin was informed that the Red Flag had been run up and that from that moment this flag had become one of the centres of the world?

The imperialist war of 1914 had cost Russia 40,000,000,000 gold roubles * and the massacre of a third of the working population; industrial production and transport were reduced to a fifth or a sixth part of the 1913 figures. The Civil War, which rent the Empire throughout practically the whole of its length and breadth, represented a further loss of 50,000,000,000 roubles. All the factories were in ruins and a great part of the public works as well. In the country, ravaged by gun-fire, half the land was lying fallow. Administration, education, all the State services were dislocated by catastrophe and by the hatred of the enemy

* Six gold roubles amount approximately to £1 at the present price of gold in England–(Translator).

in their midst. The Red Army was without rifles, without boots, without bread. The new State, which was later to be subjected to blockade and boycott, was for the moment suffering from the armed onslaught of the Great Powers. Let us draw as near as we can to that war of invasion of a quite particular kind—treacherous and underhand—the glorious leaders of which were Monsieur Clemenceau, Monsieur Poincaré and Mr. Lloyd George, the accredited enemies of popular revolutions. Let us draw near to what Mr. Winston Churchill, as Stalin recently recalled, defined as "The invasion of the fourteen nations."

The army of the White adventurer, Kolchak, champion of the Tsar, received from the French Government 1,700 machine-guns, 30 tanks and dozens of field-guns. In Kolchak's offensive thousands of Anglo-American soldiers, 70,000 Japanese soldiers and about 60,000 Czechoslovakian soldiers took part.

Denikin's Army of 60,000 men was entirely equipped in arms and munitions of war by England. It received 200,000 rifles, 2,000 guns, 30 tanks. Several hundred English officers acted as either advisers or instructors to Denikin's Army.

The disembarkation of the Allies at Vladivostock comprised two Japanese divisions, two English battalions, 6,000 Americans, 3,000 French and Italians.

England spent in the Civil War in Russia £140,000,000 and (a less important item for the people meddling with the world) the lives of 50,000 soldiers.

From 1918 to 1921 England and France never ceased killing Russians and laying Russia waste. Let us just note, in parentheses, that, at the end of 1927, there were still 450 engineers and 17,000 workmen employed in repairing the damage done *in one single oil-field in the Caucasus* by the passage of Western civilization. And the destruction wrought in Russia by the monstrous interference of the great European and American countries may be estimated at about 44,000,000,000 gold roubles.

Let us remember that in 1921—three years after the end of the war—a French Admiral installed in Russia, quite openly protected the enemies of the Soviet Government. That Monsieur Millerand, President of the French Republic and Monsieur Doumergue, another President of the French Republic, daring to do what at any rate neither England nor Turkey had dared to do, officially recognized Jordania and Tsenkely, who had been thrown out of Georgia, as the head and the ambassador of that country. And that official France, which claims to be loyal and to be democratic, had recognized Kolchak, and was about to recognize Wrangel, as Vice-Tsars.

Let us remember that the White Guards were mobilized in France, and made an armed State there within the State, developing their various organizations and their military formations under the benevolent eye of the authorities (the same authorities who expel all foreign workers who attend any non-official or non-religious demonstration and manufacture new laws whose object is to expel them without any reason). These hired desperadoes of Tsarism marched, fully armed, beneath the Arc de Triomphe, and it was they, too, who jogged the arm of the assassin Gorguloff (President Doumer having, in the opinion of the Tsarists, been guilty of insufficient animosity against the Soviets). As for the followers of Wrangel, they were widely welcomed in the Balkans, especially in Jugoslavia, where, in arms—and even in uniform—they awaited the moment to march for the holy cause of reactionary resurrections. Jugoslavia was not justified, quite recently, in reproaching Hungary for fostering the training of assassins

—the most she could do was to accuse her of competition.

Whilst we are upon this subject, let us widen this glimpse by a few more years, in order to get a better and more comprehensive view of the enormous methodical attempt over which nowadays we draw a modest veil—as though history was a drawing-room in polite society, where it were better not to talk of such horrid things, in order not to upset the well-bred company.

The sabotage of budding industry, which the U.S.S.R. made superhuman efforts to revive, has been raised to the level of an international institution, in which important personages, military officers, technical experts, political agents and the diplomacy and police of the Great Powers have all taken part. What subterranean manœuvres, what scheming and plotting! I am still bewildered by all the photographs of documents which I have seen personally. For years one could search in any corner of the Union and one would infallibly discover the English, French, Polish or Rumanian microbe of spying and foul play, mixed with the virus of the White plague. A certain amount of it still remains. The same people who blew up the bridges and whatever public works still remained in liberated Russia, gasping for breath, who threw emery into the machines and put the few remaining railway engines out of action—these same people put powdered glass into co-operative food supplies in 1933, and in December 1934 appointed one of their number to blow out Serge Kiroff's brains from behind, in the middle of the Smolny Institute in Leningrad. They unearthed nests of vipers and found that assassins and terrorists have been streaming into the country from Finland, Poland and Lithuania where they swarm, and the crimes committed by these blackguards, praised by the White Press of the "Vérité Russe," and other villainous associations, are hypocritically commented upon by the great "right-minded" Press.

What shall be said of the rôle, as ferocious as it is ridiculous, played by the Intelligence Service which covers the universe at the cost of millions of pounds sterling, with its international network of spies, of informers, of corrupters and destroyers—and of suppressers of men? Here is an example of the audacity of this poisonous penetration, taken quite at random. Monsieur Georges Valois, a member (nowadays a dissenting one) of the *Action Française*, tells, in the preface to one of Stalin's reports—without considering the enormity of the matter, and solely to authenticate a favourable opinion of Lenin with regard to him—that an agent of the Intelligence Service had wormed his way into the Councils of the Soviet Government and right into the very heart of the supreme controlling organization; that this agent made a report to the English Government, which sent this report to the French Government, which (Monsieur Poincaré) communicated it to Monsieur Léon Daudet, head of the French Royalists and grand vizier of the Pretender to the French throne, and that it was thus that Monsieur Georges Valois, who was at that time a member of the *Action Française*, heard about it.

The universal desire to discredit the Socialist State, the moral necessity for flinging mud at this living challenge to imperialism, had given rise to an amazing flood of calumnies and defamatory utterances. We will not enter here into that legendary and burlesque domain. The journey into it would be too long to be described in one book. We will note, however, as being more serious than the inanities in question (some of which have, however, stuck in the ears of our contemporaries), the agencies and perfectly appointed and equipped workrooms, especially in Central Europe, having as their object the manufacture of sensational Soviet forgeries calculated to put the new State into bad odour with the authorities and the public opinion of the Great Powers. This fact is well known and has, besides, been solemnly admitted in the English House of Commons by an important personage (who could not do anything else). The Zinovieff forgery had a very strong influence upon Anglo-Russian relations. The forgery used by Tsankoff, the Bulgarian butcher, enabled him to wave the red spectre in front of his people and gave him the means, though beaten himself, of obtaining from the victors a supplementary army with which to massacre his own people.

Of course, one can understand that the colossal "precedent" of the complete *volte face* of tsarist Russia alarmed the reactionaries, especially those of the kind called democratic (who have really cast aside their disguises in this connexion). But it is really surprising that so many sincere French Liberals have treated the Russia of the Revolution in the same way as England treated the France of the 1789 Revolution. And it is amazing that so many eminent intellectuals have remained in a state of regal incomprehension before a phenomenon of such breadth and such depth. (This is what is called the progress of ideas, in our countries.)

And, in the midst of all this hatred and all this defeat, in the midst of all this malediction, it was strange to hear the voices of people who, like Bullitt, then an obscure journalist, said things like this: "There will come a day when all the men of our age will be judged by the extent to which they have understood and defended the magnificent effort of Red Russia."

A day will come? But, in the meantime:

"Not for a short time, but over a space of two years, from 1918 onwards, you will remember, comrades," Stalin said recently, "the workers in Petrograd did not receive even a single piece of bread for several weeks at a time. The days on which they received a pound of black bread which was half oil-cake, were happy days."

This, then, was the situation which the new government had to face all around it, surrounded as it was by the capitalist menagerie. Everything to be done? It was worse than that: everything had to be re-done. It was a double task.

It seemed to be only common sense, from the moment at which it had the power in its hands, but was still hampered by the White Europeans, to try hurriedly to ward off the appalling economic landslide by making a few provisional concessions. In this economic system that was so disorganized, was there no means of contriving some scheme for permitting its gradual reorganization by making use of a certain amount of the old, still existing middle-class mechanism? To deal with the most urgent matters, to make sure of military defence, and the means of living—before launching oneself into political achievement and the restoration of economic stability? This was the clearly indicated course of action.

Yes, it was indicated economically, but quite the contrary politically. Small business men in a hurry would have acted in this way. Not Socialists creating a world. Yes, it appeared to be common sense. But revolutionary wisdom was greater than that sort of common sense. It saw further than that. It saw that, to act in such a way at that time was to put a finger into the gears of a backward-moving machine, and it decided that it was necessary, even in the terrible situation in which it found itself, to destroy utterly the political and social past and to dislocate completely and for ever the old machinery, far from wishing to fasten the new society to it in any way at all. In other words, being almost annihilated itself, to annihilate still more! A decision which was cheerful in its very boldness and which gave a sound dramatic sequel to the march of events.

The middle classes could not understand that their time had passed. It never entered their heads that somewhere, all through the old continent, capitalist sovereignty could be broken up. And, at heart, apart from the militant Socialists, few people believed in the Revolution. People met with scepticism and inertia the proclamations of this government which differed too much from other governments, which detached itself in such an exaggerated way from past tsarisms and existing tsarisms (or liberal substitutions for them). . . . "It was not only newspaper men," someone said retrospectively at the Fourth Congress, in 1922, "who refused to take seriously the most important revolutionary measures of the Workers' Government. . . . Each factory, bank, counting-house, shop, and each lawyer's office was a fortress holding out against us. . . ."

So that at that moment the alarming problem of the safety of the Revolution arose once more in all its intensity. The Revolution had to show its face and its power. The defeat of the Russian middle classes was not yet accomplished. There was still a certain amount of victory to be gained.

So, in spite of everything, this Revolution must be carried on to the bitter end. The middle classes must be completely crushed, the bridges must be cut (to undo is to create in another sense); one must confiscate and completely expropriate; commerce, industry, everything must be seized.

1917-1927. THE FIRST STONES

It meant voluntarily complicating and seriously aggravating the situation in which the Revolutionaries were struggling; it almost certainly meant risking the great increase, at certain points, of the bitter crisis of misery; it meant asking the people to make an effort which looked like being beyond human capacity and, above all, dissatisfying the peasants. And yet, where a narrow or commonplace policy would have eagerly chosen the compromise which would have irrevocably retained the middle-class régime, the men of October destroyed everything. To an already incalculable destruction they added a complete supplementary destruction. In order to defend itself and to dig its foundations deeper, the Revolution flung itself still deeper, of its own accord, into the abyss.

There was a certain amount of anxiety in the ranks and indeed, a certain amount of hesitation at the top. For instance, the former industrial magnate Urkwarth offered to take, and pay for, a concession of the Ural factories from which he had been expropriated. Kameneff and Zinovieff, in a fit of panic, were in favour of granting this concession. Stalin was against the proposal. Lenin was also against it, but he hesitated. Bela Kun, who was working in the Ural district, was summoned to inform the Central Committee of the state of mind of the workers and officials on the spot. These were against the concession, which was for Urkwarth merely a means of getting his foot once more into the stirrup, and which would mean more trouble than profit for the Republic. When the meeting that was to decide the matter took place, Zinovieff and Kameneff endeavoured to obtain from Stalin a declaration against the concession which they favoured (as a matter of fact they admitted it afterwards). But Stalin refused to speak before those who came from the Ural had put forward their point of view, which, explained by Bela Kun, led to the concession being refused and the tempting bait being rejected.

The middle-class machinery being violently cast aside, "War Communism" was instituted, that is to say the utilization of only a portion of all the economic elements which the State had appropriated to itself: "A clumsy, centralized machine, destined to extract from industry disorganized by war, by revolution and by sabotage the minimum of produce necessary in order that the towns and the Red Army should not die of hunger."

It was necessary, so far as wheat was concerned, to proceed with the "compulsory removal of the excess of peasant labour." It was a system of State rationing, "a besieged fortress régime."

So that, after the last violent upheaval, the remnants of middle-class power were really definitely eliminated and cast into the past, at the same time that the majority of the Whites and the foreigners were cast beyond the frontiers. The Revolution and peace remained alone on the historical and economic ruins. But public life was in its death-throes. Commerce and industry had gone still further downhill. Then Nature took a hand in the game: one of the most appalling famines of modern times, caused by an exceptional drought, descended on the most fertile Russian territories. The peasants who had, willingly or compulsorily, ensured as much as possible the supply of the gigantic two years' battle, were everywhere frightened, distrustful, often hostile. At certain points they revolted (1921).

As for the immense reinforcement hoped for and for which the horizon was daily scanned—the World Revolution—there were certainly no signs of it. What was the international proletariat doing? It occasionally stirred a little, but without any real result, or else it was being defeated, like that of Hungary, thrust back, it is true, into the age-old régime by Allied bayonets; and like the one upon which most reliance was placed, the German proletariat, shot down by machine-gun fire by Monsieur Clemenceau.

They had to do without everything and to realize that the Soviet State had to construct its economic system with its own resources.

And for that they had also in the immediate present, when War Communism was out of date, to consider a new transitory economic position, at the same time that the political and social struggle in the West, and in the rest of the world, was to take the equally transitory form of immediate war claims on a partial united front.

It was in these conditions that the Soviet State judged that it would be able to do quietly what it had not been willing to do at any price two years previously, and passed from the methods of War Communism to those of the market; and the New Economic Policy was created (the N.E.P.).

In our part of the world the N.E.P. has not been properly understood, and indeed people have been grossly mistaken about it (Monsieur Herriot, for instance). It has been thought, generally, that it represented a precipitate retreat on the part of the Bolsheviks, because they had rushed headlong into a socialist system of economics and that this had been found to be impracticable.

But this is very far from the truth. As I remarked earlier, the Bolsheviks had decided that it was advisable for their great organizers to put the finishing touch upon a Revolution which was not quite complete. They knew quite well that, by doing so, they were bound to increase their economic difficulties and disorder. But it was only after cleaning up the political situation to its very foundations that it seemed to them to be able to admit of a certain effort at economic opportunism. "The difference between Revolutionaries and Reformers," said someone then who had not always spoken in that vein (Trotsky), "is that Revolutionaries only admit the principle, reform, after the seizure of power by the proletariat." The formula of the budding Soviet power was: "I will make concessions, if necessary, but when I have become master, not before."

So what they did was this: So far as the peasants, and wheat, were concerned, they replaced the "removal of excess crops"—much too violent a system—by a levy in kind, authorizing the free sale of the excess. Money was again put into circulation. Measures were taken to stabilize the rouble. State enterprises were placed upon a commercial footing. Salaries were graded according to qualifications and the kind of work done. And, as the State found that it had more enterprises on its hands than it could manage itself (since it had seized them all), it hired a certain number of them out to private individuals.

After the application of this policy, which involved, as can be seen, considerable concessions on the part of the Bolsheviks—in 1922—the situation was "re-established." Thus their big railways, the property of the State (40,000 miles of line, 800,000 employees) were already supplying one-third of their pre-war service. In the country, 95 per cent. of the arable land, nominally belonging to the State, was in the "economic enjoyment" (which practically meant, in spite of limited periods of tenure and certain servitudes, "in the possession") of peasants, who payed a tribute in kind: 300,000,000 *pouds** of rye on a harvest which had then reached three-quarters of its pre-war size. As for industrial enterprises, they all belonged to the State; but the State only exploited four thousand of them (with a million workers, it is true) and hired out 4,000 (of minor importance, employing 80,000 workers). Private capital began to make its appearance and developed in the home trade. It represented 30 per cent. of the whole amount in circulation in the home trade. Foreign trade, which remained a State monopoly, represented, in comparison with pre-war figures, one-quarter as regards imports and one-twentieth as regards exports.

The market was re-organized, but the position of the Workers' State was, politically, a dangerous one, thus dragged away to the Right. Side by side with the socialist advance a new capitalist advance was taking place (especially in the country districts) and strong defensive measures had to be taken.

In the struggle which was brewing, "the proletarian power had on its side the most highly developed productive forces of the country. In short, it appeared in the market as a landowner, as a purchaser and as a vendor with much more power than its competitors, because it had the additional advantage of possessing political power" (and particularly fiscal power, which assured it of a financial weapon and allowed it to make certain supplementary profits on private enterprise). "The middle classes had on their side past experience and relations with foreign capital." (Report at the Fourth Congress, 1922.)

This was the start of a duel with very grave matters at stake and whose issue must have incalculable social and moral consequences. For both sides the great objective

* One poud = about 43 lbs.

was, in this agricultural Russia, the capture of the peasant market. The peasants, the poorer elements among whom had aided and abetted the Revolution, were distrustful at that time of the Revolutionaries who had given them the land but had taken away their wheat. The Russian peasant, a realist, but a short-sighted one, had already shown signs of violent resistance. From the point of view of good relations with the country districts the N.E.P., thanks to its few doors open to initiative and private profit, and its regulations which no longer bore the same aspect as the stern requisitions of which the country districts bore the whole brunt, was of vital importance.

The Bolsheviks, who are the least blind of men when looking into the future, knew quite well that the future of the socialist State depended upon harmony between the productive economy of the land and that of the towns (in the same way that the Revolution itself, indeed, only succeeded because the peasants as a whole had accepted it—in some cases had even assisted it—or had let it go on). But, even whilst proclaiming it expressly and even pointing out the landmarks of this great harmony that was to come, the new masters provisionally let the heavy industries remain idle, such as electrification and all the rest of it, as well as the prospects of a reasoned reconstruction of the economic system, and works of national importance. This was so that they might consolidate the Revolution by a period of graduated plans making it possible to proceed to certain indispensable repairs and to prepare the way for the future. They encouraged co-operation in the country districts as much as they could and kept stoutly declaring that they were well on the road from Capitalism to Socialism, although "actually nearer the starting-point than the finish."

It was solemnly asserted at Moscow that: "The State does not grant industrial concessions or conclude commercial treaties, except in so far as neither of them are capable of undermining the foundations of its economy."

Do you remember, my friends, the sniggers and even the roars of laughter that greeted such declarations amongst "right-minded" people? Those who, in France, kept on saying: "Have confidence in the Bolsheviks," found themselves in a sufficiently thankless situation. "Ha, ha! They're coming round, these uncompromising Revolutionaries!" murmured the wise men of all nations. "It's quite obvious: they're taking the first backward step, the return to the good old capitalist methods. It's the beginning of the end of the mad socialist experiment!"

When Chicherin met the French representative, Monsieur Colrat, in Italy, in 1921, the latter rudely interrupted the People's Commissar for Foreign Affairs in the middle of a speech, by telling him that the Bolsheviks had no right to join in conversations about political economy, in view of the economic disorganization of their own country. I have not the honour of knowing Monsieur Colrat, but his summary condemnation could not possess the slightest value or even have the least meaning unless the Bolsheviks had had time to apply their economic methods in the territory of which they had made themselves heirs—and this was clearly not the case. But Monsieur Colrat is not the only person who made ridiculous remarks. (We will pin them on the backs of those who uttered them so pompously when the laugh was on their side.)

"The State will not allow the foundations of its economy to be undermined." But one can understand that our Western Conservative Republicans, our turn-coat politicians, found it incredible that statesmen should fulfil their engagements strictly and follow unswervingly the line they had laid out for themselves. What was this new method of procedure? It belonged to the peculiar originality of these curious Oriental people. And perhaps they might even make it fashionable in politics one of these days. However that may be, when they proclaimed passionately: "We will not allow ourselves to be swindled!" these honest people were right. And it was still more honest of them to announce their intentions.

"Are they coming round . . . ?" No, Mr. Cabinet Minister. No, my lord, they did not come round. And immediately the expressions on your capitalist faces grew longer, until they were almost caricatures. Very few years after this start, it was clear to everyone that the Bolsheviks were gaining their objectives all along the line, reviving industries, gradually reducing the part played by private capital, and that they were emerging completely victorious from the period of economic labour under the ensign of the N.E.P. The compromise between Capitalism and Socialism, between private and collective enterprise—the marriage of the carp and of the rabbit—was, as had been promised, only temporary. The brightening of the face of world Capitalism before the N.E.P. was in fact, only due to a mere flash; and the *nepman* was no longer anything but a superannuated personage whose only use was to figure on the theatrical stage as a picturesque type belonging to an age which was historically defunct.

Such is opportunism and that is what is meant by it. The greatness of Lenin, and of the man who worked most closely to him in these chaotic and changing surroundings, consisted in having realized how this form of opportunism could be turned to their advantage. If you are asked: "Is opportunism good or bad?" do not answer. You can-

STALIN IN HIS ROOM AT THE KREMLIN

not do so. Opportunism—I naturally use the word in a general sense, and not in the disparaging sense in which it is sometimes used—may be good and it may be bad. It may lead to victory or it may lead to defeat. It is one's duty to grasp what may be useful to one; to neglect to do so is a mistake. In certain circumstances fanaticism is only fear of responsibility. It is often only too convenient to be a hundred per cent. unyielding and to take refuge in the ivory tower of purity, when everything is tottering and going to blazes outside. At other times one must be utterly and tyrannically uncompromising. One knows how to be honest, and mere willingness is no longer sufficient for accomplishing one's duty once it achieves certain proportions. In 1921, those who deserved to be called opportunists, in the bad sense of the word, were, among the socialist ranks, not those who approved of the N.E.P., but those who opposed it. Because the latter would have sacrificed the future to the present, whereas the correct meaning of the word opportunism should be to sacrifice the present to the future. The opportunism of Lenin and of Stalin—and of all great strategists—is a step backward in order to take two steps forward. For stupid or frightened people, and also for wavering Socialists who, unconsciously or not, are seeking some sort of loophole, it is two paces back in order to take one pace forward.

Once more Marxism teaches us that a word is merely a word; that is to say, it is nothing in itself. Formulæ are only worth anything if they are put to good use, and there may be a vast difference between two phenomena which are expressed, grammatically, in the same terms. Marxism is an example of pure relativity. It depends, in the long run, entirely upon the Marxists themselves. (Not even on Karl Marx. Marx is a great man not because of his name, but because he is the most consistent of all the Marxists.)

The fact remains that the same man who, from 1903 to 1912, had done everything with a forceful obstinacy, which "went beyond" so many of his companions, to divide the Revolutionary Party in two, even though it was being hunted and its ranks decimated by Tsarism—and who acted thus precisely *because the Party needed its whole strength*—has admitted, when this Party was victorious, that he compromised on a great number of points with middle-class methods. If you think that this is contradictory, you are mistaken—for the man in command of the situation was just as right in one case as in the other.

Thus appeared what Lenin called: "The curve in the straight line." A fine, powerful conception which does not mean arabesques, whorls and spirals, but which reminds one of the neatness of the circles of latitude or of the curvature of space according to Einstein.

As soon as possible, in the midst of all this, it was necessary to get on to the course that it was intended to steer permanently, to put socialist economy back into Socialism by the proper stages and then to develop it systematically.

In 1922, at the Eleventh Congress of the Party, one year after the introduction of the N.E.P., Lenin decided that "the retreat was at an end and that they must begin to think about reorganizing their forces." And he added that "the key of the situation lay in the choice of men." After the Eleventh Congress, Stalin was elected General Secretary of the Central Committee of the Russian Communist Party. He immediately organized, one might almost say, re-organized, the Party, with a view to setting the national socialist economic system on its feet.

The situation was still a precarious one. The Great Powers had not disarmed, or at any rate had only partly done so. The Russians had been shown the door whenever they had attempted to obtain anything from them, except by the Scandinavian countries and by Germany; with the latter country the Treaty of Rapallo had been signed, which brought about a certain stability (in misfortune). The Geneva Conference with the other Great Powers came to nothing. The pretext for its failure was the repudiation of tsarist debts by the Bolsheviks. The Great European Powers were themselves in process of reconstructing their post-war economy, by means of £1,200,000,000 which the United States had lent them for this purpose (quite apart from its previous loans for carrying on the war), and which the said Great Powers were one day brightly going to refuse to pay back to the United States when, having sensationally drawn a distinction between the money that was owed to them and the money which they themselves owed, they decided officially to forget the latter, and to relegate the receipts referring to those debts into the category of scraps of paper. And this without having the ethical reasons for doing so which were pleaded by the Soviet Power for the repudiation of tsarist debts, reasons which had, let us repeat, been solemnly advanced before the war by important Russian politicians, holding the most moderate views, regarding the loans contracted by a despotic government entirely in its own private interest, and for the purpose of crushing its people; "against its own people" in fact. It must be admitted that there is a difference between a revolutionary government refusing to be responsible for the embezzlements of a Tsar who was the enemy of his subjects, and these other governments repudiating their own signatures (after having extorted quite a considerable indemnity from the vanquished).

While the majority of Soviet citizens were living on millet-seed, around the hypertrophy of a few *nepmen*, and while the underfed leaders were growing daily thinner, they set to work to build up the future.

This work was all organized according to principles of co-operation. First of all the principle objectives had to be decided upon. Marxist theory and practice offered a very wide margin in this respect. They were carried on side by side, because only theory can teach practice what to do and how to select exactly the right starting-point. Theory gives the trajectory from the starting-point to the finishing-point. If it is correct it stretches a feeler out into the future. Stalin quotes Lenin in saying that it is the great lever of all things. All those who have seen Stalin at work recognize that his most important quality is a capacity for "grasping a situation in all its complexity and detail, for putting all that is most essential to the fore, and for fixing his whole attention on what is most important for the time being." It may be observed that when those who really know— such as Kuibicheff, who directs the State Plan*—speak of Stalin's accomplishments, they do not only say: "He did so and so," they say: "He did so and so *at the right time*."

The first great vital problem to be solved was that of the peasantry. It was, and still is, the supreme problem of the Soviet Republic.

It must not be forgotten—and must constantly be repeated—in the first place, that the two main characteristics of the Russia of that time were that it was an agricultural country and was very backward. The territory marked

* I.e., the perpetual Five-Year Plan. (Translator's note.)

out and punctuated by Petrograd, Odessa, Tiflis, Vladivostock and Archangelsk had remained until that time a feudal, disordered and muddled country around the splendours of the Kremlin, and the diamonds in the imperial crown and in the churches, whilst the grand dukes and the boyards with their suites lived a life of debauchery abroad. A short time before, half the land had belonged to 18,000 nobles, the other half to 25,000,000 peasants. The lack of coherence caused by this state of affairs was everywhere apparent. Industry, in a very backward condition, contained a few relatively wide areas which were subsidized to the extent of 43 per cent. by foreign capital.

Now it is through its industry that a modern State is enabled to grow. It was therefore through industry that a huge territory had to be transformed into a great country. Even from the peasants' point of view? Yes, even from the point of view of the peasants' progress, as much economic as political: it was only by the intervention of industry that the socialist metamorphosis of the villages could be accomplished.

Consequently "the centre of gravity of economics must be displaced in the direction of industry," (Stalin). All that is much easier to say than to do in the presence of such a vast expanse of fields, of steppes and of forests. But one must be fearless when confronted by a sheet of blank paper.

"Our country had to be transformed from an agricultural country into an industrial country, capable of itself producing everything which it needed. This was the principal point, the foundation of our general line of action."

Thus speaks Stalin, People's Commissar in the Workers' and Peasants' Survey.

But his idea, which coincided with that of Lenin, was

that it was not sufficient to say that one must proceed by the path of industry. Certain industries must be selected from the whole. "Industrialization does not mean the general development of all industry." The "centre" of economy, its "basis," the sole means of making the whole of industry progress, declared Stalin, was the development of heavy industry (metals, combustibles, transport), for this is the "development of production of the means of production."

And this also meant the production of something which, at the moment of speaking, could almost be expressed by the cipher zero, as the result of the backwardness of the centuries that had gone before, of the deluge of the last few years and also as the result of the disorganization of the constructional scheme of economy brought about by the introduction of the N.E.P., which had to be adopted for a certain time.

But Lenin had peremptorily specified that: "If we cannot find means of creating industry among us, and of fostering it, that is the end of our country as a civilized country and, *a fortiori*, as a socialist country." And Stalin made similar observations about heavy industry.

Here it is necessary to put, in parentheses, similar considerations to those which we have already examined. The question arises, once more, in this matter of heavy industries, of a policy whose results would not be apparent for a long time. Another alternative appeared to be much more reasonable: to begin—more modestly—by reconstructing and developing the lighter industries, textiles, consumption, food supply, allowing the population to be revictualled, by satisfying the immediate needs of the public, so as to silence all the more crying demands . . . and besides, the ordinary man, the enormous mass of amorphous citizens, the colossal snow-man, much prefers to appear to be starting at the beginning.

Once more a conflict began (it is only a short time since it has ceased) between the logic of the groundlings and the logic of the giants, between the far-sighted idealists with their overwhelming preoccupations about the future and the short-sighted people who carry no burden on their shoulders.

Let us start in a small way and develop gradually, said the latter. In this way you will limit public sacrifice, you will curtail the era of privation and you will facilitate internal peace, instead of hurling yourselves headlong into the system of turning villages into cities and of attacking world records when you do not possess a sufficiency of the necessities of life.

But:

"Your point of view is the wrong one, comrades."

And logic and patient anticipation of the future, answering through Stalin's lips, explained: "Yes, one would satisfy a few of the immediate desires of the urban and rural populations by beginning with the light industries. And after that? Only heavy industries can serve as a basis for the industrial revival of a country. Only the development of the heavy industries can make co-operation in the country districts possible, that is to say the achievement of great socialist ideals."

"Co-operation between the peasant and the worker is essential," declares Stalin, "but the re-education of the peasant, the destruction of his individualist psychology and the transforming of it into a collectivist mentality, can only be accomplished on the basis of a new technique, of collective labour, of production on a large scale. Either we must carry out this task and then we shall establish ourselves permanently, or we must abandon it, and then the return to Capitalism may become inevitable."

There is also the question of national defence, which needs the heavy industries. National defence is a sacred duty. Capitalism has misapplied a great many fine phrases. That is no reason why one should not give them their true meaning for the first time. National defence is an abominable thing when it means avarice and brigandage and "myself before you," when it means ruin and suicide, when it means the first stage of national warfare; but it is worth more than life itself when it means a stage of progress, lifting people out of slavery, and bold defiance against the predatory countries which are constantly seeking for a pretext to destroy living Socialism, and which have made so many definite and serious efforts in that direction that no one could honestly dispute their intentions. This duty of social defence does away with all criminal necessity for having in any way to confide in the Great Powers, and it shows that a true desire exists that the dawn of the Russian Revolution really shall be a dawn.

Stalin, on the day on which, summarizing things broadly, some years later, he said that the first foundation of the Soviet State was the alliance between worker and peasant and that the second was the union of nationalities, added that the third was the Red Army.

So heavy industry was the "first link," to employ the terminology dear to the men who, in Russia, spend their time changing abstract ideas into concrete facts.

But it was not sufficient merely to take heavy industry in hand. They increased the difficulty of the task by deciding to take it in hand quickly. Too much delay would have destroyed the value of any success they might achieve and would, moreover, have been very dangerous. To dawdle too long in the temporary sterility of vast workshops would be to invite risk of defeat. So everything had to be speeded up.

And suddenly, at this point, another almost unsurmountable obstacle appeared: there were not enough technical experts, and technics mean both machinery and manpower. Here too, in the difficulties of recruiting technical directors, strong measures were taken. There were two alternatives, Stalin has since explained (I heard this quite recently on the wireless whilst correcting the proofs of this book) ... "two alternatives: the one which consists of first training technical experts—a matter of some ten years—and, afterwards, building machinery. Or the one which consists in beginning at once by building machines and training operatives at the same time. We chose the second solution. As a result, there has a been certain amount of bad work and a certain amount of deterioration took place. But we have gained what was the most precious thing of all, namely time, and we have acquired, spurred on by necessity, the technical experts which we lacked. All things considered, we have gained infinitely more than we have lost, and once more the quiet and confident venturesomeness of Bolshevism has scored a great success." ... "We have conquered—it is only right that we should have done so," added the Stalin of 1934.

But at the time, this upheaval, added to the discarding of the old slow methods of progress, was not to everyone's taste, even among those responsible for it. Some of them made wry faces. Stalin sought them out and shook them into activity, "those philistines in carpet-slippers, dressing-gowns and night-caps who approach the problems of socialist construction solely from the point of view of the tranquillity of their existence."

So, hovering over the existing ruins, we see the mists of the future peopled with gigantic industrial silhouettes. In that country, in front of the commonplace foreground with its ruins, rise the dim shapes of lathes, blast-furnaces, dams and of huge bridge-spans rising like sombre rainbows against the sky. In the steppes, or in the fertile countryside formerly so neglected, appear, stuck on here and there as though on photographic mounts, factories and groups of factories: armoured cities. Around these oases of science and of the socialist harmony of teeming human multitudes, the cultivated plains are cut up into squares and lozenges, patterned with the up-and-down movement of tractors. And, over the whole map, a network of roads and railways is slowly appearing.

The work was scheduled to begin at the end of the Civil War and to continue by long, carefully thought out and calculated stages. 1921. 1925. 1927.

The co-operative store system was pushed forward very actively, particularly in the country districts. The co-operative system had always existed in Russia. Its activity and growth had now to be methodically intensified. "Co-operation is the high road leading to Socialism." (Lenin.) It is obvious that it attunes people's minds to the theory of collectivity and introduces an atmosphere of community and socialist habits into the practical calculations of daily life. Again, co-operative stores have the effect of gradually ousting private enterprise, by squeezing private middle-men out of existence and themselves becoming the inter-mediaries between the State trusts and the consumers. Later the co-operatives can be developed on a large scale.

At the same time the leaders decreed a whole series of measures for organization, for thrift, for the prevention of waste, for the increase of output, for the strengthening of discipline and of diligence.

... But things only really took shape and began to come to life with the development of electrification.

Electrification was the deep-rooted bond which connected the whole of the vast ideal industry to the land.

Lenin had foreseen the part that electric current was to play in the world of the future around him, at a moment when no one else foresaw it, whilst the N.E.P. was still in existence, and in the midst of the highest capitalist hopes concerning the wounds, as yet unhealed, of a tortured nation.

The idea which had sprung out of the earth was called the *Goelro* (a word made up of the first two letters of each of the words State, Electricity, Russia).

"I have read your *Plan for the Electrification of Russia*," Stalin wrote to Lenin in March 1921. "It is a masterly outline of an economic, a really *constructive* plan, a real 'State' plan, in every accepted sense of the word. It is the only real Marxist attempt of our times to put the superstructure of Russia, so economically in arrears, on a 'really true' industrial technical basis, only possible under existing conditions.... What is the good of the dozens of so-called 'constructive plans' which, to our shame, are constantly published in our Press? They are just the babblings of children, nothing more.... Do you remember Trotsky's plan, last year, his proposals to bring about the 'economic renaissance of Russia' by means of the wholesale employment of the unskilled labour of the masses of peasants and workers (the Workers' Army), in the ruins of pre-war industry? How paltry, how primitive, when compared to the *Goelro* plan! It was like a workman of the Middle

Ages posing as an Ibsen hero. My advice? ... First: Not to waste one moment more in chattering about this plan. Secondly: To *begin* carrying the scheme out immediately *in a practical manner.** Thirdly: To subordinate at least one-third of the available labour to the interests of the *commencement of this new work* (two-thirds—both of men and of material—will be necessary for 'current' needs). Fourthly: As the collaborators of the *Goelro*, in spite of all their good qualities, are nevertheless lacking in practical experience (one feels that there is a kind of professorial incompetence in their articles), practical men must figure on the 'Plans Commission.' Fifthly: The newspapers *Pravda, Isveztia* and especially *Economicheskaya Zhizn* must devote themselves to popularizing the 'Electrification Plan,' both so as to bring it to everyone's notice and to give all material details about it, pointing out, at the same time, the fact that there is *only one* 'constructive economic plan,' namely the 'Electrification Plan,' and that all other plans are only empty and harmful chatter."

Electricity has become the central pivot of future reconstruction of continents. The whole of such reconstruction will radiate from the electric pylon. Almost magical hydro-electric sources already figure largely in the great collective progress of the U.S.S.R. "Socialism," says Lenin, "is the Soviets plus electrification." An all-powerful combination of ideas and of material objects, which joins and mixes entities certain of which seem to have nothing whatever in common. One might have studied both Socialism and electricity for a long while without discovering it. It was like mixing apples and oranges, in defiance of the instructions given by teachers to their pupils in primary schools. But actually it was putting a powerful, ready-

* The words in italics were underlined by Lenin.

made framework straight into an idea. It was like an algebraic formula. It was like the great command in Genesis: "Let there be light."

This thaumaturgic plan to make thousands of horsepower spring out of every corner all over the country, this electrification proposal, seemed comic and presumptuous in the West of Europe. H. G. Wells, who has specialized in visions of the future, constituted himself the mouthpiece of those qualified to speak on the subject, whose sense of the ridiculous had been shocked by this Soviet pretentiousness. When Lenin said to him in 1921: "We will electrify European Russia and Asiatic Russia," he thought it amusing. Not the idea in itself (if England, he explained, had had an idea like that, one could understand, because England had the means of carrying it out), but in this ignorant country in which the only regular thing seemed to be the ruins, and coming from "the little man at the Kremlin," it seemed peculiar. All the more because the Bolshevik prophet, with his poor confused brain, also spoke of 100,000 tractors in Russia in the near future, whereas one could count the existing Soviet tractors on one's fingers. Wells, the literary technician of the future has, on the only occasion upon which his vision has been checked, seen the future all awry. Would that he could efface from his work that page on the subject of which the schoolboys of the U.S.S.R. are so critical of him even at the present time!

At the Eighth Congress of the Soviets, and at the Fourth Congress of the Communist International, the Electrification Plan and the Electrification Commission were enlarged and systematized into a State Plan for its economic working and a State Plan Commission. This Commission began to be especially active when the U.S.S.R., after having the existing industrial installations put into working order and after having started them going, began to occupy itself with new installations on a huge scale.

And thus began the series of Five-Year Plans, themselves sections of larger plans.

This gigantic process of "planification," which casts its net over whole countries and for long periods, is entirely a Soviet conception. But the idea has made its mark all over the world. If it has made actual material progress in the U.S.S.R., it has also made progress elsewhere, abstractly and verbally. The Soviet Union has never succeeded in borrowing money from the Great Powers. But the Great Powers have borrowed certain important things from the Soviet Union, and that among them. They have even taken from it the idea of a *controlled economic system*, ornamented with a few international affectations. "Controlled economics" are the hesitating homage of Capitalism to Socialism!

Controlled economics, yes. There is no other way for the human race to get out of its difficulties. And in it we have, indeed, the universal panacea. But control means unification and Capitalism means Anarchy (both from the national and the international points of view). If the word "controlled" has not a full national meaning, and if it has not a real international meaning, it means nothing at all and is worth nothing, either at home or abroad. A controlled economic system is like peace; it cannot exist if one begins by cutting it up into small pieces.

That the idea of the Economic Plan should be an exclusively Soviet idea is due not so much to any reason of priority, as to organic reasons. In capitalist countries, private enterprise and privileges, and the multiplicity and divergence of interests that are brought into play in the question of economics make it impossible to carry out any general concerted economic plan: the proof is that it is only by marvellous feats of skill and juggling each year, at the last possible moment and sometimes even later than that, that our budgets are given some semblance of being balanced. This is not the case with the Socialist State carrying out a strictly logical constructive plan, in the interests of the public, mathematically exact, and in which the directing body is at the same time the legislative, executive, proprietary and consuming body.

The fact remains that from the moment it was proclaimed, the Soviet Five-Year Plan, with its wealth of detail and precision, once more brought a smile to Western faces. And why? These people whose economic statistics were falling off and melting away, and who pathetically brought up the rear of the procession of world economic statistics, were serving us up amazing sets of figures . . . by placing them in the future? They boasted of huge undertakings which were not yet even begun. When they were asked: "How is such and such an industry getting on with you?" they would reply: "It will be in such and such a condition in five years' time," and they would launch out into magnificent far-off perspectives.

And we, on our side, could not help thinking, with regard to these nebulous statistics, of the lovely promises, of which our own fashionable politicians are so lavish, to all citizens in general and to electors in particular. We could not lose sight of how strange it would appear to us to have to take the promises of a minister or of a government seriously.

It was terribly hard work, in other countries, to preach confidence in these figures from Moscow. "One must be a blind fanatic to believe in them!" people said.

Others said: "The figures of the Five-Year Plan must be incorrect because they are too high. Such a shifting round of national resources is only possible in a period of war, under the threat of shell-fire."

In 1928 I wrote (It is I, Barbusse, who am speaking now) that: "In the Five-Year Plan now in progress, it was not a question of speculations on figures and words by bureaucrats and literary men, but one of a cut-and-dried programme; the figures of the State Plan should be considered more as accomplished victories than as indications and," I concluded, "when the Bolsheviks assure us that by 1931 Soviet industry will have increased by 8 per cent., that 7,000,000,000 roubles will have been invested in economic revival, that their hydro-electric stations will reach a power of 3,500,000 kilowatts, etc. ... we must admit that these things virtually exist already. ..."

... Now if, at the date indicated, the above figures were not exactly as had been foretold, it was because they were nearly all exceeded.

The "true worth" of the figures of the Plans has been demonstrated now that, with the passage of time, these figures have passed from the vague zones of the future to the photographic zones of the present. If any of the prophesied figures have not been reached, their percentage is absolutely insignificant and negligible. In a great many directions they have been exceeded. The Soviet economic plans were realized to the extent of 109 per cent. in 1922–23 and 105 per cent. in 1923–1925, on all the main heads, to speak only of the earlier Plans.

No one could really be surprised. Clearly the most intelligent Plans are always materialistic ones. And, given the rational structure of Socialism and its direct and simplified contacts with reality all along the line, it is strictly normal that the forecast of these Plans should be realized almost exactly, however arduous the programme. "It would be magic, if it were not Socialism," said Stalin.

But it is not only by human intelligence that socialist theories are thus changed into great accomplished facts, it is also by the strength of the human heart. Something beyond mere logic is necessary to carry out a logical task on such a scale. Will-power? Will-power itself is not enough either. One must have enthusiasm. Through socialist ideology and through the direct action of the Party (which is, for the masses, the master-guide and motive power), one must obtain the collaboration of the mass of the workers: quantity, and also quality. Without the voluntary definite, ardent collaboration of the working class one can do nothing. So one must "arouse in them the creative forces stifled by Capitalism," one must "arm the workers with enthusiasm for work." They must have technical qualifications, and moral qualifications as well. It is the alliance of these two forces, in any case related to one another, that makes super-work possible.

Enthusiasm for work? Capitalist economists consider that to be all humbug. "One will never get anything from the worker," they declare pompously, "except by the lure of gain." A good old-fashioned method which the capitalist system has always employed when it has been able to do so (nowadays it is becoming difficult). The formula "grow rich" always succeeds with capitalist crowds (it even succeeds in ruining them completely).

In the socialist régime, the worker is not at all in the same social status as in the capitalist régime. In the capitalist régime the worker is a convict. He works reluctantly, because he is working only for himself. It is not even hard for him to see that he is working against himself. So he must be excited by special stimulants: money, patriotic duty, Christian principles and all the thunder of the Lord. But the socialist workman works with all his might "for glory," because glory in this case means his own power and advancement. It is in materialist Plans that one finds the highest ideals.

But it was not only the Capitalists that laid down the law. There were also critics murmuring in certain strata of the Party itself. All these appeals to competition among Socialists, said these comrades, were all very fine for purposes of agitation and propaganda, but to count upon them for purposes of practical and generalized labour was going too far, and Comrade Stalin was overstepping the mark. But Stalin doggedly maintained the real value of competition to the cause and its practical economic bearing as an incentive. When, some years later, it was shown that the enthusiasm of the workers was in fact an asset of enormous importance for the progress of labour, he gained a victory which he recorded as follows: "This year we rounded a corner of the utmost importance."

It was by enthusiasm also that the question of technics was eventually solved, as we have seen. It was a difficult and very serious problem. Technical experts had to be obtained, and among those who were qualified or who could be trained as such there was a terrible percentage of traitors (both native and foreign). "The mob have beaten us in open warfare. We will beat them by science," predicted Palchinsky, the chief of the machine-wreckers. A body of Soviet technical experts was hastily put into training and these worked with such a will that there was soon a sufficient number of them who were thoroughly competent.

This spirit of competition, which results in a sort of spontaneous and intensive self-realization of each individual towards the achievement of maximum results and which, said Lenin, far from being extinguished by Socialism, is considerably increased by it, is defined by Stalin as follows: "The principle of socialist competition is fraternal help given by the more advanced comrades to those who are more backward, to the benefit of general progress."

This does not mean that in setting to work with these purely moral incentives there can be no exaggerations and no mistakes. Stalin himself has emphasized this point insofar as concerns despotic measures—too childishly despotic in a blissfully unconscious way at present—such as the mathematically equal distribution of salaries and the strict levelling of everyone—measures having a somewhat clumsy and demagogic character which make them more harmful than useful in the development, still so immature, of individual and collective social personality. We will revert later to those schemes which are mere caricatures of Socialism.

But one may say that the irresistible driving-force of the leaders and the willing enthusiasm of the workers in their masses, in their brigades and in their armies, are exceptional and permanent characteristics of the work of construction.

Another incentive and source of energy is self-criticism. Stalin was one of the promoters and defenders (on all occasions, but most particularly at a Conference of the Party in 1921) of "the safety-valve of self-criticism." It is the duty of both the militant Socialist and of the Party, individually and collectively, to make use of this right, this weapon of self-criticism. They must bring faults and mistakes out into the light of day, they must be ruthless towards shortcomings and weaknesses; otherwise they must be held responsible for them. One must be able to play the part of custodian in addition to one's own part, and one must be one's own censor. It is only in Socialism that the words of the Reformer concerning the interpretation of the Scriptures (misleading in his own mouth) really mean something: "Let everyone be his own Pope."

On a day which arrived with appalling suddenness, Lenin was no longer there.

This great bereavement took place at the beginning of 1924. Lenin died on January 21st, at the age of fifty-four. It seemed incredible to all the men who had hitherto surrounded him so closely. They could not realize the fact that they had lost the man in whom the whole Russian Revolution was incarnate—the man who had carried it in his head, had planned it, had created it and had saved it from subsequent disaster, Lenin, one of the greatest conquerors of history, and immeasurably the most sincere; the man who has done most for humanity up to the present time.

"When the Party became Lenin's orphan, when it asked itself 'What shall we do without the genius of our leader?' Stalin quietly observed that they would triumph over every difficulty." (Kaganovitch.)

Some days after Lenin's death (which brought a tremendous influx of workers anxious to join the Party, as though these workers, emphasizes Radek, "were trying to compensate, by the contribution of a multitude of brains, for the brain of genius which had ceased to create"), Stalin, in the name of the Party, at a great ceremony, addressed a farewell to the familiar spirit of the Master, which took the form of a solemn oath: "In leaving us, Lenin has left us the duty of maintaining intact the honour and purity of the noble title of Member of the Communist

STALIN WHILE WATCHING BESIDE LENIN'S BODY, 1924

Party. We swear to you, Comrade Lenin, that we will do our utmost to do your will."

From the very first moment that the Soviets came into power, Stalin had been Lenin's understudy, and he continued to understudy him when he was no longer there.

That was mainly because Lenin had long before made the Party itself his understudy. He had forged it himself, solidly, fully, and in detail, with all its powerful foundations and its irresistible momentum, and had made of it a machine productive of leaderships. To say that Lenin was irreplaceable was erroneous, in spite of Lenin's supernatural greatness, because of the very constitution of the Party. When Lenin was no more, the duties produced the man. It was the exact opposite of the animal transmission of dynastic power, which has dislocated history for two thousand years.

The rise of Stalin and the increase of his already considerable authority became inevitable, and he became more and more indicated as leader of the Party.

But there must be no misconception about the growing ascendency which Stalin exercised, and one must not throw oneself lightly into the well-known variations of the themes of "personal power" and of "dictatorship."

There can be no dictatorship in the Communist International and in the U.S.S.R. It cannot exist because Communism and the Soviet régime develop along the lines of an extremely definite doctrine, of which the most important people are merely the servants, whereas the characteristic of dictatorship, of personal power, is to impose one's own law, one's own fancies, in opposition to existing law.

There may be different interpretations of Marxism, especially in its reaction to events and, from this point of view, a particular interpretation or even a particular course of action may at any given moment predominate at the head of the State and of the International. The question of whether such interpretation or course of action is a good one is solved automatically, and the leaders prove themselves to be right or wrong by contact with logical exigencies and the sequence of events. It would therefore be a great mistake to think that there is any supreme authority in the U.S.S.R., an individual sovereignty imposing itself on this great organization by artificial means, such as force of arms or intrigues. (The tyrant who, when anyone stands in his way, makes a sign to the executioner, like the Caliphs in the *Arabian Nights*, or to hired assassins.)

By means of machinations, trickery, corruption, or else by secret service and crime, or by introducing spies into lobbies and armed forces into council chambers, or by killing one's enemies in bed at night (two at a time), one might become, and remain, king or emperor, or duce, or chancellor—one might even become Pope. But one could never become Secretary of the Communist Party by any such methods.

A man like Stalin has naturally been violently attacked and has defended himself with equal violence (indeed he has more often than not taken the offensive). Certainly, but all these noisy, re-echoing discussions took place in the full light of day, in the full sight of everyone, every argument advanced in them being exhaustively examined in the most open manner like a great public trial before a jury of the whole nation as compared with palace intrigue.

Actually, in the socialist Organization, each man takes his place naturally according to his own value and strength.

He is automatically selected for his position by force of circumstances. His degree of power depends upon how much he understands and upon how far he can carry out the incontestable principles of Marxism. "It was simply," says Knorin, "by his superiority as a theorist and his superiority as a practical man that Stalin became our leader." He is leader for the same reason that he is successful: because he is right.

Actually there is only one country at the present day where such a state of affairs can exist—but to take any different view of the position is not to understand the Soviet régime. I once said to Stalin: "Do you know that in France you are looked upon as a tyrant who acts merely according to his fancy, and is a bloody tyrant into the bargain?" He leaned back in his chair and burst out into his hearty working-man's laugh.

The leader who decides, in the plans which he prepares for the whole State, the fates of all the different races, is the same man who considers that he must "render an account" to any comrade who asks him for it, and declares that he is ready to do so at any moment.

It was nothing but the exceptional attitude adopted by Trotsky, whose public position had been a considerable one by Lenin's side, and who showed a tendency to place himself above the Central Committee, that brought the question of "the leadership" up before the Fourteenth Congress. To Trotsky's exuberant personality Stalin opposed the principle of Community-leadership. He declared: "One cannot direct the Party without colleagues. It is absurd to think that we can. And now that we have lost Ilitch it is stupid even to speak about it. Common labour, collective leadership, a united front and unity among the Central Committee, with, as a vital condition, the subordination of the minority to the majority, are what we really need at the present time."

Not so very long ago, Stalin said to a foreign visitor who was anxious, as are all intelligent tourists in the U.S.S.R. (particularly those who visit important Soviet personalities), to go closely into this question of personal power in the Workers' and Peasants' State (looking meaningly at Stalin): "No, one must make no individual decision. Individual decisions are always, or nearly always, biassed. In every association, in every community, there are people to whose opinions heed must be paid. In every association, in every community, there are also men who may express erroneous opinions. Experience of three Revolutions has shown us that out of a hundred individual decisions which have not been examined and corrected collectively, ninety are biassed. The leadership organization of our Party in the Central Committee, which directs all the Soviet and communist organizations, consists of about seventy people and it is among those seventy members of the Central Committee that are to be found our best technicians, our cleverest specialists and the men who best understand every branch of our activities. It is in this Supreme Council that the whole wisdom of our Party is concentrated. Each man is entitled to challenge his neighbour's individual opinion or suggestion. Each man may give the benefit of his own experience. If it were otherwise, if individual decisions were admitted, there would be serious mistakes in our work. But because each one may correct the errors of all the others and everyone considers these corrections seriously, our decisions have hitherto been as correct as it is possible for them to be."

This conception of collective work must be still further enlarged if it is to be accurately studied. We must not forget the energy and progressive spirit with which Stalin insists upon the co-operation not only of the representatives of the masses, but of the masses themselves, in the present history of the Soviets.

He strongly indicts "the lack of faith in the creative faculty of the masses" (under the pretext that they are not sufficiently developed intellectually). If they are properly taught they will both lead themselves and lead you. No "aristocracy of leaders with regard to the masses," because it is the masses themselves who are called upon to destroy the old order and to build up the new. Not to be nursemaids and governesses to the crowd: because, quite definitely, they learn less from our books than we learn from them. So that it is only by collaboration with the masses that proper government can take place.

"To be at the wheel and to stare blindly ahead until a catastrophe occurs does not mean leadership. The Bolsheviks do not understand the act of leadership in this way. To lead one must foresee. . . . If you are isolated, even with other comrades who are also leading, you will only see everything if, at the same time, hundreds of thousands, millions of workers are on the look out for weaknesses, discover errors and apply themselves to the achievement of the common task." It is like cleaning out the mechanism of government by making a river flow through it as Hercules did in the tale of the Augean stables.

And in dealing with the masses, persuasion, not violence, must be used. When Zinovieff defended the theory of dictatorship of the Party in 1925, Stalin rose up in arms against "this narrow point of view" and declared that there must be complete harmony between the Party and the mass of the people, and that mutual confidence should not be destroyed by any abstract and unlimited rights which the Party chose to confer upon itself. In the first place, the Party may be mistaken: and even if it is not, the masses may take some time to see that it is right.

Stalin is not at all the sort of man he is supposed to be on the "other side" of the human race, beyond the world barricade which traces a frontier of its own through the middle of official frontiers. But then this other half of the world is composed of a multitude of men born blind, guided by others who have wilfully blinded themselves.

In 1925, at the Fourteenth Congress of the Party, Stalin pronounced the watchword of industrialization. For four years the development of the Soviet Plans and electrification had been advancing by leaps and bounds. It now became necessary to apply oneself systematically to "catching up and overtaking the most advanced capitalist countries, in the shortest possible period."

However, Stalin refused to accept the conception of international stabilization. He considered it to be too rigid a conception in which the Revolution was in danger of being buried. He considered it to be more accurate to show the two different systems in working order, the two worlds side by side, the two halves of the world: Anglo-Saxon Capitalism and Soviet Socialism. At the moment at which capitalist power was at the height of its prosperity and showed no signs of declining, Stalin predicted its decline and the general slump (1928).

In 1927 the Fifteenth Congress of the Party took place. A period of construction in which the collectivization of agriculture was particularly to the fore. "Leaping from the moujik's screw on to the horse of steel"—this kind of metaphor by which Lenin expressed his thoughts in so

1927 is an important date because it marks a definite stage in development. It was at this date that the U.S.S.R. reached the level of pre-war tsarist economy. The figures of 1927 are in nearly every case higher than those of 1913, in only a few rare instances falling below them.

A most significant fact. From thenceforward the feasibility was established, not only of a purely socialist economic system, but also that of a purely socialist economic system in a single country.

In general agricultural production the pre-war level was passed by 1,000,000,000 roubles, or about 8 per cent. In industry it was passed by 200,000,000 roubles, representing an increase of 12 per cent.

The railways, the length of whose permanent ways, in 1913, on the territory now administered by the U.S.S.R., was about 36,500 miles, had increased to about 48,200 miles. For the whole of the former territory of Russia the mean increase in the workers' wages was 16.9 per cent. over pre-war figures (figures arrived at by taking purchasing-power into account).

Educational development had reached sensational proportions. Let us quote a few salient facts. In 1925 there were, in the primary Soviet schools, 2,250,000 *more* pupils than there had been in the Russian schools in 1913, and there were double as many as there had been in the technical schools. Twice as much money was being spent per head on education, and there were ten times as many scientific institutions.

The national revenue was 22,500,000,000 roubles. As for mechanical energy, the U.S.S.R. ranked immediately after the United States of America, Canada, England, Germany and France.

As regards socialization proper. In industrial production,

77 per cent. of the activity was collectivist, 14 per cent. private enterprise and the remainder co-operative. In agricultural production, socialist 2.7 per cent., private 93.3 per cent. In commerce, socialist 81.9 per cent., private, 18.1 per cent.

These were, with the immense handicap of agriculture, the sensational first steps—the result of amazing common sense, understanding and strength of mind.

Chapter Six

THE PARASITIC WAR

THE Opposition. In 1927 took place the massed offensive of the Opposition, all along the line, against the leadership of the Russian Party and of the Communist International. The Opposition had often revealed its existence and had on various occasions held itself aloof, never having ceased to ferment secretly, but it now came methodically and fiercely into the open, with a definite plan of action. Its fire was concentrated on Stalin, and the defence of the Party majority devolved upon Stalin with his indomitable energy.

Of what, exactly, did this Opposition consist? Reference used constantly to be made to it in our part of Europe. It is still quite frequently mentioned, even now. At first sight this Russian phenomenon or, rather, this phenomenon imported from Russia, is quite incomprehensible, except to the initiated. One hears that prominent Revolutionaries, militant Socialists of the highest rank, suddenly begin to treat their Party as a foe, and to be treated as foes by it. One sees them suddenly leave the ranks and fight like demons amid torrents of abuse. They are eliminated, excluded, exiled—and all for questions of disagreement on what seem to be negligible shades of difference. One is tempted to conclude that everyone in the land of the New is terribly and fantastically stubborn.

Not at all. When one goes closely into the matter one sees that what seemed complicated is really quite simple—

but that what seemed superficial is really not so at all. It is not a question of shades of meaning, but of the widest possible differences really affecting the whole question of the future.

How is that?

In the first place, let us observe that the Communist Party is, as Lenin in his great wisdom wished it to be, a Party which is uncompromising and inflexible in its principles. There is no room for fancifulness in it. The leaders of other Parties can go about with false noses and double faces without anyone insisting on any surgical intervention in their regard. But the Communist Party will not have anyone on its effective strength who is in the very least contaminated. It will not allow his mind to harbour any vague formulæ or to be content with approximations of essential facts and ideas. On the contrary, its doctrine is constantly becoming more and more clearly defined and more and more serious.

Let us observe, in the second place, that the Russian Communist Party is a State force, in the sense that it is the advance-guard of the proletariat which directs a socialist State, and that its work is done in flesh and blood. And, lastly, that it is working in a new field, and that it is an example which has no example to follow. For this triple reason, the jolt caused by the introduction of fresh tendencies is apt to be more serious than it would be in other circumstances, but, at the same time, it is terribly and vitally important that the unity and homogeneousness of the Party should be preserved, and it is always prepared to take violent measures to rectify errors and to straighten out kinks. When one reflects on the conditions under which the Party is working, and on the number of varied and important initial tasks with which it is faced, one has to recognize that this must not be otherwise.

This, then, is how the phenomenon of the Opposition is evolved. Every problem to be solved, every measure that has to be taken, admits roughly of two opposite solutions, and creates a parting of the ways, a thesis and an antithesis, a "yes" and a "no"; every decision taken involves a "for" and an "against." The answer is "yes" when it appears that there are more who are "for" than who are "against," but the "against" still subsists. It subsists partly in the facts themselves, since no measure is completely and absolutely good or completely and absolutely bad. It subsists also in the minds of those who constituted the minority opposed to the measure adopted or who were undecided about it. And a curious but pernicious sort of distortion occurs, an exaggeration of the arguments against the measure and of its evils, an exaggeration out of all proportion to the facts. In other words, the instinct of man on the war-path is aroused, develops and gathers strength and violence.

In this process, the factor of purely individual interest plays a much less important rôle than we ourselves might be tempted to believe. Animosity between individuals, though it may often have resulted from opposition, has never in any circumstances been the cause of it. And it is only in the case of Trotsky that we have to take into account a certain amount of strictly personal element, namely Trotsky's opinion of his own importance, which he possesses in a very high degree. His very self-willed nature, his intolerance of any form of criticism ("He never forgives an attack on his ambition," said Lenin) and his disappointment at not being put at the head of affairs without any associates, have a great deal to do with his hostility. Ideology is the arsenal in which this hostility naturally equips itself with a perfect armament. A man who wants to find an excuse to fight will always find it. (At the time of the Renaissance one saw princes and nations embrace Protestantism, not from conviction, but in order to give a reasonable pretext and a public ideal for their personal economic and political ambitions.) Nevertheless —even in the case of Trotsky—the opposition is, above all, a question of deep-seated tendencies. It does not rest upon facts taken by themselves. It always manifests itself in the way of general forms of thought, of habits of mind, of temperament and of intelligence, if one may say so.

One may also assert that certain individual tendencies of mind and of character are apt to identify themselves with certain political tendencies. Narrowness of mind and short-sighted aggressiveness may manifest themselves by prejudice and opposition—intellectual and moral cowardice by lower middle-class opportunism and lapsing towards Reformism and Menshevism.

It is this which gives the Opposition its great importance and its formidable scope, because it is the divergence of tendencies in question which brings about wide divergence in the interpretation of communist doctrine. Divergence from the practical interpretation of the doctrine, that is to say from Marxism, a different assessment of the "peculiar requirements of the moment," may have quite unforseen consequences, or may give a different meaning to the whole policy. A mistake about an isolated fact may be corrected like a mistake in an arithmetical sum. But an error in tendency is a general deformation, beginning at the bottom and, increasing by geometrical progression, bringing with it an enormous number of modifications of detail susceptible of changing the whole face of national

THE PARASITIC WAR

history—to say nothing of resulting in terrible disaster. It is a modification of the "line" of the great Party which is the motive force of the State.

In its origin, the Opposition is a tendential malady.

But it is a particular kind of tendential malady of the gravest possible kind, whose main symptom is lack of discipline, definite separation and drifting apart from the majority of the leaders. The opposing tendency to that of the majority is no longer a subject for discussion, but an object for war.

It is in this way that the functions of the Opposition differ radically from those of self-criticism. The aim of self-criticism is to bring all the tendencies back into a common path. Nothing is more natural than that different tendencies should exist; nothing is more healthy than clear and open discussion on any points at issue. Self-criticism ensures this maximum freedom of expression of opinion, which is the privilege of the Bolshevik Party.

But the Opposition does not follow the lines of self-criticism. Its essential and most pernicious characteristics are that it forms itself into a separate body, refuses to identify itself with the decision of the majority—the majority vote being the only democratic method and, indeed, the only sensible method of settling a disagreement until the facts can be thoroughly co-ordinated. In this case, something remains over after the vote is taken. The Opposition seizes this something and consolidates round it in a solid body. Instead of accepting the decision more or less openly, it fights it. "The Opposition View" becomes indurated and overgrown, and the State organism is attacked by a parasitic growth in its interior. In this way, the Opposition brings about what is called a split, the prelude to a definite schism. Self-criticism always remains open, but

Opposition closes itself up. The self-critic remains inside the community. With the Opposition, the figure "2" makes its appearance. And so, in this way, we see "liberty of opinion" pathologically creating a group in the bosom of the Party which takes the form of a Party itself and constitutes a permanent conspiracy. When this Opposition group considers itself to be sufficiently strong (and outside the Party it relies, like all oppositions, on the support of the various adversaries of the State policy), it goes to war and tries to seize the reins of power in order to change its heterodoxy into orthodoxy.

Lenin had very explicitly fought this particularism, by which the disease starts, at the Tenth Congress, and he had caused the following resolution to be adopted: "Each organization of the Party must keep a strict watch to ensure that the freedom of necessary criticism of the mistakes of the Party, of analysing the fundamental policy of the Party, of taking notice of all its practical experience, of applying its decisions, of considering the remedies for any errors that may be made, and everything that follows from these things, should not become the prerogatives of certain men or of certain groups collected round a definite platform but should be quite open to all the members of the Party."

On what questions was the Opposition most active? According to what has just been said, and when it becomes a question of unreasonable persistence, in the Party mechanism, of general tendencies running contrary to those of the majority, and of the consolidating of those tendencies—it is easy to understand that the Opposition showed itself in all the great administrative problems of the U.S.S.R. and of the Communist International. It always attempted to approach all these problems from an angle different to the one from which the administrative majority envisaged them and approached them.

It appears to anyone who casts a summary glance over the salient facts of the Russian revolutionary movement from the end of the nineteenth century, that two basic tendencies, namely, the reformist and revolutionary, which had brought about the schism between the Mensheviks and the Bolsheviks, subsisted up to a certain degree in the very heart of the Bolshevik Party which had come into power. Some of the leaders, Kameneff, Zinovieff and, to a certain degree, Trotsky, were, as we have seen, in certain important connexions, hostile to revolutionary methods. They would have liked to have prevented the October Revolution and, once this had been accomplished, to have avoided the dictatorship of the proletariat.

In practice they would have preferred a constitutional-democratic régime to a socialist régime. They had no confidence in the strength or the durability of a truly Socialist state in the heart of a capitalist world; they did not believe that the better class peasants could be won over to this cause. In addition, they criticized the principle of State industry which they looked upon as an enterprise of a capitalist order. They were in favour of freedom for splits and groups in the heart of the Party, that is to say, of the heterogeneousness of the Party. These points, upon which Zinovieff, Kameneff and Trotsky came together repeatedly, constitute the principal characteristics of the most important of the "Oppositions." It is the return to life of the Menshevik ferment.

So that, during Lenin's lifetime, the Opposition consisted of those who opposed Lenin's point of view, since Lenin actually ruled the Party which he "had forged with his own hands for twenty-five years," and which was his own creation. But after Lenin's death it made, if one may say so, a pretext of Stalin to intensify its offensive and to attack the same theses with the same arguments, pretending all the while to be defending the purity of Leninism.

Stalin, too, placed himself beneath the banner of Leninism, in the campaign which followed, to defend passionately the unity of the Party which was imperilled by the rebellion of the minority. To safeguard the unity of the Party became his great concern, as it had been Lenin's, as it had been Lenin's and Stalin's together, for, as we have already seen, these two never disagreed with one another on questions of either doctrine or tactics.

There was a second paragraph, a second verse as it were, to Stalin's oath, quoted earlier on, concerning the honour of the Party. "In leaving us, Comrade Lenin recommended us to preserve the unity of the Party as the apple of our eyes. We swear to you, Comrade Lenin, to fulfil this wish of yours faithfully!"

The breaking up of the Party, a schism in fact, became possible as soon as the great Master was no longer there, and had it succeeded it would have been an incalculable calamity.

The situation was altered in two respects; Stalin not only no longer had Lenin by his side, but he had Trotsky—Trotsky no longer under any restraint now that Lenin had disappeared.

The whole Opposition gravitated around the personality of Trotsky. Even if he does not personify it all, one may say that he symbolizes it. It is due to him that it became a great danger—due to the authority conferred upon him by the part he had played in the history of the Revolution and in the beginnings of the Soviet State.

To-day, Trotsky, exiled from Russia as the result of the

open war he waged on the régime, has become the victim of certain vexations of the capitalist police forces and of the sarcasm of the great newspapers, because of his old title of People's Commissar. What is being hounded down in Trotsky and what is being avenged on him beneath European skies is the part attributed to him in the October Revolution. The international middle classes, which do not investigate matters very closely, take a keen delight and pride in bullying a Bolshevik. But, side by side with this persecution which he has long ceased to deserve, he finds the support and complicity of a motley collection of enemies of the Soviet régime, and even without referring to his present political activities, one cannot blind one's eyes to the dagger-thrusts that have been aimed by him and his followers at the U.S.S.R. and at the Communist International. They really constituted an attempt to assassinate them, and an effort to destroy them.

Need one repeat that the personal factor undoubtedly very largely influenced Trotsky's attitude? Even during Lenin's lifetime, his incompatibility with all the other leaders became apparent. "It is very difficult to work with this comrade," grumbled Zinovieff, who, however, was more than once to be found in his camp. Trotsky was much too much of a Trotskyist!

Up to what point was it Trotsky's despotic character, his rancour at being supplanted, at being neglected among the others instead of shining alone, his "Bonapartism," that induced him to break with the Party and to construct for himself a sort of patchwork imitation Leninism, and to start a political war with the more or less implicitly expressed object of the formation of a new Party, namely a Fourth International? It is very difficult to say. One cannot, however, avoid remarking that Trotsky led an intensive Opposition against the Party in 1921 and again in 1923 and that, in the interval, in the year 1922, in a speech before the Fourth Congress, he defended all the points of view of the majority on the thorny question of the N.E.P. in a very concise manner. This did not prevent the Trotskyist Opposition, brandishing the theory of permanent Revolution, from endeavouring to show, on the morrow of the Congress, that the Revolution had come to a standstill and that the N.E.P. was a capitalist degeneration, a kind of Thermidor. These contradictory attitudes which followed one another at such a short interval of time seem to show the intervention of some artificial factor of an exclusively personal nature.

Whatever may have been the various causes which incited it, the great reason for Trotsky's schism is chiefly his conception of political principles. Even if the incidental cause is vanity, the fundamental cause is ideological. It is based upon a fundamental divergence of tendencies between his own and Lenin's principles of Bolshevism. It reveals a different political temperament, a different set of values and different methods. And it is as a result of the intensive and bitter development of these fundamental differences and of their exploitation that Trotsky gradually took an opposition stand against the *whole* of the official Bolshevik policy.

Menshevik to start with, Trotsky always remained a Menshevik. He may have become anti-Bolshevik because he was a Trotskyist, but he certainly did so because he was an old Menshevik. Let us put it, if you wish, that the Trotskyist aroused the old Menshevik in him.

Many people have, to the best of their ability (and it has now become a sort of tradition to do so) made comparative portraits—in the manner of La Bruyère—of Lenin and Trotsky: Lenin monolithic, thoughtful and quiet in manner, Trotsky sparkling and nervous. Jacques Sadoul, with a great deal of skill, inaugurated the series of these conventional confrontations between the man of genius and the man of intelligence. The general gist of this picturesque contrast may be considered fair enough even though it may be perilous to push such a literary exercise too far (the exigencies of a ready-made parallelism making the author sometimes leave the true path, in attempts of this kind). But, above all, the two people are not on the same scale, and in any case, one cannot reasonably put any other personality on a parallel with the gigantic figure of Lenin.

But Trotsky's very qualities had serious counterparts which easily changed them into defects. His critical sense, hypertrophied but without any broadness (Lenin's, like Stalin's, was encyclopædic), rivetted his attention upon details, prevented him from visualizing situations as a whole and made him pessimistic.

Besides, he had too much imagination. He had an uncontrolled imagination. And this imagination, jostling against its own self, would lose its balance, and cease to be able to distinguish the possible from the impossible (which, in any case, is not the function of the imagination). Lenin used to say that Trotsky was perfectly capable of producing nine good solutions and a tenth disastrous one. The men who worked with Trotsky will tell you that, every morning when they awoke, they murmured, as they opened their eyes and stretched themselves: "I wonder what Trotsky is going to invent to-day."

He saw all the alternatives too clearly, so that all sorts of doubts would assail him. The thesis and the antithesis haunted him at the same time. "Trotsky is a human shuttlecock," said Lenin. So he would hesitate and vacillate. He was unable to make a decision. He was afraid, and consequently always instinctively opposed the actual work in hand.

Again, he was too fond of talking. He would become intoxicated by the sound of his own voice. "Even when speaking confidentially to a single person, he becomes declamatory," said one of his former companions. To sum up, Trotsky possessed the eminent qualities of an advocate, of a debater, of an art critic and of a journalist—but not that of a statesman having to break new ground. He lacked the exclusive and absolute sense of reality and of life. He lacked the great straightforward ruthlessness of the man of action. He did not possess really strong Marxist convictions. He was afraid. He had always been afraid. It was out of fear that he remained a Menshevik, and it is equally out of fear that he has become unbalanced and is sometimes seized with frantic attacks of extremeness. One cannot understand Trotsky unless one can discern his weakness through his fits of violence.

In a general survey Manuilsky has given us an even broader view of the matter: "The almost uninterrupted succession of Oppositions was the expression of the retirement of the feebler elements of the Party from Bolshevik positions." All Opposition is a confession of retrogression, discouragement, incipient paralysis and sleeping-sickness.

It was the same abroad: "During the period of the actual and relative stabilization of Capitalism, Socialists began to waver and to leave the ranks of the Communist International." It is hard work having to keep on marching forward, constantly bearing that banner. After a certain time one's feet grow tired, one's fingers lose their grip—unless one has a vocation for it.

THE PARASITIC WAR

Powerful and elementary methods of action are required to make progress on the great path of history. One must know how to spurn the casuist. Faced by the quintessential arguments of the Eleatic philosophers against the reality of movement, Diogenes, surly and silent, gave proof of its reality by getting up and walking. Crowds prove the futility of this or that objection by walking over it. When 100,000 people act together there must be some intelligence in what they do. ("Intelligence," according to Descartes, being that modicum of reasoning power which everyone possesses.) In spite of any argument to the contrary one must agree with them. It is because of the platitude, the bustling pettiness and the impotence of Menshevism, because of what Stalin has called "the dissolute character of the Mensheviks in the matter of organization," that Trotsky was beaten. If Trotsky had been right he would have won. In the same way as the Bolsheviks who, at the dawn of the New Era, opposed the Mensheviks in the heart of the Social-Democratic Party and forced a separation, would themselves have been beaten—if they had been wrong.

The Opposition naturally applied itself first of all to the most important problem of the Russian Revolution: the possibility of building up a Socialist System in a single country.

Lenin had taken up his position with regard to this problem even before the Revolution. At that time he wrote: "The development of Capitalism differs entirely in each country. From which we arrive at the incontestable conclusion that Socialism cannot conquer in every country simultaneously. It will start by conquering one or more countries . . . and this will not only arouse irritation, but also a direct tendency on the part of the middle classes of other countries to crush the victorious proletariat of the socialist State."

The victory of the October Revolution brought the victors face to face with two tasks: the socialization of the world and the solid construction of Socialism in one place. Which was the one by which to begin or, rather, from what side should this dual task be approached?

Lenin considered that the more important task was clearly that of building up a socialist society where it was possible to build it up, namely, in Russia.

Trotsky was afraid that this would lead the Revolution to a dead end. This advance over a single sector on the whole capitalist front seemed to him to be doomed to failure. He was afraid and the Menshevik in him was resurrected, or, rather, aroused. Under those conditions, he said, the Russian Revolution must be considered as a provisional one only.

It will be recalled that during the Sixth Congress of the Party, in the middle of 1917, Preobrajinsky had attempted to have it laid down that the socialization of Russia should be dependent upon the establishment of Socialism in every other country. And it is because Stalin had risen vigorously against this that no vote was taken upon the amendment, inspired by Trotsky, making the possibility of founding a Socialist society in disaffected tsarist Russia depend upon the success, in the first instance, of the World Revolution.

Karl Radek, whose opinion in the circumstances is all the more interesting because he allied himself—for a time —to Trotsky's outlook, says in this connexion: "Trotsky returned to the point of view of the Second International, which he had himself formulated at the Second Congress of the Russian Party, before the split—namely that the

STALIN ADDRESSING A CONGRESS

'Dictatorship of the Proletariat' should mean the power of an organized proletariat representing the majority of the nation."

So that, unless the proletarian Revolution could command half the votes plus one, there was nothing to be done. For Trotsky, not only the victory of the proletariat in a single country, but even its victory in this single country unsupported by an absolute majority, reduced itself to an "historic episode." Trotsky, then, became clearly a partisan of this "civilized European Socialism" which the Second International opposed to Leninism. The Social-Democrats placed no confidence in the Revolution. The Social-Democratic leaders thought that socialist-revolution was only possible in a country of highly developed Capitalism, not in Russia, because of lack of a solid foundation of labour. They only believed, for Russia, in a middle-class revolution, which would have been, like all middle-class revolutions, nothing but a ceremony for the transmission of hegemony from autocracy to the middle classes (reinforced at the edges, and specially adorned, by the skilful grafting on of a few picked workers), by which the workers' and peasants' class as a whole would be just as much trampled on as they were before. Stalin has already told us that this incorrect estimate of the real revolutionary capacities of Russia resulted in the deplorable abstention of the Social-Democrats from the 1905 Revolution.

We know that other "Oppositionists," such as Zinovieff and Kameneff—the most important figures in the Party with Lenin, Trotsky and Stalin*—abounded in the Trotsky sense. "By predicting the building up of Socialism in a single country, an opportunist state of mind was cultivated in the Party," and "all this led to the abandonment

* And Sverdloff, who died in 1919.

of the positions captured by the revolutionary proletariat," and, lastly, becoming warmed up to this thesis, "the international tasks of the Revolution were abandoned." And then big words and sweeping gestures—the battle of windmills came into play.

Trotsky's general theory (and that of Hilferding) consisted in establishing the doctrine that the socialist economic system in process of construction is completely dependent upon the world capitalist system, from whence follows a gradual fatal capitalist degeneration of the Soviet economic system, in the midst of a capitalist world. Radek also said—at that time: "We have no power in face of World Capitalism." These, and others, were afraid. One can detect the breath of apprehension, the access of panic which gathered this Opposition group into its eddy.

Lenin and Stalin themselves took an entirely different point of view of the matter and they unquestionably put it into its right place. Construction in a single country is a force of which advantage must be taken. "Give me a sufficiently powerful lever and I will raise the world," said Archimedes. And Radek—Radek himself again—says, very expressively: "The possibility of construction in a single country is the fulcrum of Archimedes's lever in Lenin's strategic plan."

Lenin never lost sight of the world organization of socialist policy. Lenin never lost sight of anything. He had indeed that end in view when he began with Russia. In the last articles that Lenin wrote before his death, he declared that the socialist reconstruction of Russia (which has every form of primary commodity at its disposal) was quite feasible by virtue of the law of the unequal development of Capitalism, notwithstanding the "cultural" backwardness of the country and in spite of the condition of the peasantry.

Stalin, whom both Trotsky and Zinovieff reproached bitterly for his narrow-minded theory of nationalism, has never ceased to proclaim that "the development and the support of the Revolution in other countries is one of the essential tasks of the victorious Revolution." He even goes so far as to lay it down that, so long as the U.S.S.R. remains politically isolated in the world, it will not be able to be considered as a thoroughly stable power. But there is a difference between "transitory" and "provisional." And he sets out to show the effective strengthening which construction in one country constitutes for the revolutionary principle in general. And he points out the terrible, inevitable, lightning-like, reciprocal repercussions of Soviet reconstruction on the interior situation of nations and of the reinforcement of the Communist International on the borders of other established régimes.

"One must not see," says the author of *Questions of Leninism,* "one must not see in the triumph of revolution in a single country a purely national fact. But neither must one think that the Russian Revolution is an inert thing that can only be helped from outside." It is not that one of these alternatives depends upon the other, but that they are interdependent.

As for the barriers, the Great Walls of China, which people point to, he solves the whole problem and points to a few guiding facts.

Dependence on foreign Capitalism, you say? Let us examine that. . . . Stalin has cleared the ground: Comrade Trotsky has said in the course of his speech: "That in reality we find ourselves constantly under the control of world economics. Is this right? No. That is the dream of capitalist sharks, but it is not the truth." And Stalin goes on to show that this supposed control is not exercised from the financial point of view, either on the nationalized Soviet banks, or upon industry, or upon foreign commerce, which are also nationalized. Neither is this control exercised from the political point of view. So that it is not exercised in any of the practical meanings of the word "control." All these people keep parading a bogey of control. On the other hand, "to broaden our relations with the capitalist world does not mean making ourselves dependent upon it."

Manuilsky (in 1926) emphasized the error of the "law of heredity" which Trotsky tried to use for his own ends by evoking the tsarist economic system. This did indeed make Russia dependent upon world Capitalism, because the Russian capitalist economic system was an integral part of the world capitalist economic system. The situation is quite different for Revolutionary Russia so long as it maintains the essential principles which differentiate it from other countries.

Finally Stalin lays great stress, as a conclusion, on the necessity for persuading the workers' classes in capitalist countries that they can dispense with the middle classes in putting a new society upon its feet.

No doubt the sequence of events has now brought into the realm of accomplished fact things which at that time were only dreams, and we possess experience which allows us to take short cuts. Nevertheless, this discussion seems to us to be strange enough, even for its time. For to what other methods could the Russian Revolution have recourse, since it was evidently incapable of immediately imposing the proletarian Revolution upon the other countries of the world, than to build up Socialism to the best of its ability

THE PARASITIC WAR

in the only territory occupied by it? What else could it do? Leave the conquered territory to stagnate whilst it devoted itself to the future conquest of the rest of the world? An extravagance of the so-called reformist brain. Besides, how could the spreading power and the power of attraction of socialist achievement in one particular part of the world be ignored? By reflecting ever so little on this simple and absorbing question, one arrives at the conclusion that it is precisely because revolution in countries developed and exploited to the uttermost limit by Capitalism would encounter special difficulties to the extent to which they are under foreign control, that the existence and stabilization of a socialist State is an important trump card in helping to make the proletarian victory a general one. But one still had to believe in the possibility of the constitution of this continental revolutionary reservoir, and to be far-sighted enough to discern it in advance.

In the midst of this muddle which put the Soviet Communists at such loggerheads, two men of common sense and clearness of vision seem to move about among the shadows. Lenin and Stalin were faced with a host of inconsistent adversaries whose want of confidence, of energy, of courage and—as one of them who was afterwards converted remarked—whose incredulity resulted in their losing the northern provinces and upset them so much that they gave utterance to the most puerile and paralysing inconsistencies.

Here Stalin and Trotsky really appeared as the exact opposite to one another. They are two types of men situated at opposite poles of contemporary humanity. Stalin relies with all his weight upon reason and practical common sense. He is impeccably and inexorably methodical. He knows. He thoroughly understands Leninism, and the part played in government by the working classes and by the Party. He does not try to show off and is not worried by a desire to be original. He merely tries to do everything that he can do. He does not believe in eloquence or in sensationalism. When he speaks, he merely tries to combine simplicity with clearness. Like Lenin, he is always driving the same points home. He asks a large number of questions (because they show him the temper of his audience) and he relies largely on the same words, like some great preacher of old. And he has an unerring way of putting all the strong and all the weak points before you. He has no equal in ferreting out reformist complacency and opportunist laziness in a man. "With whatever veil," says Radek, "opportunism covers his miserable body, Stalin tears it aside." (You, who call yourself orthodox, you are nothing but a Conservative disguised as a Communist!)

This great question, the building up of Socialism in a single country, is fairly representative, let us repeat, of the position which the Soviet protagonists occupied in the series of ideologico-political duels which took place during the first phase of construction of the U.S.S.R. It also explains fairly simply why it has been said that Stalin's defensive offensive, when he dared to attack Trotsky, who was regarded, especially after Lenin's death, as taboo, "purified and rejuvenated the Party by ridding it of the remains of the pollution of the Second International." The struggle against Trotskyism is the struggle against a muddled, meddling and cowardly lower middle class—in a word, counter-revolutionary in the heart of the Party.

Shortly afterwards another opposition group appeared on the Right. The ruling majority was caught between two fires on the question of the peasantry. The Trotskyist Opposition (on the Left) did not appreciate the rôle of the peasantry in the Revolution, and Bukharin's Opposition (on the Right) lost sight of the rôle of the proletariat with regard to the masses of the peasants—the former haunted by the spectacle of the rich peasant and the blot made by the N.E.P., the latter by the spectre of the trouble that must necessarily follow any re-adjustment and, for fear of fire, throwing cold water on the war of the classes. A policy of not falling down either to the Right or to the Left, and of accurately gauging the importance of people and of things. So far as the small peasants are concerned, to say: "They will be devoured by the *kulak*" was to underestimate the case. But to say: "They will devour the *kulak*" was to overestimate it. The wisest course was clearly to stay exactly where one was, and do nothing at all.

Not only Kameneff and Zinovieff, who were at first hostile to Trotsky, allied themselves to him, but we also see Zinovieff joining Bukharin in considering that the peasant question was the chief question of Leninism. "Be quiet!" cried the majority. "When you talk like that, you Russianize Leninism and deprive it of its international value." "And you will find yourselves," says Manuilsky, "moving along the path traced by Otto Bauer (Austro-Marxist Nationalism, called National Cultural Autonomy).

Tirelessly, Stalin began at the beginning, put each principle in its proper place, and once more laid it down that "the fundamental question of Leninism, its starting-point, is not the peasant question but the question of the dictatorship of the proletariat, the question of the conditions of obtaining it, and the conditions of its retention. The question of the peasantry as allied to the proletariat in its struggle for power, is a subsidiary question."

Then he turned to the Right. It was Stalin's idea to put

on to the agenda of the Sixth International Congress not only the question of the struggle against the deviations of the Right (who wanted to check the readjustment of the situation resulting from the N.E.P.) but also the struggle against the conciliatory tendencies towards them.

How did events actually develop? Let us note systematically the various phases of this conflict.

The first signs of Trotsky's secession had placed the Party in a difficult position ("The Party is feverish," said Lenin) during the Brest-Litovsk period and that of the Syndicates. The wavering in the Party at that time and the attacks on Lenin facilitated the Kronstadt rising.

After Lenin's death, Trotsky first directed his attacks against the Party with a certain amount of reserve, but later he delivered more and more open and severe attacks on the occasion of the discussions provoked by his essays *The New Current* and *Lessons of October*, in which he presented the part played by the Party and his own part in a biassed and inaccurate way. The famous letter of the Fifty-three (1925) puts the question "of the country going to ruin."

The reports of the meetings of the Party bear witness to the fact that it acted with a great deal of circumspection and of patience towards Trotsky. In 1923, during Lenin's illness, Trotsky was again the head of the Political Bureau, the supreme executive organization. The Party endeavoured to influence Trotsky by every means in its power, whilst he himself was notoriously striving to turn to his own advantage the discontent which cropped up here and there, to make a group of the discontents and to be their leader. This vague group hostile to the Party refused to criticize Trotskyism and adopted Trotsky's divergent line.

When, after Lenin's death, Stalin resumed the struggle, he began, in dealing with Lenin's old adversary, to employ the pedagogic method instead of taking repressive measures (Jaroslavsky). These attempts at persuasion came to nothing and the question arose as to whether Trotsky could still remain in the leadership of the Party, or even in the Party at all. The question became all the more urgent when Trotsky adopted the doctrine called "Clemenceau's doctrine": namely that in the event of war the government should change. This theory, applied to the U.S.S.R. and to the strongly united and harmonic organization of the governing machinery, constituted a real appeal to schism and to civil war.

In December 1925, when the Bolshevik Party held its 14th Congress, Zinovieff and Kameneff presented themselves to it at the head of a thoroughly organized Opposition—mostly consisting of delegates from Leningrad—and armed with the theses enumerated higher up (construction of Socialism impossible in a single country, under-estimation of the better-class peasantry, comparison of the sector of Socialist production to State capitalism, complete liberty to split). This Opposition received the name, which was however little justified, of the "New Opposition." Its mouthpiece, Zinovieff, insisted that side by side with the Central Committee's report (with Stalin as reporter), a report of his own should be presented. This was permitted, and it meant the official declaration of hostilities.

Stalin energetically counter-attacked this offensive, all of whose faults were the result, in his opinion, of "one fundamental fault," namely, lack of faith in the triumph of Socialism.

In 1926–27 occurred the phenomenon of the Opposition combining to form a sort of trust of their doctrines, a strong attempt at concerted action, at decisive action, and high-handed methods.

This Opposition, gathered round Trotsky, issued a memorandum of their grievances, a "platform." Everything was classified in order and it formed a complete programme, a statement of policy, intended to show that the leadership of the Party had completely abandoned Leninism and was pursuing the wrong track in every direction. At the same time, these former adversaries of Stalin, now become his open enemies, pursued abroad a campaign of disparagement of the Soviet Union and of the Party in their existing forms.

In order to deal with this challenge and these repeated attacks, the Central Committee decided that the Political Bureau should publish their own case one month before the Congress of the Russian Communist Party in December 1927, and that the Opposition might furnish all the replies they wished—and that these should be reproduced in the Party Press and sent out to all organizations. In this way, decided the Central Committee, the discussion would remain open for a month upon all points.

But, on September the 3rd, 1927, the Opposition launched its "platform" of 120 pages and insisted upon its immediate publication and despatch to local committees and organizations. The Party refused to accept this infraction of the decision it had taken, and to spread the discussion over four months, judging that this was a luxury which the constructors could not afford to allow themselves at the height of their unremitting labours.

One must know this work (the "platform") thoroughly if one is to understand all the meanderings of the Opposition. All these fragments of criticism and accusation pieced together make a sort of protective covering for the

THE PARASITIC WAR

Opposition, and this bulky address, which deals with all the essential chapters of the doctrine, of the life, and of the actions of the Party and of the Government, puts forward a code which amends the existing forms of Leninism from beginning to end, in the name of a new kind of Leninism.

It is impossible to reproduce this encyclopædic attack, even in an abbreviated form. It contains too many faces and facets.

However, now that the question of Opposition to the U.S.S.R. has almost entirely lost its vital importance, it is no longer necessary to examine each paragraph of this parallel Leninism through a magnifying glass. Many of the problems of the Opposition were solved immediately. A peremptory and historic reply was given to them. The subsequent course of events and the significant progress of socialist construction have played havoc to-day among the Opposition arguments and have removed any excuse for the existence of most of them.

And further—a fact which extinguishes the judiciary action of the critic—nearly all the important members of the Opposition, convinced by the turn matters have taken, have since made honourable amends (honourable for their powers of discernment and for their character).

Let us not forget, however, that the Opposition, being a manifestation of deep-rooted tendencies, still exists—quite apart from Trotsky's continued activity and other secret activities—though in a latent and dangerous form, even though it has no longer any chance of asserting itself.

Moreover, even though its case is hopeless, hatred persists and is always trying to strike. We have recently seen that the terrorist organization calling itself the *Centre of Leningrad*, which charged Nikolaieff to kill Kiroff, was composed of the "decayed remnants" of the old Zinovieff-Kameneff-Trotsky Opposition, allied to tsarist assassins and foreign paymasters, and that one of its aims was to strike down by murder the actual leaders of the U.S.S.R., in order to avenge itself for the defeat of the Opposition and to bring about national and international complications.

That being so, a close study of the large number of charges, which constitute the historic platform of the Opposition of 1927, suggests the following considerations, which it is well should be put down in writing, in order to put a dissension which was so very serious into its proper perspective and close the subject.

Let us note once more that the facts put forward are there as *examples*, alleged by the Opposition, of the employment of bad methods or of the wrong employment of good methods. The challenge is to the methods, tendencies, administrative ideas (the current expression *deviation* appears in every line in all the arguments on both sides). The fundamental question was therefore one of more or less accentuated divergences—to the Right or to the Left —from the principles and tactics of Leninism.

In the first place, many of the precise details (statistics) upon which the Opposition relies in framing its accusations of deviation and its predictions of headlong disaster are indisputably inaccurate, either because the figures given are incorrect, or because they are misleading owing to all the elements of a particular question not having been taken into consideration.

For instance: the so-called increase in industrial and transport shortage in relation to demand (this was the main complaint); the delay in the increase of wages in proportion to the work done; the shortening of the working day; the increase in the difference between the wages of men and women; the lowering of the wages of youths; the increase of unemployment; the amount allocated to the unemployed; etc. . . .

In the second place, many of the charges are brought without any proof, while in other cases they are in direct contradiction to earlier decisions of the Party and to results already achieved. For instance: the disguising of the progress made by the *kulaks;* the suppression of democracy within the Party; the abandonment of the idea of industrialization (in the shadow of the N.E.P.); the attempt to oppose co-operation in electrification (also in connexion with the N.E.P.).

In the third place, a great number of the proposals of the Opposition are quite obviously dangerous, clumsy and likely to produce disastrous results. All this category of definite proposals shows a lack of appreciation of realities, and possesses a character of bluff and demagogism, either because the proposals are bad in themselves, or because they are inopportune and premature.

For instance (apart from the too obvious criticisms of the disadvantages of the N.E.P., the exploitation of that temporary state of affairs brought about by immediate necessities, and the demand that it should be put an end to immediately): That support should be given to the nationalist deviations to the Right, which might have the effect of breaking up the Soviet Federation. That wholesale prices should be increased (the Fifteenth Congress pointed out the formidable repercussions that would eventually result from such a measure, which the Opposition adopted without considering the mechanism of Socialism as a whole, but solely in order to secure the goodwill and support of the peasants). That restrictions should be placed on production (the closing down of factories and over-organization). That measures, equally demagogic, of mass exemption from contributions of the poor peasants and the withdrawal of State capital from co-operative schemes should be adopted (which would mean the reinforcement of private capital). That surtax should be levied upon the rich, tantamount to confiscation, and that private capital should be suddenly abolished and the N.E.P. liquidated before it had entirely done its work. That supplementary requisitions of wheat should be made (infallibly provoking the crash of the whole struggling credit policy of the U.S.S.R.).

It is clearly a great temptation for anyone who wishes to play to the gallery to suggest such measures, but all they could achieve would be a reckless adjustment, on paper only, of problems which in actual practice can only be solved gradually and not without a certain delay.

It is obviously easy to brandish evidence like the *kulak* danger, the growth of unemployment, the shortage of housing for the workers and the fatty degeneration of the bureaucracy. It is also easy to say in nearly every case: "Things ought to move more quickly." But the question is whether it is possible to move more quickly and whether the relative, not actual, slowness of progress is or is not the fault of the Party leadership, and in any case whether this is a sufficient reason to make radical alterations in its whole policy.

Is the Party to be blamed, for instance, because it is unable to procure the vast sums of money necessary for the complete reconstruction of the workers' dwellings? And in the great major drama of the industrialization of the land (which is known to be necessary but which is being retarded both voluntarily and involuntarily), is it not putting the cart before the horse in the most ridiculous way to stifle the co-operative system of commodity distribution, which is actually in existing working order, by potential electrification? It may be observed that this antinomy of "co-operation as against heavy industry" presents itself in almost the same form and with the same details as the antinomy of "Socialism in one country as against World Revolution." The question at issue is whether one ought to abandon an objective that is half reached for another—a greater one—which is not yet attainable. The alternative one has to decide is: either to do something concrete, or to begin at the end.

It is, in any case, notorious that many of the measures of salvation feverishly put forward by the Opposition are the very ones which the Party itself recommends and applies. In these cases the Opposition is merely discovering America. It is playing the part of the fly on the coach-wheel (and a tsetse fly at that!).

Invest 500,000,000 roubles in industry, enjoins the Opposition. But the curve of investment in industry, continuously mounting, was already 460,000,000 roubles in 1927 when this injunction was launched. Some of the proposals of the Opposition—as, for instance, those relating to a better distribution of agricultural produce, to the assistance of poor peasants and small contractors, to the charter of adolescent workers—are copied from resolutions already passed and put into force.

The question of "democracy," that is to say of everyone working in common and of the participation of the masses in the fruits of labour—of the respect for minorities in the political plan—was in the first instance the chief concern of Lenin and of Stalin. Actually, no government is compelled to furnish so many accounts and is so subjected to the control of a Party, itself intimately connected with the people, as is the Soviet Government. The chronology of the public life of the U.S.S.R. bristles with the roman and arabic numerals of International Congresses, Party Congresses, Soviet Congresses, Conferences and "Plenums." The layman is lost in this mass of figures which are, nevertheless, worked out with the utmost care. As soon as any subject comes up for discussion, it automatically comes out into the open and is thoroughly aired.

Bureaucracy? Yes, no doubt one is always right when one abuses it. It has a deplorable tendency either to become sterile and fat, or thin to mummification. But, all the same, the Administration has a broad back and very often one blackguards it with theatrical violence and with one's eyes shut, solely because one wants, for one reason or another, to attack the government. More than twenty years earlier, in 1903, Lenin replied to the Mensheviks and to Trotsky: "It is obvious that outcries against the bureaucracy are only a method of showing one's dissatisfaction with the composition of the central organization. You are a bureaucrat because you were elected by the Congress, not by my wishes, but in spite of them. . . . You are acting in a barbarous, mechanical way because you take orders from the majority of the Congress of the Party and pay no heed to my desire to be personally consulted. . . . You are an autocrat because you do not wish to restore the power into the hands of the old group of your colleagues, which defends its own ideas all the more energetically because it objects to being disregarded by the Congress." Thus Lenin expressed himself, and he was an amazingly good psychologist with a hundred piercing eyes.

The Plenum of the Central Committee and of the Control Commission, which met in 1927 before the Fifteenth

Congress, made a supreme effort with Trotsky and Zinovieff. It asked Trotsky to renounce his theories on the change of government and his calumnies on the "Thermidorian" character of the central power, and to come into unconditional line with the rest of the Party. Trotsky and Zinovieff rejected the possibility thus offered to them of definitely re-establishing peace within the Party. In consequence, they were excluded from the Central Committee, censured, and warned that if they went on they would be expelled from the Party itself.

Trotsky and Zinovieff (the latter being particularly influential at Leningrad where he was President of the Council of the Soviets) went on with the war. They tried to excite the Young Communists against the Party. There were more and more secret meetings, secret printing-presses and tracts: they seized meeting-places by force and, on November 7th, 1927, for instance, made demonstrations in the streets. At the Fifteenth Congress, a special report was presented on this intense political conspiracy against the central power. This made it abundantly clear that Trotsky and his followers had decided to create a party with a central committee, district committees, and town committees, a technical apparatus with its own funds and its own Press. And the same thing on the international plan, with the object of supplanting the Third International. Orthodox members of the Central Committee were prevented by force from being present at Trotskyist meetings (this was so, for instance, in the case of Jaroslavsky and some others, who were "physically" ejected from a meeting at Moscow).

The Fifteenth Congress attempted to clear up this deplorable and dangerous state of affairs, urged Trotsky to dissolve his organizations and, once more, to renounce his bellicose methods which not only overstepped the bounds of what a militant Bolshevik could be allowed to do, but even those of "Soviet loyalty," and finally, once for all, to put an end to his systematic hostility towards the points of view of the majority. But the counter-proposals of the Trotskyists, signed by 121 people, so far from being conciliatory, accentuated the attacks and the split. Trotsky and his followers were expelled from the Party. Even this decision left a door open, namely the possibility was considered of their being individually taken back into the Party if they would alter their ideas and would adjust their behaviour accordingly. This is a long way from the Trotskyist caricature showing comrade Jaroslavsky, President of the Control Commission, as a fierce, bloodthirsty watch-dog held in leash by Stalin.

One might be tempted to say: "Has not the Opposition, in any case, been useful in drawing the special attention of the leaders to weak spots and in putting them on their guard against such and such a danger?"

No. In the first place, in principle, self-criticism was an infinitely more efficacious method than a duel to the death for keeping the leaders on the look out.

Again, it is patent that the curve of the regular and gradual achievements of the Soviet State bears no trace whatever of the intervention of the Opposition. The Opposition lost no opportunity for correction; on the contrary, it put obstacles in the way which had to be steered round; and that is one of the reasons why the great rise of the U.S.S.R. dates from the moment at which the Opposition was reduced to harmlessness. The present leaders of the U.S.S.R. deserve to be given credit for the fact that since the October Revolution they have not modified their attitudes and their points of view in any particular, and that everything they have done since Lenin has been done according to Lenin, and not according to modifications and counterfeits of Leninism.

I will delve, rather at a venture, into far-distant times, into the days before the Revolution, right back into the last century: Vano Sturua tells of an illicit visit paid by Stalin to the big workshops at Tiflis in 1898—not yesterday, it will be noticed: "Sosso was remarkable for his decision and firmness"; and he found violent fault with the "slackness," the "hesitation," "the irritating spirit of compromise," which he observed among many of the comrades, and the same Sosso (aged nineteen at the time) already foresaw the defection of a number of intellectuals "of whom a good half actually passed over into the Menshevik camp after the Second Congress."

That is how Stalin appeared then, and that is how he appeared, some thirty years later, when confronted with the Opposition crew. He was the same man; the man of action, confidence and progress, as opposed to those of theory, pessimism and marking time.

The Opposition did everything it could to discourage the Revolution and cast over the world (with all the force it could muster) doubt, the spectre of ruin, desolation and perdition, and a shadow of decadence and of surrender.

"Shake up our Opposition," said Stalin, "throw aside its revolutionary phraseology, and you will see that at the bottom of it lies capitulation!"

And on another occasion: "Trotskyism is trying to inject a lack of faith into the forces of the Revolution!"

Trotskyism, which has to some extent spread over the globe, attacking the network of the Communist International, has done everything it could to destroy the work of

October. Around Trotsky, all sorts of people from all sides, persons who have been banished, renegades, malcontents, and Anarchists carry on a campaign of systematic detraction and machine-wrecking, a struggle which is exclusively anti-Bolshevik and anti-Soviet, absolutely negative and containing every possible form of treason. All that these turncoats wish to do is to become the grave-diggers of the Russian Revolution.

One is quite justified in considering Trotsky as a counter-revolutionary, although that obviously does not mean that Trotsky harbours all the ideas of middle-class reactionaries against the U.S.S.R.

Stalin once said: "The Opposition will end by hurling itself into the arms of the Whites." Some people were inclined to think that this prophecy went too far and was the result of the fierceness of the struggle. The bloody events of December 1934 have justified it in the most sinister way. Will this be the only justification of it that we shall have?

If the Opposition had won, the Party would have been split in two, and the Revolution would have been in a sorry state. Ordjonekidze wrote: "The triumph of Trotskyism would have meant the ruin of all the constructive plans of the Soviets. The victory of Stalin over Trotsky and over those of the Right is like a fresh success for the October Revolution."

Stalin was not content to settle the problem of the Opposition in the heart of Communism and to cut the Gordian knots of these political complications. He had helped the other Communist Parties to overcome the hesitation of the Right, and to rid themselves of the pernicious seductions of Opportunism and Reformism; the Polish Party

THE PARASITIC WAR

after May 1926; the English and French Parties which had, in 1927–28, "to place their electoral tactics upon the rails of true revolutionary policy." Towards the same period, the opportunist offensive invaded the German Party. But Communist Germany dropped the Brandlerians, as did Czechoslovakia the Haisists, and the United States the Lovestonians and the Pepperists. In 1923 the Bulgarian Party had eliminated, thanks to him, the bad tendencies that made it skip from the Left to the Right—from demagogism to opportunism. "The proletariat must have a clear objective (a programme) and a definite line of action (tactics)," said Stalin, who always acts according to his words.

It is interesting, as proof of the accuracy of foresight to which a broad clear mind can arrive, to recall that in 1920, in spite of the imposing effective strength of the German Social-Democratic Party (the most important after the Russian Party), and in spite of the united front, Stalin had offered an opinion full of doubt and of reservations on its actual unity, which he considered to be "more apparent than real." Those who have followed the contemporary historical tragedies, can realize how wise and how weighty were those words which, twelve years later, events showed to have been so terribly true.

Since those days, Stalin has watched more jealously than ever over the unimpaired greatness of Leninism, which he had saved from intrigue at a moment when the great experiment of liberty, which had never ceased to make progress, had nevertheless not yet quite reached its full maturity; at a period at which the Soviet Revolutionaries and the proletariat were eagerly yet slowly giving life to the monumental new organism by a self-sacrifice comparable to a transfusion of blood.

Chapter Seven

THE GREAT WATCH-WORDS, 1928–1934

THE last contemporary period of the Russian Revolution. The period of the 1928 Five-Year Plan.

The only people of their kind, the people who were so terribly new, the stranger nation among the nations, attacking the forces of nature. They had arrived at electrification, dimly perceived through defeat and storms, and they were working around it.

The Plan which embraced the years 1928 to 1933 and which was replaced at the end of 1932, at the end of four years, by a fresh Five-Year Plan, because it was considered that the old one had been completed, was imposed upon the towns and in the country districts at the same time. It consisted of the reinforcement of industry—a great step forward—and the victorious socialization of the country districts (two great vital questions which are closely linked together by the anatomy of machinery). It was necessary to raise this Russia, which was at the bottom of the industrial ladder of the world, by completely socializing it.

Let us consider once more the fundamental aims, spreading out further than the eye could reach, as they were defined by Stalin: "We have to change backward Russia into a technically modernized country—so as not to be dependent on capitalist countries, so that Soviet power should be solidified and so that Socialism should conquer, so as to allow of the elimination of the *kulak* and the transformation of the little private agricultural farm by collectivizing agriculture, and so as to have an adequate military defence." And all this building up in a single country had to be done without foreign capital.

In spite of the remarkable results achieved by the single country in question, after a fierce and at the same time methodical struggle lasting for ten years, the opinion of the world had not changed and had not forgiven it for having left the "old order"; and the great capitalist newspaper Press (which is by no means an informatory Press) persistently pursued its dishonest tactics, which consisted in either denying the results with a stroke of the pen, as one denies a commitment, or else, in cases in which it was too absurd to deny these results, of attributing them to an abandonment of socialist principles. From the time that the last Five-Year Plan was embarked upon, until its achievement, the same splenetic irony contorted the utterances of the official journalists. Here are a few extracts collected by Stalin himself:

"It's not a plan," said the *New York Times*, "it's a speculation" (November 1932). At the same time: "Complete insolvency!" announced the *Daily Telegraph*. The *New York Times*, already referred to, went further: "Ignominious Defeat." "Deadlock!" declared the Polish *Gazeta Polska*. "The catastrophe is obvious," pontificates the Italian *Politica*. "Breakdown of the Entire System," the *Financial Times* feels itself constrained to remark. The American *Current History* is no less categoric on the subject of the Five-Year Plan: "Breakdown of its Objectives; Breakdown of its Principles."

"In the U.S.S.R. the Five-Year Plans only exist on paper. They never succeed," wrote a Russian—an ex-Communist, expelled from the Party for filthy behaviour. This same individual informs us, in addition, in a book written in 1931, that "in the U.S.S.R. prison is the only place in which one does not die of hunger," and also that "every Soviet citizen has holes in his shoes and despair in his face," "I care nothing for the World Revolution," Stalin was supposed to have said, in 1927, to a Mr. Campbell, an important American farmer, who at any rate has had the effrontery to assert it, in another book.

Whilst we are on this subject, let us add, if you please: "In the Moscow hotels they cook children on spits and eat them," or, at any rate, so it is asserted in various places by a great many respectable people nowadays.

Now the 1928 Five-Year Plan, supported by colossal figures, ended in four years by an achievement of 93 per cent. of its objects. As regards heavy industry, the achievement in four years amounted to 108 per cent. National production trebled between 1928 and 1934. Pre-war production was quadrupled by the end of 1933.

From 1928 to 1932 the number of workmen employed increased from 9,500,000 to 13,800,000 (an increase in important industries of 1,800,000, in agriculture of 1,100,000, and in commercial employees of 450,000) and, naturally, unemployment has become a thing of the past there.

The part played by industry in total production, that is to say in relation to agricultural production, was 42 per cent. in 1913, 48 per cent. in 1928, and 70 per cent. in 1932.

The part played by socialist industry in total industry at the end of four years was 99.93 per cent.

The national revenue has increased during the four years by 85 per cent. At the end of the Plan, it was more than

45,000,000,000 roubles. A year later 49,000,000,000 (½ per cent. being capitalist and foreign elements).

The amount of the workers' and employees' wages rose from 8,000,000,000 to 30,000,000,000 roubles.

The number of persons able to read and to write has risen, for the whole of the U.S.S.R., from 67 per cent. at the end of 1930, to 90 per cent. at the end of 1933.

Pause a moment and compare these figures, which testify to a progress unique in the annals of the human race, with the virtuous prophecies which figure above—Insolvency, Deadlock, Catastrophe, Breakdown—all of which were uttered at a time when the Plan was almost realized already —in spite of universal opposition.

New branches of industry have been started, from making machine-tools, motor-cars, tractors, chemical products, electric motors, aeroplanes, agricultural machinery, powerful turbines and generators, high-speed steel and iron compounds, to synthetic rubber and artificial fibre. Two years ago I travelled from London to Leningrad in a large boat in which everything, absolutely everything, in the machinery and fitting out, was of Soviet construction (even to the pianos, one for the passengers and one for the crew). In Moscow I saw a gigantic aeroplane (inside this colossus one received the impression of being in a machine-room in a factory), in the construction of which there was nothing that had not come from the U.S.S.R. and had not been manufactured there—except the tyres of the landing-wheels.

Thousands of old-fashioned factories have been reconstructed. Thousands of new enterprises have collected in multiform and multicoloured groups round gigantic enterprises of which many take their place, in size, at the head of all contemporary industrial civilization: Dnieproguès,

Magnitogorsk, Cheliabinsk, Bobriki, Uralmashstroi, Kramachstroi.

Systematic scientific expeditions enable all the resources of the soil to be located. Enormous new centres have risen all over the country, in the Ukraine, Northern Caucasia, Transcaucasia, Central Asia, Kazakstan, Buriatomongolia, Tartary, Bashkiria, Ural and Western Siberia, the Far East.

"In four years," says the *Nation*, "about fifty new towns have sprung out of the earth, each of from 50,000 to 250,000 inhabitants, harmonic and specialized industrial centres." An immense town covers the banks of the Dnieper with an architectural scheme of concrete and metal, beside one of the most powerful hydro-electric stations in the world (and which, in a few years' time, will be only in the fifth or sixth rank).* In the main basin of Kusnietz, six new towns have suddenly sprung up, with 600,000 inhabitants. In the extreme north, owing to the discovery of phosphate deposits, a town suddenly appeared which, at the moment, has 50,000 inhabitants.

Pierre Dominique who, in other respects, has given vent to a number of fairly puerile general reflections as a result of the mania he has for treating Socialism as a racial question, gives us, basing his observations entirely on a solid foundation of facts, a glimpse of the immensity of the rise of industry in Soviet Asia. ". . . Beyond the Ural Mountains, there are three great industrial centres, of which our own three centres of the Nord, of the Lorraine region and of the basin of the Loire give rather a feeble idea in the sense that the Soviet centres are each as large as France.

---

* Dnieproguès produces 750,000 horsepower, but the Beauharnais Saint-Lawrence, in Canada, produces more, and the Hoover dam, in Colorado, produces a million. Well and good. But the Chaman, in Siberia, will produce 2,000,000 and the Bratsky Ostrog 2,600,000. Even the Titans, we are told, only succeeded in piling Pelion upon Ossa!

There is the Ural centre with Magnitogorsk, Sverdlovsk and Cheliabinsk, the Kusnietz centre with Novosibirsk, both in full operation, and the Angarastroi centre, as yet unexploited. There, around new towns which have arisen out of the steppes during the past three years, and of which two have already populations of 300,000, new nations have been organized with rapidly increasing populations; an entirely new Red Asia is being created; the second scale of the great Soviet balance is being filled with new wealth."

What must be constantly noted and repeated is that the extent to which this industrial exploitation has been organized over a country twice the size of the United States, or of Europe, or of China, and the number of whose inhabitants is increasing at the rate of ten millions every three years.* All this formidable mobilization of individual effort has been carried out with an eye to the whole general scheme. Every detail of execution and every wheel in the machinery fits together. The single centralized management never loses sight of the nation as a whole. It apportions the work and regulates it.

It need hardly be added that this method of working entirely for the general good, which must necessarily give the maximum result, is not possible in countries in which capitalist Anarchy reigns, with its conflicting aims labouring under the burden of private profit and the fantastic disorder of private enterprise. Formerly, rice used to be cultivated in one particular region. The experts and the specialists reported that the conditions were unsuitable and that cotton would give much better results. So rice had to be cultivated somewhere else and vast fields of cotton were planted in its stead. To make use of the cotton, cotton-mills

* The population of Europe is increasing about two and a half times more slowly.

had to be built—several cotton-mills. Motive power had to be adapted, created on the spot if necessary, and the new centre had to be linked up with the lines of communication. Whence we see appearing a hydro-electric powerstation, a railway line, railway stations, roads, canals. In addition to these, an apprenticeship and technical school for the workers and engineers, various centres of work and of culture, instructional establishments and organizations for children and for adults, sport, radio, theatres and cinemas, laboratories and hospitals. That is how the enormous and complex Soviet molecule is constituted: the combine—and the synthetic city, the vague city suddenly springing up as the result of a natural law, around its mechanical centre. It is thus that towns spring up intelligently in the right place, at the exact place required by the combination of local needs and of national needs. It is thus that economic foundations join together and form one solid base.

Other perspectives open out, calling for urgent attention. "We have," said Stalin at the Seventeenth Congress of the Party, in January 1934, "laid the foundations of the Ural Kuznetsk combine, uniting the Kuznetsk coal with the Ural iron ore. The new Ural economic base has thus become, from being a dream, a reality." And Stalin also announced: "The foundations of a new and powerful oil industry have been laid on the western and southern slopes of the Ural Mountains, in the region of Uralsk, in Bashkiria and at Kazakstan."

And the lighter industry of commodities? The one that had been deliberately shelved to make way for the macromegalic industries, which made the housewife sigh and the citizen grumble (Hell take it! One has to wait half an hour to buy butter and three days to get an overcoat!). It has come back into its own and complaints are everywhere dying down. In four years the production of light industries has increased by 187 per cent. Shops are regularly increasing in numbers. The restaurants are feeding 20,000,000 people to-day. The figures representing the retail and food trade which in 1928 were 12,500,000,000 roubles were, in 1932, 40,000,000,000 roubles. And, indeed, you have only to take a walk through Moscow, and you will see perfectly appointed shops the whole way along the streets, and the same assortment of all kinds of merchandise as you would see in other great capitals. This is a fairly recent state of affairs and a great visible sign of progress, even when compared with conditions of last year.

And now for the financing of all this. The problem presents itself here in a peculiar form of its own. "Substantially," explains Stalin, "in capitalist countries the funds invested in big industrial schemes are obtained either by foreign loans, or by spoliation." (War indemnities, colonial confiscations, unfair exploitation of labour.)

The U.S.S.R. does not employ these methods. It is unable to borrow, and it leaves the employment of spoliation methods to "civilized" countries. So that it has to find the capital to invest from its own resources.

The Soviet State has resources because, quite independently of taxation, it possesses all the monopolies. These resources are mainly represented by the levying of a percentage on the receipts of the State services (commerce,* transport, postal and telegraphic services, etc. . . .), on the profits of the social organizations, and on the resources of the population, not so much in the form of obligatory taxes

---

* Let us note that the U.S.S.R. has suffered from the effects of the economic depression. Certain of its exports, although increasing in volume, have diminished in value during the past few years, as, for instance, petrol.

as in the form of loans, participating shares, savings banks (thus it is that the annual contribution of the population, namely 8,900,000,000 roubles, only includes 3,300,000,000 roubles obtained by obligatory payments, taxes, or insurance).

Grinko, People's Commissar for Financial Affairs in the U.S.S.R., tells us that the financing of the Five-Year Plan in four years represented a sum of 116,000,000,000 roubles instead of the 86,000,000,000 predicted.

And Grinko adds: "We have completely exploded the middle-class theory according to which the Soviet countries could not put their prodigious programme of socialist construction into execution without the help of foreign loans. . . .

"The principal reason that enabled us to accumulate so much capital lies in the primary fact that waste of national revenue, such as takes place in capitalist countries, does not exist with us. We have got rid of the parasitic classes which in all capitalist countries consume an enormous portion of the national revenues without producing anything. . . . We do not go in for imperialist politics. . . . There is no anarchy in our social production. All our resources are applied almost exclusively to the building up of our economic and cultural systems. . . ."

Great words, whose solemnity and deep significance can hardly be exaggerated and which, pronounced in 1934 by a Minister of Finance actually in office, strikingly reveal a complete change in the collective mechanism. These words, which have all the weight and all the wealth of the definite facts of which they are merely a statement, should be read over and over again and pondered over by all mankind. "With us there are no loopholes and no side-tracks, so there cannot possibly be any fraud. The infectious parasitism of middlemen, speculation, and the scandals which eat away the structure of other great countries are unknown to us. Our policy is an open one and an honest one, and the whole mechanism works well and smoothly for the mutual benefit of each and all."

Let us make a few comparisons with foreign countries so as to fix these ideas in our minds.

In 1933, as the result of a slight revival in business, the United States and France had slightly improved upon their pre-war economic production: the United States figures were 110.2 per cent. of the pre-war figures, France 107.6 per cent. England (also after the revival) had reached 85.2 per cent., Germany 75.4 per cent., and the U.S.S.R. 391 per cent.

Let us endeavour to see, by casting a glance over a few apex figures, what this means in pure figures and what the graph of world statistics shows at the present time.

In 1929, the year of the apogee of capitalist industrial production, the Soviet Union ranked fifth on the list of nations, after the United States, with production equivalent to 139,000,000,000 gold roubles, after England and Germany, each with 39,000,000,000 and after France, with 29,000,000,000.

Since then capitalist production has fallen 36 per cent. and with its 33,000,000,000 gold roubles production the U.S.S.R. comes up to the second place in the list of producing Powers, after the United States.

In agricultural machinery and locomotive construction the U.S.S.R. to-day holds the world record (in agricultural machinery alone her annual production represents a value of 420,000,000 gold roubles, against that of 325,000,-000 in the United States).

The U.S.S.R. occupies the second place in the world for the production of general machinery, and also for the production of petrol, iron and steel; the third place for the production of electric energy (after the United States and Canada), the third place, also, for boot manufacture, which I quote as an example because people have constantly delighted in talking of the worn-out boots or absence of boots of the wretched Russians; in that branch of industry they are still behind the United States and Czechoslovakia from which the late Batta covered the soil of Europe with new soles.

If we endeavour to visualize the titanic highway that would be made by the great factories of the world placed end to end, we would see in that evocation of the supernatural: Magnitogorsk (metallurgy), not yet quite completed, and which, when it is completed, will equal the American Gary Works which holds the record for size at the moment, Cheliabinsk (heavy tractors), the Stalin Automobile Works in Moscow, Kramatorsk, in the Dombass region, (heavy machinery), the Kaganovitch factory in Moscow (ball bearings)—which are giants of their species in a world of giants. The Lugansky locomotive factory is the most powerful in Europe, and masses of other factories (machinery which makes machinery and works metal) bear the numbers 2 or 3 in world magnitude.

Some other comparisons with foreign conditions:

Unemployment.—During the period of the Plan, when unemployment was eliminated from the U.S.S.R., the number of unemployed rose, in England from 1,290,000 to 2,800,000 and in Germany from 3,376,000 to 5,500,000. In France the number of unemployed, which has not stopped increasing, save for a short period at the end of 1933, is to-day 1,600,000 completely unemployed and (after the dead, the wounded), 2,900,000 working on short time.* In the United States, according to the Alexander Hamilton Institute, the number of unemployed in March 1933 was 17,000,000. In Italy there are 1,300,000 unemployed. In Spain, there were 650,000 unemployed in September 1934 (23,000 more than in January).

We are told that in many of these countries unemployment has decreased. Let us observe that in the same places in which they talk of the reduction of unemployment they also talk of the reduction in the total amount of wages. But it should be particularly observed that there is no bluff or deception in the world more shameless than those which surround the official figures of unemployment in all capitalist countries. It is impossible to humbug the public more deliberately than the competent authorities do in juggling with words and figures to disguise the true situation. No capitalist country admits its unemployed. Entire categories of workers, and of industries not having a certain proportion of workers, are "forgotten," and whole districts are "neglected." After performing the operation which consists in cutting working hours in two so as to give the half day obtained to an unemployed man, this unemployed man is removed from the list, whereas no change has really taken place at all, for twice one-half still makes one (United States). To say nothing of public works done on credit which deepen the abyss for the future, or of the paper transactions which alter words without altering facts. . . . And to say nothing of the goitrous growth of munition factories (everywhere, but especially in Germany and in Japan). . . . It is thus that unemployment fades away be-

* For France, these figures were obtained by applying to the total number of industrial workers the percentage of unemployed furnished by the investigations by the inspectors of labour and of mining engineers.

fore the fascinated (fascisized) eyes of the masses. *A fortiori*, only an outrageously small proportion of unemployed are supported in capitalist realms. The rest live as best they can.

"Three years ago," declared Stalin in 1933, "there were 1,500,000 unemployed in the U.S.S.R." Nowadays the number of workers has increased by 4,500,000.

Wages.—During the four years in question they have sunk in the United States by 35 per cent., in Germany by 50 per cent., in England by 50 per cent. In Italy, between 1929 and 1931, by 24 per cent. to 45 per cent., taking into consideration, naturally, the purchasing power of money. In the U.S.S.R. wages have increased by 67 per cent., the mean wages of the industrial worker being 991 roubles in 1930 and 1,519 in 1933.

Quality of work done and output.—In the United States of America the increase in output was, during the period of prosperity, 25 per cent., according to Mr. Stuart Chase. During the best economic period in England (1924–1929) it was 11 per cent.; in Germany, between 1913 and 1931 (Monsieur Kuezinsky) 27 per cent. In the U.S.S.R., whilst the above-mentioned countries were crumbling away, an increase of 40 per cent.

Let us pass over the enormous assistance given to scholars and to scientific institutes and to their many-sided activities, and let us merely say a few words on the subject of public education. The population of the U.S.S.R., we have seen, is growing at the rate of more than 3,000,000 a year. This is also the figure of the yearly increase of pupils. Without entering into details of the "cultural" sector which is so advanced among all the sectors of the life of the U.S.S.R. (Education is broadcast there; one finds it at every street corner. Every enterprise is a centre of culture, every barracks is a school, every factory a factory for moulding men's minds)—let us merely observe that in the U.S.S.R. there are 60,000,000 pupils of all sorts whose education is financed by the State—one person out of every three in the Union. As for the Republics, I will quote one or two among the many: in Tartary the number of schools, which was 35 in 1913, was 1,730 in 1933. The Cherkesses (Western Caucasus) possessed 94 per cent. of illiterates in 1914; nowadays there is not one single one—0 per cent. There were twenty-six times as many schools in Daghestan in 1931 as there were in 1914 and thirty-eight times as many in Kazkistan. Seventy different languages are cultivated in the U.S.S.R. Twenty of these were not written and had to be stabilized by being given alphabets.

The last Budget estimate for public instruction in the U.S.S.R. shows an increase of 20 per cent. over the previous one. Whilst in England, the same estimate suffered a decrease of £11,700,000 and in Germany the estimate has fallen successively from 1930 when it amounted to 690,000,000 marks to 590,000,000 in 1931, and 570,000,000 in 1932. (Since 1926, the German credits allotted to public instruction have been decreased by 1,000,000,000 marks.) In North America the schools are emptying. In Switzerland and in the United States, they are beginning to give up theories of child education.

The Press.—In 1929 the daily circulation of Soviet newspapers was 12,500,000; in 1933 it was 36,500,000.

And what of the question of Art?

Apart from the continuous search for new and direct formulæ for the theatre and for theatrical production, apart from the subversive creations of the Soviet cinema, there is a great deal to be said concerning Soviet literature, since in that direction really fine constructive progress has been made, and since, also, Stalin has always taken the keenest interest in the development of literature and of the Arts. In the Social State the rôle of writers, whom Stalin has called "the engineers of the soul," raises a problem which not only concerns the homogeneousness of socialist society, but which nowadays also concerns, in the very highest degree, the progress of Art itself, by introducing new elements into the portraying of contemporary life. These are vast perspectives, visual, theoretic, and dramatic, of *collectivity*, and also the sense of human duty, which is the reflection, in every active creature, of human progress. Soviet literary culture consists in enriching and developing the man in the writer, as André Malraux has very justly observed.

At the present time, when one cannot say that Soviet literature has even completely passed its groping period, quantities of important works are accumulating, which by their insight into the national life, their comprehensive range over the work of everyone and their mental stability, are preparing a great new phase in literary history. Here are some of the best-known names, which carry the most weight in their various fields: Gorky, Serafimovitch, Gladkoff, Fedin, Tikhonoff, Ivanoff, Penfieroff, Pilniak, Ehrenburg, Fadeyeff, Sholokhoff, Vera Imber, Tretiakoff, not to mention all the non-Russian Soviet writers, and a large number of eminent critics and journalists, such as Radek and Bukharin. (That clever and brilliant man Lunatcharsky died in 1933.)

Many of the writers of the old Western countries are unaware of the formidable competition with which they will one day have to deal, all along the line, from this powerful body which is so far practically unknown to them, but which, although its style is, in places, less refined

STALIN'S SECRET LIBRARY, NOW IN TIFLIS MUSEUM

than that of our own literature, brings a great deal more substance and a great deal more thought to bear upon the problems with which it deals.

It has repeatedly been found necessary to control that latent potential force which literature represents in a community of workers. Under the influence of Stalin, the Communist Party has enlarged the writers' movement in a remarkable manner, first by checking political sectarianism in literary organizations and then by completely suppressing this sectarianism (which had brought a dangerous sterility into national production), by means of the famous decree of April the 23rd, 1932. This decree founded the Union of Soviet Writers of the U.S.S.R., replacing all other existing literary organizations, on the basis of a united and comprehensive front of men of letters, from the official revolutionary writers downwards. "Sectarianism must be abolished in literature," said Stalin, "and even the reactions which it has hitherto caused."

The members of the Union of Soviet Writers undertake to direct their energies towards "socialist achievement" and towards the defence of the U.S.S.R. The National Congress of Writers, which took place in August 1934, at Moscow, and which was for many of us a revelation regarding the richness of national Soviet literature, gave its solemn blessing to this programme. All the Soviet writers adhere to it with immense enthusiasm.

The great idea is to confer upon the writer (while at the same time enlarging the scope of his work), the mission of setting out, as clearly as possible, the scientific and moral evidences of socialism—but without paralysing literary activity by pinning it down exclusively to political propaganda. This application of the social sense to creative work implies the definite abolition of "art for art's sake," and of individually selfish art with its narrowness and its pessimism. (We in Europe and America ought also to organize the occasional efforts that are being made in the same direction.)

In our older countries, which are still cynical enough and stupid enough to pride themselves upon their spiritual mission, everything which has anything to do with the mind is, in reality, despised and sacrificed. One has only to note how science and education are degraded by being pressed into the service of war and of the preservation of the existing social order. Writers, artists, scholars, all the intellectuals are impoverished by the power which is anxious to divert all public assets into the abyss of armaments. There is practically no future nowadays for students, and what little there is is deprived of all its dignity. They are monopolized and trained—either as inventors or as educators—in the theoretical and practical preparation for war, and for the exploitation of the proletariat. They are compelled, whether they like it or not, to become war-material manufacturers with their brains (poor relations of the great armament firms), or the police officers of Reaction.

Let us turn our eyes in other directions. Formerly, the death-rate in Russia was very high, being more than 30 per 1,000. During the past four years, it has fallen from 27 per cent. to 17 per cent. The U.S.S.R. death-rate is still higher than those of England and of the Netherlands (16), of the Scandinavian countries and Australia (15–14), and of New Zealand (so privileged in that respect: less than 10)—but it is now lower than that of Spain and Hungary (26), of Rumania and Austria (25), of Italy (22), of Germany and France (20).

National Defence represents 4.5 per cent. of the total

THE GREAT WATCH-WORDS, 1928–1934

Soviet Budget (in Japan it is 60 per cent., in France 40 per cent., and in Italy 35 per cent. of the whole State Budget). The Red Army consists of 562,000 men. The Japanese Army contains 500,000 men. Hitler claims 300,000 like France, but he has really 600,000 under his command, according to the most conservative estimates, for a territory one-fiftieth the size of that of the U.S.S.R. Soviet armament has progressed considerably. Vorochiloff declared at the beginning of 1934, that mechanical transport and armament represented 2.6 horse-power per Red soldier in 1929 and 7.74 horse-power in 1934.

During the time that Soviet production was being mobilized and its retail trade increasing by 175 per cent., forty-eight other countries saw their trade fall to 42 per cent. of its 1929 figures; and the workers' wages fell, for the period 1929–32, from 43,000,000,000 to 26,000,000,000 marks, from 53,000,000,000 to 28,000,000,000 francs, and from £381,000,000 to £324,000,000 in the countries of the mark, franc and pound sterling respectively. Since the time that these statistics were published, matters have grown worse.

Between 1930 and 1932, five thousand banks failed in the United States (a dead loss of $3,500,000,000, in spite of a subsidy of $850,000,000).*

In 1932, in Germany, the State (through the medium of the taxpayer) had to produce 1,000,000,000 marks to put five banks on a sound financial basis.

At the same period, in France, and by the same procedure, 3,000,000,000 francs were given to respectable banks which had gone bankrupt. Let us take a paragraph at random from a conservative paper and we find a tale of 300,-

---

* As a quiet contrast let us note that the film star Greta Garbo earns about £200,000 a year at Hollywood.

000 unemployed, of 150,000 intellectuals destitute—there were 120,000 failures in 1933 in Paris and the Département of the Seine alone.*

The Budget deficit was, in 1930, $900,000,000 in the United States and 2,800,000,000 francs in France; the following year the American deficit multiplied itself by three and became $2,800,000,000, the French multiplied itself by two and became 5,600,000,000 francs; the last Budget showed a deficit of 9,000,000,000 francs.† In Italy, a deficit of 4,000,000,000 lire. And to-day America is a State network of codes just as severe as they are useless, over which a lot of men of superior intelligence are puzzling their heads. And in France, apart from the immorality of a permanent lottery, we have political inflation and proclamations which allow the Frenchman, caught by the throat, to work in peace in order to make him disgorge his savings. The deficit goes on increasing in spite of the enforced raising of taxes, in spite of all the lowering of wages, of salaries, of unemployment relief, of pensions, in spite of the lamentable cutting down of credits allocated to scientific development, social services, education and progress. And in spite of the New Economic Morality which consists in not paying one's debts. In France, not to pay America has become a point of national vanity with those who blackguard the Boche because he does not want to pay £8,000,000,000 which he never owed. French comic-song writers ridicule Uncle Sam in the most light-hearted way because he has had the bad taste to complain that he has been

* To-day—the end of 1934—there are 375,000 unemployed in the Paris area.
† The French National Debt amounts to 64,000,000,000 gold francs, not counting the Municipal Debt. The Treasury deficit, not counting the railway deficit, is about 12,000,000,000 gold francs. (Monsieur Caillaux, President of the Commission of Finances of the Senate, in December, 1934.)

swindled. And lastly, in spite of the prohibitive customs barriers which are being piled one upon the other—in a sort of Customs race—and the mad system of outbidding one another, by which the Nations attempt to solve a problem which could only be solved by an international understanding, which is quite out of the question under any form of Capitalism, either in general or in detail.

A fairly typical example of the absurdity, as grotesque as it is terrible, of Customs duties and of the grabbing that goes on at the frontier *at the expense of the national consumer*, is the one of coffee in France. Coffee is not a luxury product, it is really part of the food of the public, a product of primary necessity. Neither is there any particular question here of defending the agriculture of the country, since French colonies produce an almost negligible quantity of coffee as compared with the total consumption of the French Empire. Coffee costs 320 francs for 100 kilos (360 with the retailer's profit). But each 100 kilos is burdened with 321 francs Customs duty, 180 francs commodity tax, 100 francs licence duty and a certain number of other taxes and surtaxes, amounting to 630 francs in all, nearly double the purchase price. This is the usual kind of knockout blow, in direct defiance of common sense, that the voracity of the effete Exchequer system deals to the consuming citizens in our own countries.*

Whilst all this is going on, mass destruction of coffee is

---

* The consumer is the taxpayer, and the only use of the taxpayer is to pay taxes. There are, of course, three forms of taxation, namely direct taxation, indirect taxation and disguised taxation. It is purely and simply rifling the pockets of the public to invent work to occupy the unemployed, who are thereby condemned to perpetual unemployment, to give wine rations to soldiers imprisoned in their barracks, in order to benefit peasants who are allowed to be exploited by middlemen; and to lower the price of the transport of wine for the benefit of the big wine merchants.

taking place in Brazil. And a journal of economics recently announced in carefully chosen phraseology: "At the end of the present campaign, Brazil will have freed the market of 32,000,000 bags of coffee in order to keep up the price." 32,000,000 bags represent one and a half times the world's total yearly consumption of coffee.

That is the situation over there—where society is modelled on the needs of everyone. And that is the situation here where the needs of everyone are modelled upon the existing state of society.

For reasons which a child could understand, here there is nothing but disorder and decline.

Over there everything is order and progress. All things considered, since man has been man no one in this world has ever carried out such a comprehensive task and still less a task involving such colossal organization. As Stalin says: "The eddies of enthusiastic rhythmic progress are perpetually widening." And he also says: "Each period of national development has its epic. To-day, in Russia, it is the epic of construction." Never has any task been organized in such a monumental manner! The 1928–32 Plan is the greatest proof of the supremacy of human intelligence and willpower that has hitherto been given.

The question naturally arises as to whether there are any weak points. Of course there are weak points, but they are being carefully watched. There is still an insufficiency of transport . . . the U.S.S.R. has only 52,000 miles of permanent way, whereas France, one fortieth of its size, has 25,000 miles. Even though railway traffic has increased during the past three years from 113,000,000,000 tons to 172,000,000,000 tons, and river and canal traffic from 45,-

000,000,000 to 60,000,000,000, there is a lag in this respect which cannot continue without harm resulting from it.

Again, the Soviet experts declare that the prices of raw materials have not come down sufficiently. They did not, in fact, come down at all during the four years of the Plan. The lowering of these prices will therefore be the first task of the next programme. And there are many other shortcomings which will have to be strenuously attacked!

And what, to-day, is the attitude of the great middle classes and of its maid-of-all-work, the great Press, towards the balance-sheet of Soviet experience?

The late Monsieur Poincaré gave his opinion in the Argentine newspaper *La Nación*. To explain the capitalist crisis (which is a crisis of overproduction proceeding from countries which live together at daggers drawn under a system of tariff warfare), Monsieur Poincaré lays the blame on the criminal attempt of the U.S.S.R. to put its economic house in order. According to him it is the U.S.S.R. that is responsible for the failure of all the economic systems in the other five-sixths of the world; for "in the U.S.S.R. everything is subordinated to carrying through a Five-Year Plan which allows dumping to spread rapidly to manufactured articles. By this system, the U.S.S.R. proposes to introduce into other nations, to their increasing economic embarrassment, discords and dissensions which make it impossible for them to arrange for their own defence." When one thinks that this truly idiotic appreciation of the situation was uttered by a man who had played a really important part in politics, one is amazed. Long before this, one had been forced into the belief that Monsieur Poincaré had relapsed into second childhood.

Besides enemies, there are friends of a peculiar kind.

There are journalists like Monsieur Mallet, author of a very recent report in which utter disparagement is concealed beneath the flowers of flattery and under a semblance of impartiality which is really too clumsily transparent. Monsieur Mallet does not quote one single result, not one single piece of progress, without afterwards attempting to destroy it with a poisoned dagger, or else by declaring that it is, after all, merely a piece of honest Capitalism saving the situation.

There are also the big, noisy politicians like Monsieur Herriot, representing Western Capitalism, the accredited supplier of radical labels to reactionary governments—Monsieur Herriot who makes prodigious efforts to try to dwarf Soviet Socialism to the dimensions of his own electoral programme, resurrected for the occasion.

I know quite well what I shall be told: "If you were to say as many bad things about Russia as you say good things, we might believe you. Monsieur Herriot, for instance, in his last book, makes a balanced, objective report, in all its light and shade, whilst you are prejudiced and make a panegyric."

Quite right. But it is only the truth that makes it a panegyric. We have not invented any argument.

The prejudiced man is the one who, being the servant of a bastard and mediocre conception of capitalist Republicanism does not see the breadth and depth of creative originality put into the activities over there. He does not place the Soviet facts into their true settings of time and space, into their world and historic settings and in their repercussions upon the human race. He is not telling the truth.

Now the real facts are these. The most poverty-stricken state in Europe (in spite of its vast size), ignorant, fettered,

THE GREAT WATCH-WORDS, 1928–1934

ill-treated, starved, bleeding and shattered, has, in seventeen years, become the greatest industrial country in Europe, and the second in the world—and the most civilized of all, in every respect. Such progress, which is unequalled in the history of the world, has been achieved—and this too is unequalled—by the sole resources of the country of which every other country has been the enemy. And it has been achieved by the power of an idea, an idea which was directly opposed to the ideas of the rulers of all other national societies—the idea of fraternal and scientific justice.

To say, merely, that such a fact (such a triumph of the human mind) is "interesting," and that "one must not condemn it in principle," is either not to understand it or deliberately to mislead people. To place the few patches of shade in this extraordinary picture on the same plane as the high lights, to compare their institutions with our own, is really to insult human intelligence.

But let us leave the procession of one-man bands, like Monsieur Herriot, of minor quantities like Monsieur Poincaré, of amiable Jesuits like Monsieur Mallet. Listen to the great newspapers. They have a bitter pill to swallow.

Le Temps, in its number of January the 27th, 1932, says: "The Soviet Union has won the first round by industrializing itself without the aid of foreign capital." The same paper, some months later, in April, observes: "Communism seems to have leaped in one bound over the constructive stage which in a capitalist régime has to be crossed very slowly. To all intents and purposes, the Bolsheviks have beaten us in this respect."

The Round Table: "The achievements of the Five-Year Plan constitute a surprising phenomenon."

The *Financial Times:* "There can be no doubt about

their success. The Communists' exultation in the Press and in their speeches is by no means without foundation."

The *Neue Freie Presse* (Austria): "The Five-Year Plan is a modern giant."

Mr. J. Gibson Jarvie, president of the United Dominion Trust, said: "Russia is advancing at the moment at which we are retreating. The Five-Year Plan has been left behind. . . . Soul and ideal. . . . The youth and the workers of Russia have something which we lack, namely, hope."

The Nation (United States): "The four years of the Five-Year Plan show a really remarkable series of achievements. The Soviet Union has devoted itself with an intense activity, more appropriate to war-time, to the construction of the foundations of a new life."

Forward (Scotland): "What England did during the war was a mere bagatelle beside it. The Americans recognize that even the feverish period of the most intense construction in the Western states could offer nothing comparable to it . . . a degree of energy unprecedented in the history of the world. A brilliant challenge to a hostile capitalist world."

Chapter Eight

THE PEASANTRY

The work accomplished in the country districts was even more important.

It was a greater struggle and a greater victory—because it was necessary to modify radically a tradition whose bonds were much stronger and had been so long undisturbed.

It cannot be claimed that the peasant question is permanently settled. But a substantial start has been made. The most important task has been accomplished—the definite victory, the invasion which must now be consolidated—the reasons for which must be driven more and more into the head of the son of the soil.

Let us cast a last glance over the limitless panorama of the fields.

"The struggle for the conquest of the peasantry runs like a scarlet thread through the whole of our Revolution, from 1905 until 1917," says Stalin.

It had been comparatively easy to persuade the majority of the peasants to sympathize with or at any rate not to be antipathetic to the Revolution, owing to the miserable existence dragged out by most of them during the former régime: they never hesitated to choose between Tsarism and the Revolution. But once the Revolution was an established fact, the Socialist reconstruction, which had been made possible by political and economic circumstances, encountered a formidable obstacle, namely the huge proportion of agriculture in the economic whole.

"One of the great difficulties of socialist reconstruction," Lenin stated bluntly, at the very beginning, "is that Russia is an agricultural country." And Lenin also observed that the small peasant proprietor is, in principle, more inclined towards Capitalism than towards Socialism.

How were the country districts to be included in the general scheme of construction? In the case of large properties, the problem was immediately solved by the expropriation of the large proprietor, the common enemy. There remained the small properties—divided up into millions of individual strips—and, like all peasants of the soil, the moujik has a fundamental longing, with his whole heart and soul, to possess *his own* land.

When the country was struggling in the N.E.P., rather like strong swimmers who have been shipwrecked, Lenin announced that "the essential task, the task which will decide all the rest, and to which everything must be subordinated, is to establish a point of contact between the new economic system which we have undertaken to build up, perhaps badly and clumsily, but which we are nevertheless building up, and the rural economic system in which millions of peasants subsist."

This point of contact had to be found in the common interest, in the material profit of the peasant. It resolved itself into a question of personal advantage or disadvantage, not one of big words.

"Nothing in any way mystical will ever drive the peasants to Socialism; the only thing that will do so is their own personal interest."

They had to be shown that their interest lay in Socialism. But how? We know the answer: by mass cultivation. Mass cultivation, vastly improved cultivation, demands that the fields should be held in common and that the workers should labour for the common cause—when it produces far more than the other method. In this way, it directly identifies the interest of the individual with the socialist conception. The Russian peasant, who is much more of a realist than a mystic (he is chiefly mystical in hard facts), is easily persuaded by figures—as soon as he notices that the portion which comes to each one in collective exploitation is at the same time much larger and much more certain than the profits of individual piece-meal exploitation. The moujik believes in the talisman of numbers.

The problem was that of the poor peasant, and especially —because the very poor are always easily led owing to the fact that they have nothing to lose—for the moderately poor peasant and the small peasant farmer. At the Fifteenth Congress of the Russian Party, Stalin dealt entirely with the problem of the small peasant farmer. He dwelt on the fact that "the small peasant farmer, during the period of the October Revolution, did actually turn to us when he was convinced that the middle classes were overthrown for ever, that this meant the end of the *kulak*, and that the Red Army was beginning to win on all the Civil War fronts."

A solid alliance with the small peasant farmer was necessary—an alliance "which should not in any way yield to his prejudices," but which should tend to make him understand and admit the change which was taking place "in the way of the collectivization of Soviet economy in general and of rural economy in particular"—and in the way of driving *kulak* parasitism out of existence. For such conquests of the masses can only be brought about by persuasion, not by force.

It was the quite natural extension to production of the

co-operative system, which had already made considerable headway and prepared the ground for further development in the department of commodities and retail trade.

So, whilst the large unoccupied estates were transformed into *sovkhoz* or pure and simple State farms (which give the example), the private individual exploitations must be changed into *kolkhoz*, or co-operative farms.

After four years of the Plan—at the same time that over 80,000 more square miles of U.S.S.R. territory were under wheat—224,000 *kolkhoz* and 5,000 *sovkhoz* had been created.

Sixty-five per cent. of the agricultural exploitations of Soviet territory and 70 per cent. of the peasant lands gravitated into *kolkhoz*. The percentage of collective cultivation in the peasant colonies has risen by the following degrees: 1929, 4 points; 1930, 23 points; 1931, 52 points; 1932, 61 points; 1933, 65 points, comprising two million peasant undertakings. One can see the deliberate conquering of the vast plains advance by waves. The *kolkhoz* and the *sovkhoz* between them now own 85 per cent. of the grain fields of the U.S.S.R.

And all these estates are of imposing proportions; whereas in the United States farms of a thousand acres or more only represent one per cent. of the total number of farms, the average size of the *kolkhoz* is about 1,070 acres and that of the *sovkhoz* nearly 5,000 acres.

The material advantages of collectivization have been confirmed, in the course of the present colossal introduction of socialism into the country districts, by certain characteristic facts. I will mention one: it is recognized nowadays that, in the Ukraine, the employment of the wide resources of the community has enabled the great dangers with which the harvest was menaced by drought to be averted,

THE PEASANTRY

and has also enabled the whole Union to enjoy a better harvest in 1934, than that of 1933, in spite of unfavourable weather conditions.

The State has helped the peasants:

(1) by organizing for them 2,860 machinery and tractor stations, at a cost of 2,000,000,000 roubles;
(2) by a loan of 1,600,000,000 roubles to the *kolkhoz* (it must be understood that these are loans that pass from one form of collectivity to another form of collectivity, from everyone to everyone, and not, like French loans to the railways or the shipping trade, royal ministerial subsidies of which a considerable part goes to the higher officials or the board of directors, to say nothing of all the agents and intermediaries;
(3) by the loan of grain and seed-corn amounting to over 4,000,000 tons; and
(4) by taxation and insurance relief for the very poor, amounting to 370,000,000 roubles.

And in return: in 1929–30 the "individual peasants" gave the State 780,000,000 *pouds* (1 poud = about 43 lbs.) of grain and the *kolkhoz* 120,000,000. In 1933 the proportion was reversed: the *kolkhoz* 1,000,000,000 *pouds*, the individual peasants 130,000,000. It should here be noted and remembered that there has been an enormous rhythmical accumulation of institutes, of laboratories, of science schools, of expeditions and of agronomic tours of inspection. This carefully prepared organization of agriculture with its huge classifications, its researches and selections, its experiments in methods of cultivation and manuring, and its system of distribution, itself provides us with amazing statistics.

At the end of 1934 the economic prosperity of the U.S.S.R. was so great that the Soviet Government annulled the debts of the *kolkhoz*, which represented the tidy sum of 435,000,000 roubles—and was even enabled to give bonuses and material advantages to those *kolkhoz* which had paid off their debts. "What other government in the world could have allowed itself this luxury?" asked the Radio Central of Moscow the other evening.

Another, even more typical, fact: On the proposal of Stalin, the Central Committee of the Party has decided to abolish ration cards for bread and flour (December 1934). These had been instituted in 1929, at a moment when 86 per cent. of the corn came from "individual" farmers, and when there were 215,000 private shops (which have now disappeared) in existence. This service had necessitated a very great deal of very heavy administrative work, but it had ensured that the workers and employees should have sufficient bread at the lowest possible price (in spite of the very high prices prevailing in the towns and markets). Now that industry has been triumphantly launched both in the towns and in the country districts, that 92 per cent. of the corn is delivered by the *kolkhoz* and the *sovkhoz*, that it possesses 283,000 State shops, "that the resources of the State have increased in unheard-of proportions as regards commodities as important as bread—the hour has come to consider, as a great new victory of the Soviet policy, the general and free sale of bread and of flour." (Molotoff.)

Can we attempt to compare the situation of the peasantry in the U.S.S.R. and in our own countries? We have just heard a debate in the French Chamber of Deputies on the question of corn. The President of the Council confirmed a fact which, important as it was, did not teach anybody anything, namely that, between the peasant producer and the consumer of bread, there are middlemen who fleece both the one and the other and make a daily profit in the country of *ten million francs*. Moreover, the French peasant sells his veal at 2.50 francs the kilo; the same veal, in the same village, is retailed at 10 francs the kilo, and in the towns, at 20 francs. The vine-grower sells his better-class wine at 1.50 francs the litre in the market, and the wine merchant sells it back to him, if he is thirsty, at 4 francs. If he goes into the towns he finds it costs him 15 francs, or, in a smart restaurant, 20 francs. How can this situation be dealt with? Only by provisional measures. It is impossible to do so in a lasting way in a capitalist régime in which individual caprice and fraud cannot be controlled, and in which they manipulate to their own profit the system of taxation as well as that of the freedom of the market, and laugh at what is printed in the *Journal Officiel*. Only laws which make a pretence of looking after the small producer can possibly issue from our government offices.

As examples of the increase in agriculture, it may be stated that the production of Soviet cotton has leaped in three years from being one-thirtieth of world production to one-fifteenth, and that the cultivation of sugar-beet, which in 1929 was one-third of the cultivation in all other countries together, in 1932 was more than half as much again as the rest of the world production.

There are two forms of *kolkhoz:* the Commune and the Artel.

In the Commune, the *kolkhosians* own the entire concern in common, but that is all that they do possess, and they live in communities. In the Artel, each *kolkhosian* has his own house, his own farmyard and, if necessary, his own cow; he retains private ownership of a very small portion of the vast area whose cultivation he shares in other respects with the others.

The Artel form is the one which Stalin very strongly recommends. "Concessions! N.E.P.! Abandonment of Socialism!" people cried, or wanted to cry.

But wait one moment. Socialism, contrary to the legend which those who do not wish to know the truth spread about among those who are ignorant, was not invented just to annoy people, and to pursue them perpetually with cries of "You must!" like a creditor, but, quite on the contrary, to get them out of a mess. Its object is by no means arbitrarily to deprive every man and every woman of everything that gives them satisfaction and thus to make them pay too dearly, by personal restrictions, for the political equality, the social justice, and the security of livelihood which it brings them. Restriction on private property is not an end in itself, but a means of arriving at a state which is much more advantageous, everything considered, *for everyone*. It is not a question of multiplying these restrictions indiscriminately, but of reducing them to the necessary minimum. The means of production are to be socialized, so let us socialize them. And then what?

Then? Public opinion, which is in process of changing by force of circumstances, will have changed—by force of circumstances. One will look on these questions in quite a different light to the one in which those people look upon them who nowadays still have their feet planted in the past. One will naturally prefer the purer and more complete forms of collectivism. The Commune will no doubt take its revenge on the Artel. In any case it is the deepseated interest of the community which will decide. In the meantime, the Artel does not clash with the true idea

THE PEASANTRY

of equality, but only with the narrow (and anti-Marxist) formula of levelling.

And we may even envisage "the welfare of every *kolkhosian*" (this expression is actually a watch-word). "You want your own cow, comrade," says Stalin. "Then you shall have your own cow." And he points out that the watch-word "Comfort for the *kolkhosian*" no longer has the dangerous significance which it would have had at the beginning of the N.E.P., when it would have been the first cog in the return to Capitalism, against Socialism itself. Nowadays, in the midst of socialization, it is merely a useful and loyal stimulant. Besides, the whole of Socialism itself tends strictly towards "Maximum of good with minimum of effort."

At the present time, the heaviest work is over in the country districts. But it has by no means been easy, and now it is necessary to consolidate and to keep a vigilant eye open. There was real opposition, centred on fierce and desperate resistance by the *kulaks*. And, besides, there were all the necessary disappointments of the apprenticeship period of such an enormous undertaking to be endured. At one moment, the Government was actually losing ground! It had gone too quickly. Stalin's article on the subject: "Dizzy with success," has become world famous. Something had to be done. So Communists and technical experts were mobilized, and the country was flooded with them—on the principle that to get a concern into good working order again, whatever its dimensions, the whole of the leadership and all points of departure must be got back into one's own hands and then, after strengthening the foundations, one starts again. Each tractor station has become a fortress of ideas from which to invade and enlighten the minds of the peasant hordes. So 23,000 chosen

Communists, 110,000 technical experts and 1,900,000 drivers and mechanics went off to the rescue and succeeded, for the moment, in their aims.

Criticism persisted. The majority of the *kolkhoz* refused to come into line. And even certain of the Communists frankly suggested that this onerous experiment should come to an end.

Once more our steadfast leader showed his breadth of vision in bitterly opposing such a summary and shortsighted solution of the problem. Above all the din his voice rings out:

They will not come into line? It was the same with the individual factories in 1920; they will yield in time (besides, many of them have done so already). But "they are, above all, the basis of the whole structure, the foundation of the system. . . . One cannot consider economic output from the mercantile point of view, without considering the circumstances of the moment. Economic output must be regarded from the point of view of the whole national economic system, and over a period of activity of many years. Only that sort of point of view can be called really Marxist."

Which is why it is the Stalin point of view.

If Stalin lifts his voice against the deserters, the bunglers of the Right, he also rails against the "twaddlers" of the Left and the leaders who allow themselves to be caught napping by circumstances. Thus he mercilessly indicts the Communists in the agricultural districts who did not take measures to ensure that, in 1932, when the harvest was good, the State reserves of wheat should be put safely away before the sale of wheat took place in the *kolkhosian* market, which was much more lucrative for the peasants.

He even criticizes the Council of People's Commissars

THE PEASANTRY

which, even though they did issue instructions in this connexion, did not do so, in his opinion, with sufficient clearness and emphasis.

The results obtained by *kolkhosization* are remarkable, he observes, but it would be a grave mistake to imagine that all that was necessary was to let matters drift. There are still severe difficulties to be faced.

Care has to be taken to see that the peasant does not put his share of the work on to the other members of the *kolkhoz* (we are not dealing here with the workers, who are full of energy). "The responsibility for the exploitation is shifted from the peasants, considered individually, on to the leaders of the *kolkhoz*. . . . So the Party must take charge of the management of the *kolkhoz*. . . ."

There is often not sufficient contact between the Party and the peasantry. "The government officials sitting snugly in their office arm-chairs do not quite realize that collectivism is going on outside their offices."

In certain cases, the Communists have rested on their laurels. These are the ones who have overestimated the *kolkhoz*. "They have made idols of them," and Stalin storms against them just as he had stormed against those who wanted to abolish the *kolkhoz:* "They think that since the *kolkhoz* exist as a socialist form of economics, there is nothing more to be said."

But, emphasizes Stalin (and on this particular point he reveals the key-note of the whole of Marxist self-criticism), the *kolkhoz*, like the Soviets, represent the shell of socialist organization, either economic or political, but they only represent the shell. Everything really depends upon the contents. In 1917, the Soviets were led by the Mensheviks and the Social-Democrats. . . . "Soviets without Communists" was the watch-word of the counter-revolutionary leader Miliukoff. The collective form of *kolkhoz* gives certain commodities to the counter-revolutionary elements which are partisans of "*kolkhoz* without Communists."

Stalin says further: "The old, simple struggle against the classic *kulak* no longer has any reason for existence. The form of the struggle has changed. If certain *kolkhoz* have not developed sufficiently, and if the stocks of wheat have fallen short of expectation, the fault lies not with the peasants but with the Communists. Many people are members of the Party, but are no less fools for that."

And he is merciless towards comrades who sit, like "great lords," and wait for things to happen by themselves, and towards the chattering comrades who "could drown any enterprise with their verbiage." He tells of a conversation which he had with a worthy comrade who was responsible for a certain district: it was as follows:

I. How is the sowing of the crops getting on in your district?

HE. We have mobilized the sowing, Comrade Stalin.

I. Yes, and then?

HE. We have gone into the question energetically.

I. Yes, and then?

HE. There is a change for the better, Comrade Stalin; we shall soon see a change for the better.

I. Yes, but what then?

HE. We have many improvement schemes on hand.

I. But look here! How is the sowing getting on, in your district?

HE. Well, for the moment, we can't do anything about sowing, Comrade Stalin.

Still, definite results are accumulating and, in spite of everything, the face of the countryside is no longer the

THE PEASANTRY

same. Even if it is not changing as rapidly as our enthusiasm and our thirst for the future would have it do, nevertheless it changes. The appearance of the villages has also changed. Stalin has said: "The old village, dominated by its church, and with the fine houses of the chief of police, the priest and the *kulak* in the foreground, and its tumble-down mud huts in the background, is beginning to disappear. In its place the new village is springing up, with its public and economic service buildings, its clubs, its wireless station, its cinema, its schools, its libraries and its nurseries; with its tractors, its reaping-machines, its threshing-machines and its motor-cars. The old silhouettes of the notables, the slave-driving *kulak*, the blood-sucking usurer, the produce-speculator, the 'little father'—the chief of police—have all disappeared. The notables, nowadays, are the men of the *kolkhoz* and of the *sovkhoz*, of the schools and the clubs, the foremen tractor- and reaping-machine-drivers, the chiefs of the shock-brigades for work in the fields and for breeding, the best brigadiers, male and female, of the *kolkhosian* village."

Gone for ever, relegated into pictures or on to the stage, are those glittering coloured church decorations which dazzled the poor human herds, those streets and market-places as dirty as chicken-runs—and those winding roads down which from time to time a chaise would pass drawn by horses surmounted by a kind of circumflex accent. Gone are the luxurious and overbearing personages shut in them as in boxes: the noble lady descending, at long intervals, from a sleigh, proudly clad in the ancient style and surrounded by glossy greyhounds with streamline profiles; the rich peasant, pitiless in his wealth, and the uniforms—servants in gold-lace at the top, and prison-warders below—and gentlemen of the cloth, with their hypocritical features framed in a mass of tangled hair.

Gone. Now the scene is one of spaciousness and machinery, and the people who pass by and are in command are men in overalls whose faces are frank and resolute, proud and happy.*

One is even beginning to see in some of the greatly improved *kolkhoz*, like that of Kabarda, geometric forms which must be very like what the peasant city of the future will be: a large open space in the form of a semi-circle along whose base runs the main road. From this semi-circle radiate streets which divide the territory into sectors, each having its own speciality: here the hangars and silos, there the tractors and motor-cars, there the primary schools and technical schools. . . . In a word, the architectural organization of the "town-village." It is planned like half a huge rosette, shaded at the border.

Whilst the Soviet country districts are, not without difficulty, daily improving and becoming idealized, let us turn our eyes towards another great continent, trampled under foot by the extremest form of Capitalism, the United States. The sowing of wheat there has been cut down by one-tenth. The value of agricultural produce has fallen from $11,000,000,000 in 1929 to $5,000,000,000 in 1932. In two years the value of the farms (land and machinery) has fallen by $14,000,000,000. Forty-two per cent. of the

* Monsieur Victor Boret, in his book: *The Infernal Paradise*, considers that the position of Soviet agriculture is critical and menacing because of the relatively very small area of land under cultivation (about 350,000,000 acres for 168,000,000 inhabitants). Monsieur Herriot naturally supports this point of view. But if Soviet agriculture still does not produce a sufficient return, either in quantity or in quality, so much the better! This gives it a vast margin for future prosperity (it lacks neither space nor progress). It would be much more serious if the opposite were the truth.

farmers have mortgaged their goods and the fact that in 1932 there were only 258,000 foreclosures, was due to armed revolt on the part of the farmers.

And the N.R.A., that capitalist brain-wave, can think of nothing better than of applying Malthusian principles to the crops, which is a suicidal policy: a reduction of 8 per cent. of the area under cultivation, compensation for the peasants owning land which they cease to cultivate, and compensation for the planters who bury 25 per cent. to 50 per cent. of their crops. If a hurricane lays the harvest waste there is joy as for a national victory!

The French newspapers announce that the abundance of the vintage "threatens" the vine-growers in Champagne. . . . In order to improve matters there, and here, therefore let us have floods, frost, hail and phylloxera!

We have already mentioned the wholesale destruction of Brazilian coffee. Similar measures, which seem like criminal folly, deserve that we should pause to note them, with a shudder of horror. Especially as they have become more and more common during recent years. It is not a question of isolated facts; it is a matter of methodical capitalist policy.

Following the example given by the United States, in their policy of rewarding destruction and abortion in agriculture and industry, we are already witnessing in France the prohibition by law of the use of certain vines which bear too many grapes, and of the use of improved processes in Public Works (in certain large contracts, the use of mechanical scoops is forbidden). In *Le Capital* itself, Monsieur Caillaux suggests, as one of the means to be employed to fight the depression, that the renovating of old material should be discontinued.

So that, in order to make progress, we must apparently use mediæval implements.

We are looking on at a scene which is taking place all over the world, in every department of labour, and which is like some macabre farce: they reap the unripe corn in the north of France. In the south they throw cart-loads of fruit on to the rubbish-heaps. In Lombardy and elsewhere the peasants are burning their silk-worm cocoons. All over the country holocausts of corn and other cereals are taking place: the grain, which was sown so that it should germinate and come to precious maturity, is destroyed and buried. Acres of sugar-beet are destroyed and buried, and herds of cows and pigs. Streams of milk are poured into the rivers in America (and not only in America). Boat-loads of fish are cast into the sea. Thousands of new, fully equipped motor-cars belonging to *General Motors* are being smashed to pieces by means of specially constructed monster machines.

And these carefully arranged catastrophes, these mass executions, are taking place at a time when there is a serious shortage of these destroyed commodities somewhere or other, whilst famines are decimating crowds of people, whilst in China and in India hundreds of millions of human beings are eating grass and tree-bark, and whilst the unemployed and undernourished swarm over the very land where these murders of commodities and manufactured goods are taking place.

The last results of Capitalism: it assassinates nature and it assassinates things! One can bring no more infamous accusation against a régime than this self-mutilation practised on a large scale which is a glaring proof of the topsy-turviness of the world and the return of mankind to barbarism.

ENOUKIDZE, STALIN AND MAXIM GORKY, 1931

There is no room for such distressing extravagances in the U.S.S.R., where all excess of production in one district is automatically sent where it is lacking. "If anyone suggested such a procedure here," declared Stalin, "he would soon find himself in a lunatic asylum."

Returning to the U.S.S.R., and passing from inanimate objects to men—from whom events often get their origin and always their guidance, one notices that the rapidity with which all these things have been achieved is due to one particular incentive. Output has exceeded all expectations, owing to the intense enthusiasm aroused by "the idea." Socialist competition was the formidable unknown quantity which weighed so much in the balance of success.

Soviet workers are men like any other men. And yet, as I have already said, their outlook and their work differs from that of men working in capitalist countries, in which they are constantly struggling against the owners, whereas in Russia they are working for themselves. The look of pride and of happiness that shines from the faces of Soviet workers was the "change" which struck Gorky most when he returned to the U.S.S.R. in 1928 after a long absence. "This is what the Soviet workers have done!" is the phrase one hears uttered most often—and uttered with such an accent of pride!—in crowds of workers, as they refer to achievement after achievement and success after success, following one another with the artistically arranged rapidity of a cinema film over the boundless stretches of the ex-Russian Empire, whilst the whole of the rest of the world is going backwards.

These people confuse joy and glory when they evoke the reward for the good work they have done. They have given a more definite and a deeper meaning to the expression "the joy of living." In the old days the joy of living conquered, in spite of superhuman privations, in spite of all the death and destruction around them. Nowadays this joy of living still conquers and, according to the fine expression of Knorin, it remains a sign of faith in Socialism.

The extraordinary feats accomplished and the really superhuman efforts made, both in large and in small matters, in the colossal hive of Soviet industry, furnish the material for a whole series of epic poems (and, indeed, contemporary Soviet literature has become the cycle of songs about the achievements of this age of heroic labour of the men who have been reborn into liberty). A terrific spurt lasting for months and for years, teeming with figures—and terrestrial monsters rising rapidly tier by tier towards the clouds. One's qualifications and one's proper sphere of activity become quite clear in a moment in such an atmosphere. Mr. Cooper, the American technical adviser who was engaged on Dnieprostroi, told me at the inauguration of the titanic dam there that all records and even all calculations had been beaten by the workers, in the most difficult and unexpected circumstances, and that nothing like the economy of labour that took place had ever been seen before. Besides, 20,000 qualified workers sprang fully armed from that enterprise (on the whole work front of the Four Years' Battle, 800,000).

These things are perfectly logical. Everything for and by the workers. It is the algebraic formula of crowds—when they can once be got moving.

There is a spirit of latent competition everywhere, in the minds of all the manual workers and of the intellectuals. Everyone is always thinking of possible progress (and in that way they discover short cuts to achieve it). Everyone is constantly striving to make some improve-

THE PEASANTRY

ment or other. They all become persistent inventors working at high pressure. Vorochiloff, People's Commissar for War, revealed the fact, a few months ago, that in the course of one year, he had received 152,000 communications from private soldiers, containing suggestions, ideas and inventions in connexion with organization and technique and, added Vorochiloff, most of these suggestions were interesting and worth being studied and noted.

The organizer of this effort of 100,000,000 hearts, is the whole Socialist Party, the unsullied Socialist Party—the Communist Party, of which one may either say that every member is a servant or that every member is a leader. Communism has created in the world an almost inconceivable number of apostles. In Russia, and also in other countries, a great number of these apostles have become martyrs without ceasing to increase. The Communists have shed the bright red of their blood over all the lands of the Earth. Do people realize that the age-old martyrology of the Jews is gradually being overtaken and passed in numbers by that of the pioneer Socialists? Count them: in the past eight years the accumulation of dead, wounded and condemned has reached more than 6,000,000.*

Who knows what goes on in all the capitalist gaols of the universe, and who can give us an insight into the thousands and thousands of hellish and bestial scenes for which the guardians of class order and their sadistic genius for human suffering are responsible! Italy, Germany, Finland, Poland, Hungary, Bulgaria, Jugoslavia, Rumania, Portugal, Spain, Venezuela, Cuba, China, Indo-China, Africa. One has only to watch any middle-class society and its police

* 6,021,961, from 1925 to 1933, according to the eminent directress of the "International Red Aid Society," Helen Stassova. Of course they are not all Communists, but we know that they are mostly Communists.

myrmidons at work to proclaim: This is the age of blood. But in the universal chaos we have heard the beauty of the accusing voice of a man like Dimitroff! And in the same quarter we see the great Thaelmann crucified on the Swastika like a symbol and a sign of light!

As for the U.S.S.R., if one wants to know how much a man must sacrifice himself for an idea, one must go through the annals of the Party, in which a few well-known examples represent thousands of examples which are not known and never will be known. Whatever his profession may be, the Soviet Communist is also a soldier, and is also a teacher and when a hero is needed, he is there also.

And yet, these men who are content for themselves to live a dull, often ascetic, life, are by no means fanatics on the subject of levelling, as many people think. With us, the average man—whose brain does not yet know how to digest ideas properly and whose head is filled with a strange farrago of headings of social and political doctrines—has three great grievances against the Communist, grievances such that they transform the said Communist into an ogre. They are that he is anti-patriotic, that he wants to deprive everyone of his possessions, and that he wants to turn society into a vast disciplined and equalized barracks, and to level everyone's intelligence like paving-stones. But the Communist Internationalists are, on the contrary, all in favour of national expansion, on the sole condition that it is not obtained by war, and is not put into the hands of so-called business men. Their general theory of the suppression of private property only harms a negligible number of social parasites and profiteers, and it brings with it enormous benefit to all the other inhabitants of the Earth. (All public evils result, beyond any question, from

THE PEASANTRY

the moral and material chaos brought about by the general struggle to grow rich.) As for levelling, they are its avowed enemies as soon as it goes beyond that great law of justice and of equity (the basis, in fact, of Socialism) which consists in giving each human being precisely the same political power, that is to say, in effacing the artificial and pernicious inequality on the threshold of destiny. It would be easy to show that Socialism is, of all régimes, the one which cultivates individuality the most and the best. "Just as Socialism cannot ignore the interests of the individual" (Stalin), in contrast with the pathological hypertrophy of certain individual monopolies.

There is a certain amount of confusion on this point, arising from an excess of spiritual zeal, in the minds of many Socialists. Stalin, actually speaking of the Statute of the Land, calls the "two hundred percenters" to order and urges them not to drivel about the "levelling principle" popularized by middle-class writers. They must not make the same stupid mistake, and "Marxists cannot be made responsible for the stupidity and ignorance of middle-class writers."

Stalin is very insistent on this point: "By equality, Marxism does not mean the levelling of personal requirements and conditions of existence, but the suppression of classes, that is to say equal enfranchisement for every worker after the overthrow and expropriation of the Capitalists. . . . The equal duty of everyone to work according to his capacity, and the equal right of all workers to be remunerated according to the work they do (socialist society); the equal duty of everyone to work according to his capacity and the equal right of all workers to be remunerated according to their needs (communist society). Marxism starts from the fact that the needs and tastes of men can never be alike nor equal either in quality or in quantity, either in the socialist or the communist era. Marxism has never recognized and does not now recognize any other form of equality."

Stalin recalls the fact that in the *Communist Manifesto*, Marx and Engels scoffed at primitive utopian Socialism, qualifying it as being reactionary, because of its propaganda of "universal asceticism and clumsy levelling." Besides, the Soviet phenomenon shows conclusively, whatever may have been said, that Socialism means intensive cultivation of each one's faculties and resources.

But it is among the youth of the country that the Party looks for the greatest competition. Soviet youth forms, as a mass, the storm-troops of Socialism. Youth has spread itself through the country districts to overthrow and break up the spectres of the past, and religious and social prejudices. All these adolescents, young lads and young girls, with their lithe bodies and their faces fresh and clear as mirrors—brought up in a teaching which has not had to fight any poisonous traditions, have cultivated the minds of the peasants over wide areas, like phalanxes of tractors.

Everywhere else too, the bright leaven of youth has done its work. It presents an unforgettable spectacle when it fills the Red Square with its immense elastic quadrilaterals, or crams the Dynamo Stadium with its 45,000 seats.

Youth, which as a rule is incomplete in itself, and on many points innocently ignorant, counts for nothing if it does not incorporate itself into the great mechanism of well-organized society. Then, it intuitively forces straight ahead, matured by the thought of the future before it, and it deserves respect from everyone, both for its powers of expansion, and because the future belongs to it, and for its helpful wisdom.

THE PEASANTRY

Can we say, let us repeat, that there are no dark spots in the picture? No doubt there are a few. I would enumerate them all, if I also enumerated all the successes, for, in common fairness, one must always give the true proportion between good and evil—which is never done, so far as the U.S.S.R. is concerned, when criticism is inconsiderately levelled at it without paying the least attention to the point of view of the other side.

But the point of view of the good leader is different from that of the impartial critic: he must concentrate mainly on faults and omissions. For instance, when considering the development of rural economy, he is haunted by the position of cattle-breeding—a side of it which has made no progress at all, so much so that the present-day figures are hardly any higher than those of 1913.

So particular attention must be paid to the question of live-stock (only pig-breeding is making any headway). A watchful eye must be kept on this, as upon the transport question, iron and steel works, coal, light industry, the cost of raw materials—and, of course, upon the eternal question of bureaucracy.

Bureaucracy (or, rather, officialism) is a phenomenon of human nature which constantly tends to increase and seems to resist any form of progress; it even seems to imply an immoderate respect for tradition. In the organization department the same thing is happening that is happening in the theoretical department with regard to formulæ, namely a tendency to lead a separate existence, quite independent of its original aims and objects. Bureaucracy is a sort of tumour which ends by growing eyes and ears.

So: "The sources of all our difficulties to-day are officialism and the paper administration of the social services, twaddle about the 'principles of leadership' (instead of actual constructive leadership), the absence of personal responsibility, the lack of individuality in work, the levelling system in wages, the absence of any systematic inspection of results achieved, the fear of self-criticism."

The best method of coping with these difficulties—which Stalin defines in a very clear-cut way, is "to raise the level of leadership to the political level." That is to say to have the full meaning of what one is doing, and of the place it occupies in the whole scheme of things, constantly in one's head.

Let us go straight ahead, glancing neither to right nor to left. I beg your pardon, I should have said, on the contrary, looking carefully to right and to left—to mark carefully any deviation to right or to left, always ready to make a sudden leap forward or to hold back a little. (The traitors of the Left are a little more dangerous than those of the Right, explains Piatniski, because they put one on the wrong track.) Stalin is very insistent about the reality of these dangers and he goes so far as to consider that the fact of not combatting one of these deviations amounts to a concession made to the other.

And besides, we do not get excited about our success. To do so would distract us on the threshold of the future. It might compromise or disturb our greatest and most powerful possession: our line of policy. This honest line of policy belongs to the Revolutionaries because they created it and because they have maintained it. "To have an honest line of policy and to know how to advance along it is a very rare event in the life of governing Parties. Look at the neighbouring countries, and see how many Parties in power have an honest policy which they follow. Actually there are no such Parties in the world, for they all live without perspective, wandering amidst the chaos of the world crisis and unable to see the way out of the morass. Our own Party is the only one which knows how to go forward and to carry on its labour progressively and victoriously."

Those who listen and who pay heed to this considered judgment which the extraordinary events of our own times have led a statesman to utter, must come to the conclusion that, in order to respect this great line and to keep it intact, one must remain in a constant state of vigilance and combativeness. One must not hang back, and one must make no mistakes.

Chapter Nine

WHAT OF TO-MORROW?

IF ONE wishes to see the full force of U.S.S.R. life and energy, one must see it in perspective, or, in other words, in the shadow of its future plans. All the descriptions of this swiftly moving picture grow out-of-date before our eyes—they have to be loaded with postscripts.

In the solemn atmosphere of the Seventeenth Congress of the Russian Communist Party, which took place in January 1934—"the Congress of the Victors"—dominated by Stalin's monumental report on the 1928–32 Plan—Stalin also opened the door into the endless future. The Five-Year Plan is dead; long live the 1932–37 Five-Year Plan!

The period of economic reconstruction is virtually at an end, said Molotoff, President of the Council of People's Commissars, one of the most important workers of the Union. Now they are turning to the question of developing, in quantity and in quality, the production of commodities, and to general improvement in everyone's standard of living.

On the foundations of the prodigious decentralization begun in the bosom of the Soviet world, the key industries will become twice as vast and as heavy (the production of means of production will reach 43,400,000,000 roubles, or 209 per cent. of the amount achieved by the last Plan).

The manufacture of machine tools, and the production of coal and of petrol, will be doubled; tractor, locomotive

WHAT OF TO-MORROW?

construction, foundries, steel, copper and chemical works will be trebled. The timber industry itself will be nearly doubled (176 per cent.). Five times as many trucks and eight times as many motor-cars will be manufactured. Electrical energy will attain 38,000,000,000 kilowatts (or 283 per cent. more).

The new Five-Year Plan has also provided for an increase of more than double in the manufactured goods industries (54,300,000,000 roubles, or an increase of 269 per cent.), namely, light industry, food commodities and industrial co-operatives.

Particular attention is being paid, in this new period, to improvement in quality and technique, and to replacement of machinery. The electrification of all industries, necessitating a great deal of very hard work. Enormous progress is to be made in the electrification of the country districts and of railways, and in the conveyance of power.

The output of labour should be raised—by 1937—to 63 per cent. as against 41 per cent. in 1932. The cost of raw materials (to which, in the meantime, a decrease of 4.7 per cent. in 1934 over that of 1933 has already been assigned) should decrease by 26 per cent.

The increase foreseen—and decided upon—in agricultural production is to be 105 per cent. (26,000,000,000 roubles). The number of tractor depots shall be increased from 2,446 (in 1932) to 6,000. Mechanization of agricultural work: an increase of 60 per cent. Total tractor power, 8,200,000 horse-power.

Railways should nearly double their traffic. River and maritime transport should nearly treble theirs. Motor transport is to be multiplied by 16. (For the railways, 3,000 miles electrified, 6,000 miles changed from single to double line, 12,000 miles of lines relaid; 7,000 miles of entirely new lines.)

The canal between the White Sea and the Baltic is to be completed, and also those between Moscow and the Volga and the Volga and the Don. By 1937 130,000 miles of new roads are to be made. Lines of civil aviation 53,000 miles (instead of 20,000 miles to-day).

Investment in industry: 69,500,000,000 roubles; in rural economy: 15,200,000,000 roubles; in transport services: 26,300,000,000 roubles. New undertakings to be begun and others to be reorganized together represent an expenditure of 132,000,000,000 roubles. (This is the largest figure that has ever figured in a budget or in any industrial scheme of any sort.) I will not even undertake to enumerate the principal objects it is hoped to achieve in this chapter of the Plan. . . .

As far as the factories are concerned, workers' dwellings with a floor-space of about 54,000,000 square yards are to be constructed.

The actual wages of the workers will, in 1937, be two and a half times what they were in 1932.

Illiteracy is to be completely abolished—as completely as unemployment was under the preceding Plan; every citizen in the Soviet Union will be able to read and to write.

The total number of pupils in schools and institutes will be 197 per 1,000 of the population, instead of 147 per 1,000 as at present. The funds of national insurance will be doubled.

"It is a fantastic Plan," people will say. "What has not already been said about the Plan on whose firm foundations we are now standing!" replied Molotoff quietly.

The Union of Socialist Soviet Republics will become in

this way the most powerful of all the States in the world in the principal branches of economics.*

In the great sane and heroic dream of resurrection which the U.S.S.R. is realizing under the leadership of the Communist Party, itself led by Comrade Stalin, there is, however, mixed the nightmare of war.

We know the tragi-comedy of the history of "official pacifism" in the post-war period. The equivocal position of the pompous League of Nations and its almost legendary incapability of ensuring peace being the least of the criticisms inspired by that institute of pacific ceremonies which sprang from the Treaty of Versailles to give some stability to its provisions,† and in which Germany has given up playing the part of the brigand who is always beaten by the other brigands, and in which Japan has, on its side, given up its own dishonest and lying rôle under the converging beams of international limelight.

Aggression against the U.S.S.R.—with the immense economic outlets and active volcano of Socialism—evidently enters into the calculations of Capitalism at bay, and the Soviet leaders are much too serious to commit the error of believing in the sincerity of the theatrical peace procla-

* Let us add that the results attained at the end of 1934 already indicate that the current Five-Year Plan will attain its colossal objectives. The national revenue has risen by 6,000,000,000 roubles in one year and was, in December, 55,000,000,000. The amount of electrical energy produced *has increased by one-third* as compared with 1933, and has reached 12,500,000,000 kilowatts. In the year 1934 the amount of iron smelted *was 50 per cent. greater* than in 1933. The triumph is tremendous, and Stalin is justly proud of it. But he says: "Do not be too proud, comrades, for you must remember that the production of steel has not increased in the same proportion." (This is only 40 per cent. more than that of last year.)

† As regards the carving-up of territory, not as regards the solemn clause stipulating that the disarmament of the conquered countries was to be the signal for general disarmament.

mations of the great mouthpieces in the pay of imperialist countries. But they believe that they have a part as censors to play against these dangerous artistes.

We know how unsuccessful were the first dealings of the U.S.S.R. with the League of Nations, and the outcry provoked at the Disarmament Conference by Litvinoff's proposal, which seems logical enough, for complete disarmament, or if that were not possible, at least partial disarmament.

But the U.S.S.R. has persevered in its unwavering peace policy. Soviet diplomacy, conducted in a masterly manner, formerly by Chicherin and nowadays by Litvinoff (but always by Stalin), has presented a constant and stubborn front of pacifism. (Defining what constitutes aggression, the strengthening of the Disarmament Conference which is in jeopardy and moribund, and its transformation into a permanent Peace Conference; refusal to exploit the revision of the ill-omened Treaties of Versailles to the sole advantage of belligerent profiteers who are just as worthless as those who actually profited by the said treaties; non-aggression pacts offered to everyone and many even accepted; solid diplomatic relations established with the United States and with France.) This positive and enlightened peace policy has been recognized by everyone except those whose definite interest it is to deny it.

"We are a factor for peace in the world," Stalin declared at the Seventeenth Congress. And he added with sufficiently terrible accuracy: "Around us are collecting and cannot help collecting, all the states who for some reason or other do not wish to make war for a more or less extended period."

Finally, at the request of thirty-two states, the U.S.S.R.

was admitted into the League of Nations. This is certainly some guarantee of peace, because it practically ensures the alteration of the attitude of the League of imperialist Nations under the influence of Soviet collaboration forced upon them by circumstances.

But it is not a complete guarantee—very far from it. The danger of war remains.

This is quite clearly indicated in the attitude of Japan. It is perfectly obvious that Japan wants to invade a very large part of Asia, especially China (from which it has already seized Manchuria and Jehol), by breaking its Soviet backbone and attacking the U.S.S.R. Indeed Japan proclaims this openly and is constantly adopting a provocative attitude. She has transformed Manchuria into a fortified camp which she fills with military stores, aviation centres and strategic lines of communication. In the field of foreign policy Japan and Germany have an understanding and are violently and clumsily friendly.

Before what the popular soldier-minister Vorochiloff calls "the cynical frankness" of Japan, the attitude of the Soviet Union has been the courageous, strong and noble one of granting all the concessions that it can.

But at the end of these concessions there is a boundary limit upon which is written: "We do not want one foot of anyone else's land, but we will not yield an inch of our own." (Stalin.)

If war breaks out, the U.S.S.R. will defend itself and all that it represents in the way of human inheritance. The war in question will become general and, from being an imperialist war, will transform itself, in many ways, into a revolutionary Civil War. This is not so much dictated by Party policy as it is a matter of inevitable historical destiny. Here, there, wherever the war passes, Revolution will pass. What occurred during the last war shows us clearly the turn that matters will take, but in a greater and stronger way, during the next war. Even when people try to destroy progress, they only hasten it forward.*

Whatever may happen in the unknown future, if war is declared, one of the greatest causes of confidence among the Soviet people will be, Stalin. Vorochiloff, Commissar for National Defence, is very much loved, but the Commander-in-Chief is and will be Stalin. He will gather into his own hands the whole political and military leadership. Or, rather, he will continue to do so when war breaks out, and that is considered by everyone in the U.S.S.R. as "an assurance of victory."

* It is not out of place to observe here that a terrible and significant discovery arose out of the great aerial manœuvres which took place recently in England and in France, namely the impossibility of putting up an adequate defence against an attack by bombing aeroplanes. One of our most respected military experts, Lt.-Col. Vauthier, observing (in a book with a preface by Maréchal Lyautey), "that Paris may be annihilated during the first hours of war," recommends the complete demolition of Paris and its reconstruction elsewhere under improved armour plating. . . . "And he is not trying to be funny, as one might be tempted to believe," observes Paul Faure. Moreover, Lord Londonderry, the British Air Minister, and Monsieur Pierre Cot, the former French Air Minister, have publicly declared it. "It is asserted that no human power in the present state of scientific knowledge is capable of preventing the dropping of tons of high explosive sufficient to destroy London and Paris." (Paul Langevin has calculated that a hundred tons would be sufficient. Now at the British manœuvres four hundred tons were potentially dropped on London.) The only recourse left for the country which has its capital city destroyed is to send a squadron of its own to disrupt and asphyxiate the enemy capital. What is true in the case of towns is true for military centres. "There is only one exception," said Monsieur Pierre Cot, "and that is the case of Russia, whose territory is so vast that the greater part of it is protected from raids of this nature. The U.S.S.R., whose immensity once beat Napoleon at the height of his power, is therefore in an exceptionally privileged position (Japan is, on the contrary, particularly vulnerable)." So that it is not solely in its own interest that the U.S.S.R. is fighting when it fights for peace.

Chapter Ten

THE TWO WORLDS

THIS then is where we stand in the dawn of a new era—at this era at which, as Kaganovitch says, oceans are flowing beneath the bridges.

Every nation but one is rushing headlong to ruin by way of Fascism, and they are all rushing into war. The situation is tragic. But it is not a complex one; it is, on the contrary, quite a simple one.

In the nineteenth century, as a result of the sweeping away of all previous political situations, active humanity resolved itself roughly into two Parties: Conservatives and Revolutionaries—those who wished to retain the capitalist form of society and those who wanted to change it and make it more equitable. The struggle began in various quarters, with a tendency to become general, between these two massive forces.

In actual fact it was, on one side, the working class partially organized into an international army (political and trades unionist) and all its sympathizers; on the other side, the ruling middle classes—the universal legacy of the French Revolution—their State forces, their advocates and defenders of all kinds, and also all non-revolutionaries of any kind.

For at first sight it might appear as though there were intermediate positions, but in reality there were none. Between the two essential parties all other political parties played out their incongruous, fleeting comedies. From such a state of affairs it became evident that there was no third world that mattered. There was no third path. There was no compromise. Everything which was not Revolutionary was Conservative—even the Reformists were absorbed, to a certain extent, in the question of social conservation— even neutrals and apathetic people added their dead weight —the half-hearted Revolutions themselves fell back into them and died there of inanition. If one does not obtain everything, one obtains nothing.

Consequently, the illusive middle-class Liberalism which has so many adherents, like all "middle courses," and whose slogan is: "Neither Reaction nor Revolution," and all the variations of this same theme, rest upon a grossly mistaken interpretation of the truth. The exigencies of present-day circumstances insistently demand "Either Reaction or Revolution." Those are the only two alternatives. By force of circumstances and by force of logic the intermediate formations fall either to the Left or to the Right (nearly always to the Right). There is no way of escaping from this mathematical truth (and besides, all our contemporary history confirms it). Let us repeat, to drive the point thoroughly home: If he is not a Revolutionary, the non-Conservative, whatever he may say or do, is a Conservative. The middle-course Reaction hiding its face. And the two groups remain: Capitalism, which obtains by artificial means (lying propaganda and abuse of the power it possesses by reason of the position it has acquired) the double anarchic dilation of the individual and of the nation, and which is a perpetual muddle of injustice, spoliation, corruption and war—and Socialism, which withdraws private profit from the scheme of things, and returns it all into the hands of the producers (i.e., the manual and intellectual workers) and says that the nation is not the last step,

THE TWO WORLDS 251

but the last step but one in the unification of the inhabitants of the world.

Nowadays, there is still the same universal division, with the same fundamental characters, but presented in a different way.

New events have occurred—and what events! A general reinforcement of the workers' movement and of the revolutionary conscience. Several Revolutions took place as a result of the war—a war whose tens of millions of victims and whose thousands of millions of pounds' damage cannot be estimated, and which had no real reason to take place. One of these Revolutions succeeded, and a Marxist State was formed in a vast territory. Gone, in the first quarter of the twentieth century, is the time when the capitalist stomach had the Equator as its belt. And, at the same time, the weapon of world Socialism, the International, was forged anew.

Then, immediately afterwards, the world economic crisis took place. "A temporary crisis, like the others," said the misguided pontiffs, "the seventh or the eighth." But no, it is the organic crisis of Capitalism, a crisis of decadence, of old age and dry rot, with all its methods outworn and all its outlets blocked up. (They cry out, "Produce, produce! Sell, sell!" But all the customers are vendors too, jostling one another on the frontier boundaries. Its merchandise falls back on the producing country and stifles it.) Commerce dies of a miscarriage. This is the quite natural result of the whole principle. It is not over-production that should be indicted, *for, actually, the whole world does not produce enough for its needs*, but the disorder in the distribution of produce as a result of economic nationalisms. It is also quite natural that swindling should be rife behind the scenes in all great industries.

So one can no longer quote as a model of management the method which sows misery, cultivates bankruptcy and puts robbers at the top, the régime where work brings famine in its track (to say nothing of war, threatening once more from every cardinal point). And again, people can no longer quote as a model for the joys of slavery the American workman, the gilded workman; that explodes one of the great arguments which keep crowds quiet.

Capitalism, to continue to be Capitalism, has had to disguise its aims. It has done so with a great deal of false modesty. As Stalin expressly said, some time ago, Capitalism cannot emerge from the crisis with "its head held high," it can only emerge from it "on all fours."

Faced with the progress of Socialism and the advance of their own decay, the middle classes soon pulled themselves together. They improved their programme of conservative seizure (having the material means of doing so), and to-day they are rising to the surface again, carefully disguised. The capitalist system is discreetly tucked away into the background, and is no longer visible in the foreground at all.

That disguise called Fascism—which, without being a necessary adjunct to middle-class power, does in fact occur almost everywhere (and has become the new uniform of Capitalism)—has as its main objective the division of the enemy and especially the *isolation of the working classes* and *Socialism* at the same stroke, by getting the workers who do not belong to the labouring classes on its side. This scheme was very carefully prepared by continuous, intensive, very carefully prepared propaganda starting soon after the end of the war, at a period at which the ruling classes were crippled and were rapidly losing their hold over the masses.

Discontent, resulting from all the disillusionment and all the hardships of post-war existence, has been fostered and exploited by Capitalism through a certain democratic demagogism and by certain ideas dishonestly borrowed from socialist terminology. Capitalism has extracted from these a compound of all the bitterness, all the disillusionment and all the anger, and has diverted it and directed it against a few cock-shies set up by itself.

One of these cock-shies (apart from Socialism) is the parliamentary system which, it is declared, must be swept away, in addition to Socialism, so that the last semblance of liberty may disappear (liberty itself having already vanished). So the parliamentary system (which really thoroughly deserves it!) is accused of all the sins of Israel, thereby cunningly shifting them from the shoulders of the middle-class system itself.

And they have all the other scapegoats they need. Present-day Reaction has protested louder than anyone else against the scandals, frauds and semi-official embezzlements with which its own methods are so filled, and it has gone out of its way to incriminate with these misdeeds of the capitalist system, not indeed all capitalists, but only those who have at length grown weary of the colossal complacency of class legislation.

And by thus playing with words (as, for instance, with the elastic word "régime"), the new-fangled Reaction has created a certain anti-Capitalism with excellent demagogic scope. It is the only means of preserving Capitalism: suppress parliament and install in its place a dictatorial government, and prosecute the villains who have committed the crime of being found out, and Capitalism becomes unassailable.

This activity in defence of Capitalism, with its rudiments of a superficial and negative programme, emanates from all sorts of different organizations only differing from one another by their titles, and forming a solid opposition group to the workers' movement.

The peasant classes and the lower middle-classes are set against the workers; officials are set against manual labourers; and everyone is set against the officials. The taxpayers, all the ex-soldiers who do not understand the situation, and the very young men, are dazzled. The controlling idea is to gather all those who are not already organized, the floating population, in fact, into a new organization over which control can be kept, and to smother the worker in it.

Socialism—the threadbare, mangy author of all evil—is decried at the same time as the parliamentary system, by putting it in an entirely false light. People are horrified by being made to believe that Socialism is plotting their destruction.

People say: "Socialists have been in power in England and in Germany. See what they have done." They omit to add that the people in question were perhaps socialist in name, but that they never applied the principles of Socialism. And indeed it must be recognized that this piece of sophistry is partly reinforced by the very real disappointment which certain Social-Democratic leaders, by their actions during and after the war, gave to the workers. All their pandering, whether disloyal or merely childish, and their actual betrayal of the workers, have to some extent discredited Socialism, and have appreciably weakened it among certain classes of workers which are not yet ripe for ruthless and uncompromising Communism.

So we see Mr. MacDonald, a Socialist converted to the virtues of Capitalism, being exhibited with pride, "much as a reformed drunkard is exhibited by a temperance society," says Mr. Snowden. As for the achievements of the U.S.S.R.. these are hidden, and stolen from the people.

The neo-Reactionaries are particularly virulent (as is natural) against trade unionism. We know what Mussolini thinks about it, and we also know the sentiments of those who prompt Hitler with what he has to say. And not long ago, Monsieur André Tardieu explicitly said: "To overcome the world crisis, all that is required is effective control of trade unions." The Corporate State systems which flourish in Italy, in Germany, and (in disguise) in France, are based precisely on this principle. It is the system of intimidation and of new militarism—which fills Herr Krupp with enthusiasm; it transforms every worker into a soldier —a machine tool or a rifle on two legs.

But the great weapon of Fascism against Socialism is Nationalism.

National unity and greatness, prophesies Fascism, can only be acquired if Internationalism, which is the principal element of disorder, misery and perdition, is crushed. So down with foreigners, naturalized aliens and Jews!— down, above all, with Socialists and Communists.

Nationalism is the principal driving force of Fascism. It is a kind of chauvinist intoxication which makes this timely regrouping of Capitalism proceed. It is its leaven.

A powerful leaven, indeed—the simplest, the most terrible and the most dynamic of all. Its passion inflames hundreds of millions of people. The myth of national interest or national honour inflames the dullest and most apathetic of citizens—and how much more so empty-headed, loud-voiced youth! It is the most stupid of all evil instincts because, being highly contagious, it blindly paves the way for every calamity.

"Ourselves, ourselves alone!" A comprehensive formula which avoids all deep reflection and foresight. A most valuable key-formula. One which appeals to the vital interests of the rich, of military men and of churchmen, and at the same time to the stupidity of everyone else.

Social preservation then, takes the form—for the final struggle—of so-called moral and national reconstruction trampling Socialism and the free citizen underfoot, and of a strong power which raises itself, with its soldiery, above any criticism. It is the capitalist police converted into a party.

This is the dope which Fascism has served out and is still serving out to the taxpayers—consisting of claiming to be able to put an end to the crisis and the depression by the help of the same methods that brought it about. The various forms of Fascism differ among themselves superficially; but underneath they are all the same.

However much it may establish a sort of farce of democracy, a sort of caricature of Socialism, and however loudly it gives expression to revolutionary sentiments and ideas of controlled economy—and even anti-Fascism—and however much it climbs up upon proletarian principles in order to raise itself higher, this so-called doctrine of popular reconstruction, which has installed itself in Italy, in Germany, in Hungary, in Poland, in the Balkan peninsula, in Portugal, in Austria (where the liberators have met with the most frightful butchery and the most appalling tortures), and which at the present moment is recruiting adherents among the youth, the lower middle-classes and the faithful of the churches of France and of other countries, is no more democratic than it is new. It is the old Capitalism be-

THE TWO WORLDS

plumed, tin-plated and militarized, and it consists of the same enormous fundamental contradictions running through a doctrine that is so vague that ordinary people can—at first—be made to believe that they are being pushed forward when they are really being dragged back.

It achieves nothing. Fascism is not and never will be anything but a veneer, and the only really imaginative or original things that Fascists have ever done have been to decide upon the colour of their shirts and to persuade the people that one can live on smoke.

It still remains that form of society in which one only prospers in proportion as one ruins someone else, in which one only lives by killing other people, that form of society which invades new continents in order to steal weak countries and to make the natives pay for the very air they breathe, that abject form of society in which one cannot be honest without being a fool, where the elections violate the will of the people, where men exploit each other, assassinate each other, and the payment of all the great social debts is indefinitely postponed by illusive appearances of settlement, and the people are perpetually dancing over a concealed volcano.

Such a system cannot possibly put an end to the crisis; it can only make it worse, because the more Nationalism develops, the more it proceeds to its own destruction.

It produces nothing—except, perhaps, a death sentence. The "order" proclaimed by middle-class rule is that of the cemetery.

What can be the outcome of it all? Only war. And once more we shall have snout-like gas-masks, train-loads of soldiers—hearses full of living men—masses of people rushing headlong to get themselves killed, fields turned into heaps of scrap-metal, villages into stone heaps, and whole peoples asphyxiated in subterranean prisons.

But war is also social revolution scattered broadcast in the furrows of the trenches and over every hearth in the cities.

In the meantime, the chances that this spectral programme, the programme of blundering delusion and of annihilation, has of taking root everywhere—apart from its pretence of democracy—is that it has on its side brute force, the force of the State. Because all European and American governments are either fascist or pre-fascist.

Capitalism, dragged down in the landslide of statistics, in the melting away of figures, and economically ruined, is still strong politically. Its bankrupt partisans are armed to the teeth. They can no longer keep their feet but they possess machine-guns, tanks, bombs, armies; they have crowds of policemen who would look well in an agricultural show. They control the law courts (the prisons), the newspapers, the schools, diplomacy and aggressive alliances. Legality belongs to them alone and they coin laws as they do money, inflating them as they inflate their currencies.

They have all they need in order to sweep away men of independent thought, to plunder the weak, to exploit civilization to their own evil ends, to instil national confidence to a point of wildest enthusiasm into a part of the lower middle-classes, even to death itself, to squander the efforts of the people and to maintain for a little while longer the era of decadence and destruction.

So there are six Parties in the world: the five old ones and the new one. In every country, except in the Soviet continent, the government is the enemy of the people.

THE TWO WORLDS

All the people penned up in the various countries, like prisoners in concentration camps bounded by frontiers, are all as good as one another, and they are all as good as the Soviet people. They are all great and all deserve our respect. The living mass of humanity is sacred. The hatred that one has for capitalist governments which seem like fools when seen from a distance and like criminals from nearby, forms part of the respect that one has for the people: the great German people, the great Italian people, the great English people—and all the rest of them (let us rather say: the entire undivided people of the world).

The governments which, on all sides, abuse the power which they would no longer possess if things were properly and sincerely adjusted, either torment or cajole or hypnotize the poor into the belief that their conditions will soon improve. And in their intercourse with one another they act with a casuistry and a charlatanism so complex as to amount almost to burlesque—because one cannot pursue in the light of day a political system in which the advantage of one side depends so outrageously upon the disadvantage of the others.

And all that ends, after numerous preliminary conferences and agreements, with a general increase of armaments. And, as the armament manufacturers are given a free hand, they have the effrontery to sell their goods to possible future enemies as well. (Moreover, let us recollect, as an excellent precedent, that, during the war, French soldiers were blown up on the Bulgarian front by French 75's. During the Riff war in Northern Africa, French soldiers were shot down by French rifles. Monsieur Schneider, of the firm of Creusot, controls and exploits the Czech armament firm *La Skoda*, which furnishes armaments to Germany, and is rushing Hitler into war. Latterly, at the Radical

Congress, Jean Sennac declared, without being contradicted, that Schneider had sold 400 tanks to Germany, and that a certain French factory in the south-west was selling to the Germans products which entered into the manufacture of explosives. In other particulars, also, these two-sided orders are proceeding, and only a short while ago China and Japan went together to interview one of their common munition suppliers to induce him to reduce the price of his instruments of death. And this is the truth, not an exaggeration or a caricature.)

From the Baltic to the Mediterranean, the nations lie in bondage in the height of capitalist ruin.

It began with Italy. The workers and Revolutionaries were butchered and a period of abject terror began, a period of persecution and of torture worse than those of the Inquisition, the details of which tax one's imagination: the people were cowed with revolvers and tanks, and with lingering death in disease-infested prisons.

Mussolini, the loud-speaker of world Reaction, appeared on the social scene—as a pure Socialist—at a moment when foreign capitalists were still rolling in money, and when one only needed to betray enough people in order to obtain the means of pushing one's way to the top. He now benefits by that heavy conspiracy of silence which is the characteristic and the shame of our age. He has inoculated Italy with his glory.

The chief of the Blackshirts, the Black King of the Italians, has merely redecorated the façade of Italy, but, apart from this, he has accomplished nothing positive unless it be to diminish the number of Italians. Ruin has never ceased to spread in that country which is to-day, economically, the most miserable State in Europe after Germany. (Fascism, the world regenerator!) In Italy, where the school-master teaches lessons in uniform, where the workers—even those who are not unemployed, have not enough food for their families—canonizations are organized in order to give a fillip to trade. It is true that the country is quiet, but that is because it is muzzled; to the tourist's eye everything is in perfect order.

Not long ago Mussolini declared that Italy was at the lowest ebb, "that she could not sink lower." ". . . Doctors, midwives, schoolmasters and engineers are luxuries. If every district called for them they would be spoiled," declared the fascist dictator who had formerly made such dazzling promises to his compatriots.

Take Germany with its Swastika (two interlaced gibbets). The working classes have resisted heroically there, but they have their entire destiny to reconstruct. Hitler—with his little moustache, and the whims of a moralist—was jockeyed into power by Hindenburg and Clemenceau—and the absurd mischief made by the Treaty of Versailles is the only argument that makes any sense in his reasoning.

Hitler is nothing but a loud-speaker and the agent of Capitalism, even though he does plunder the Jews. Now that he has had himself consecrated super-Emperor, his policy consists of disowning the National-Socialist programme which raised him to the throne. So as not to displease the powerful Reichswehr, he has eliminated from that programme everything which might have appeared to be democratic to the eyes of a Germany fallen into second childhood.

The Reichstag fire and the burning of books marked the beginning of his rule, and he may set fire to Europe.

He may possibly succeed in doing so. The tower from the top of which Hitler holds forth contains certain terrible machinery. All the strength, all the resources of a great nation which, although half-smothered, still contains enormous vitality, the encyclopædic German administration, the unswerving confidence, born of discipline, which still exists among a large part of its dense population—all that has been feverishly put to the service of re-arming. It is absolutely necessary for them to arrive at some definite and spectacular result before economic ruin overtakes them. The German worker, when he is employed, receives less money to-day than the unemployed received a few years ago. The Communist Party sees its moral influence increasing over the scandal of Germany. War is the only recourse for Hitler, who has no constructive programme. As soon as he feels himself sufficiently armed and sufficiently supplied with allies, he will cast off his mask. Never has any country been so inevitably dragged towards disaster.

In Austria the Government will not allow any foreign banditry, but only its own. The workers must be officially killed by the national army and police or officiously by the Heimwehr and in no other way.

In the Balkans, the White Terror has reigned for some fifteen years, as it has in Italy. Bulgaria, with its official banditry, its mass slaughters, its forest of gibbets (so many thousands of people hanged, dismembered, burned alive, hewn in pieces, mutilated: their nails and their hair torn out, their bowels crushed, red-hot irons thrust into the stomachs of men and women—and many other similar methods which have been employed in nearly every other European country, the incredible enumeration of which rises like a cry of malediction against our age).*

* The great newspaper Press pretends to know nothing of these tortures. Executions are made the occasion for public holidays. In Hungary

At the head of a precisely similar régime sat the late Alexander of Serbia, the ruler of the Serbians and of the people who were handed over higgledy-piggledy to Serbia by the Entente, and who was only king because a few cut-throats climbed one night through a lavatory window and knifed a man and a woman. Serbia had already furnished the pretext for the war of 1914: Sarajevo. It is starting all over again, by trying to pick a quarrel with Hungary, or, rather, with the Government of Horthy, giving as its reason the hurried mourning which the suppression of Alexander imposed on the Jugoslav population. But the occasion did not seem to be quite opportune and the pretext was rejected. Higher up on the map we had Pilsudski, who so deliberately betrayed France when France, in straitened circumstances, ceased to support official Poland. And elsewhere again there is Masaryk, the wise President whose love of democracy and of legal proclamations is only equalled by his hatred of the working classes. And Switzerland is distinguishing itself to-day, not only because peace is rusticating there and because it is the seat of the League of Nations, where they talk of nothing but peace in the same way as in churches they talk of nothing but love, but also because Switzerland has become just as fiercely inhospitable as England. Moreover, Switzerland had already begun her rôle of mediator during the war, by acting as intermediary between the belligerents in the matter of traffic in war material.

In France, Monsieur Doumergue has disappeared from

---

great ladies flaunted themselves at the hangings like the middle-class Frenchwomen who put out the eyes of the prisoners of the Commune with their sunshades as they were being taken away. At Sofia, the execution of Friedmann among fifty thousand people, condemned without any proof for the attempt on the Cathedral, was actually filmed for the news-reels.

circulation and no one but himself regrets it. It is not that he meant badly: jealous of the laurels of old swashbuckling Hindenburg and having, like him, "a back shaped like a pair of steps," Monsieur Doumergue, with Tardieu by his side, was obsessed with the idea of plenipotentiary powers, and broadcast mawkish appeals on the wireless for one's money or one's life. He firmly pursued the policy of increasing war estimates and police estimates, and the policy of State reform formerly concocted by Monsieur Tardieu, which was an already recognizable relative of the fascist régimes let loose among her neighbours.

But he tried to go too quickly. Threatened with the dissolution of Parliament, he was compelled to throw in his hand. His successor carried on the programme of this great bogus national figure more deftly. Flanked also by Tardieu and by Herriot, now become inseparable, he keeps up the system of legal proclamations. If he does not insist so much upon State reform, he places the words "National Economy" much more prominently upon his prospectus. What can one word do in such an emergency? The people vote in favour of remedies for the crisis which will last just as long as it will take to see that they are of no use. They do not grapple with the crisis, they flee from it, and this Government will be no more successful than any of those which preceded it in throwing any light on the Stavisky affair, which is too rich in complications. In foreign politics it will merely be a revival of the imbroglio of closer connexions with foreign powers and of markets and of *a parte's*.

What of the French Empire and the French colonies? A vast imperial French conference has been convened with great pomp and ceremony just in order to grind as much as possible out of nations that, having been vanquished, are now being punished for it. Their actual output is negligible. And yet the native has long since been expropriated and condemned to exhausting, annihilating labour, throughout the whole of Africa. He is the beast of burden, the military, tax-paying animal. In the Gaboon, whose population is visibly shrinking, the negro is frequently obliged to sell his wife to pay his taxes. In French Equatorial Africa and French West Africa, non-payment of the tribute exacted by plundering civilization entails massacre and the destruction of villages. In Morocco, women are taken as hostages for the payment of taxes. In Indo-China, railways are built for the use of colonists under such conditions that it has been said that each sleeper represents a native corpse. And if any patriot dares to raise his head, the scoundrel is struck down in the name of patriotism.

Other countries, not yet officially fascist, are struggling to become so, from the upper strata of society, of course.

In Spain, the monarchist régime was swept away four years ago in a sudden fit of anger on the part of the Spanish people, to give way, alas, to a gang of Republicans who have, towards anything which is in the least tinged with red, the mentality of bulls. They began by dealing with strikes by means of rifle fire, decimating the workers and peasants who had placed them in power. Nowadays the Revolution, which has been revived by the shameless fascisization of the Lerroux Government, is being ferociously drowned in blood. Gil Robles and his "Popular Action," which is both Catholic and fascist, is to-day the heir of the 1931 Revolution and the successor of the cadaverous Alfonso XIII. The 1934 Revolution, which progressed so far and so deeply in the Asturias, was stopped—the victim of the weakness of the Socialists and the desertion of the Anarchists—but was not extinguished. It was not even disarmed. The soil of Spain still trembles beneath the trampling of the masses.

Official England is pre-eminently imperialist and its policy is that of selfishness and of the traditional voracity of a middle-class Empire. Great Britain will be the last stronghold of Reaction in the world.

Terror and hatred of the emancipation of workers and of the freedom of mankind are clearly visible through the sober hypocrisy and ecclesiastical prudence of the speeches of the English leaders—of that terrible areopagus of great business tyrants which crushed with its weight the leader of the Labour Party when he threw his lot in with it. They protrude through the so-called Liberalism of Lloyd George and other gentlemen of the same kidney. The imperial knavery of British diplomacy, the suzerain of the *Intelligence Service*, differs only by its imperturbable consistency from the fantastic policy of a Mussolini, anxious above all to polish up his personal prestige and to keep himself well to the fore, in contemporary annals of history, as the great parasite of Italy. Sir Oswald Mosley collects his Blackshirts, but it seems unlikely that Fascism will get hold of England in this form so soon: mainly because the masses are strongly united, and also because ruling Imperialism has no need of it at the moment.

In India, where the British Government sows civilization from bombing aeroplanes (or, at any rate, so the English newspapers assert) and which makes gaps and rivers of blood with its machine-guns and iron-shod sticks in the immense multitudes standing by, mute, unarmed and passive, the restraint imposed by Gandhi has been as good as a carnage. Gandhi, a servile dreamer and an enemy of progress, has betrayed 350,000,000 human beings. The man who might have been the saviour of India has done nothing. Preserve us from those who destroy nations so as to prevent them from shedding blood!

And elsewhere? Japan, in the clutches of its military caste, has become a deformity, with its whole interior economy warped by belligerence. It blows itself out and labours to become the greatest power in the world, both on land and on sea. It is the chief purchaser of war munitions and engines of destruction in the world market. Only the worst can be expected from those poor soldiers steeped in fanaticism—when the Military Party considers itself to be ready. This military clique which rules over the Japanese Empire suffers from the Washington Pact, which gave it the number 3 as its co-efficient of naval armament, whereas England and the United States were each given the number 5. Japan wants the same number and denounces the Pact. But in addition to this it wants the Empire of the East, that is to say, it wants to be the uncontrolled master of the Pacific. It pursues this dream, verbally, by declaring itself to be invested with the "sacred mission of maintaining peace in the East" (being itself the slaughterer of China), and, in practice, by trying to prejudice England against the Soviet Union (in which it has already been successful) and also against the United States, which will always be its acknowledged enemy so long as there are not two Pacific Oceans in the world.

In the United States Mr. Roosevelt gathers a few solemn people round a table, as at a spiritualist séance, in order to solve the problem of squaring the circle of economic balance under the capitalist régime. And he employs all sorts of eye-wash and fascist dodges to produce an appearance of success. He cannot help using these methods, and these methods cannot possibly end in success. How can anyone imagine that national economy can be put into proper order, in the public interest, so long as it continues to be submitted to the arbitrary dictatorship of great private interests? Society, just like a house, must be built from the ground up and not from the roof down. Mr. Roosevelt's effort, which can only have superficial and momentary results, means beginning the social-economic building by the roof. It is all theory and paper. It is worse: whether childishness or trickery, it is, in the end, basing everything on Capitalism.

Stalin explained all this very clearly in a recent conversation with H. G. Wells, to whom Mr. Roosevelt's system appears as the last word in putting "Anglo-Saxon Socialism" (?) into miraculous practice. Stalin appreciates "the will-power and courage" which Mr. Roosevelt displays so as to "reduce to a minimum the downfall of Capitalism," but he calls attention to the fact that he does not destroy the fundamental *anarchy* of Capitalism. Moreover, he cannot do so, because the United States are, in reality, in the hands of private people, and Mr. Roosevelt is powerless. If he really went against capitalist interests he would be deposed. Nothing can come of such half-measures, which produce nothing but squibs of noisy publicity, in which Capitalism only apes socialist methods so far as they are necessary for it to continue to rule.

But there is something else. There are the sane and healthy forces. Millions of eyes are opening under the influence of the new life.

If only the mobilization of the people could be hastened! We all respect sincerity, but we are reaching the point at which ignorance becomes shameful. For the first time an appreciable portion of humanity has radically altered itself. All eyes are turned in the direction of the U.S.S.R., noting its difference from other countries which are at the same time more advanced and more backward. It is one's duty to understand all these things at the same time.

If, in the course of our survey of a world which contains so much suffering created at will by parasites, we allow ourselves to be led into anger and invective, our excuse lies in the constant evidence of this suffering which we have before us, and the necessity for shouting for help. But let us pause a moment to reflect quietly, as a thinking creature should, and let us make a sort of wager with ourselves:

What will the future be? Fascism or Socialism? What *must* the future be?

Fascism, which means general nationalist reaction? What does that mean, since each nationalist party only considers the question of its own development in relation to and in opposition to all others, and since there are about eighty of these on the face of the earth, and since the development of machinery tends to equalize the methods of destruction for all? ... What unions can there be amongst them but unions of hatred and destructive unions for purposes of gain? The extermination of the human race has never been so scientifically planned as it is in these perspectives.

And on the other side? Is the general Soviet formula capable of achievement? Yes, and it is for the advantage of everyone, and it is the only one which is for the advantage of everyone and it is the only possible one. From whatever angle one approaches the question, one cannot succeed in laying a single one of the public misfortunes with which we are burdened, or which are hanging over our heads, at the door of Soviet society in which everyone looks after everyone else, which makes men rely upon one another, and which gives a finer meaning to frontiers and removes their hostility. In the meantime, the proprietors of things and of men, the hangers-on, the speculators, the swindlers and the pimps, are floundering in the great old-fashioned current of Reaction, streaked with republican catchwords: and not only is the organized mass of the Workers' State resisting this current, but also in all other countries one-half of the population is rebelling and straining at its bonds. All over the world a latent "Second Power" of justice and the righting of wrongs is vigorously asserting itself.

(There can be no lasting States except those constructed on an international plan and the only possible international plan is that of Socialism.)

These revolutionary forces are constantly increasing. The socialist struggle in our own countries at the present time takes the broad and redoubtable form of "a united front." That is to say, of a more or less continuous (tending to become permanent) uniting for action of all the workers of all the "Left" parties, and also of those who are unorganized and belong to no party, and also of the various grades of peasants and of the lower middle-classes (these last three form the majority of the population of all the countries in the world).

We are entering—with such widely spread organizations as the "Struggle against War and Fascism" movement, which arose out of the Amsterdam Congress of 1932, and the Paris Congress (at the Salle Pleyel) in 1933, and which is the soul and the specific organ of the united front on the international scale, the general instrument of co-ordination —upon an era of mass movements of a loyally and logically revolutionary character. Their object is to prevent war and to repel Fascism and fascisization—all of them direct results of Capitalism—by the general alliance of all exploited and oppressed people, and by fighting against Capitalism itself. And this is to go on all over the world, side by side with, and apart from, the frontal battle waged by the political parties. (These parties are also forming an united front among themselves, as the French, Austrian and Italian Socialists and Communists have already done, to begin with.) Thus an agitation and a stirring up of the multitudes is brewing which threatens the imbecile and ferocious "old order."

This movement aims at rousing living people against the dead weight of governments and the deadly weight of profiteers.

There are no other expedients for the submerged, for the threatened and for the damned, than revolutionary expedients, since it was middle-class tyranny that began by counter-revolution as a preventive measure. The counter-Revolutionaries have on their side the control of arms and of the public services and are able to lie on the wireless. The Revolutionaries have on their side the fact that they "are right." The struggle to come will be a conclusive one.

And one of the objectives in all these teeming offensive-defensives, must be the safeguarding of the Soviet Union.

All human brains and all human hearts are made in the same mould. What we tell them is very simple: either men must give up living together or they must start again in a different way and they must be guided by a definite example, by the light of fire and of the dawn of a new era.

The Russian people is the first that undertook the task of saving the people. The U.S.S.R. is the only real socialist experiment that has ever been made, and it affords a real concrete proof that Socialism is feasible in this world. The results of Socialism are there; you have only to look at them. You must not let clowns and rascally politicians persuade you that they are somewhere else. That is the country in which, by the hands of two super-men, have been united "the practical genius of the American and the enthusiasm of the Revolutionary," the country of intelligence and of duty—with its yearning for truth, its enthusiasm and its youth. It stands out from the map of the world, not only because it is new, but because it is clean.

The Soviet socialist administration is the only one which has created prosperity and which has created civic virtues —which have nothing in common with the sinister code of honour of people of the Mussolini or Stavisky type, who shine side by side in every capitalist city. The October Revolution really did bring about a purification of morals and of the public spirit, which no other religious or political reform ever before succeeded in doing—neither Christianity, nor Protestantism, nor the "Civic and Civil Rights of Man" of the French Revolution.

To the world-wide group whose eyes are turned towards the future, events show, more and more, that the interests of all the workers—labourers, peasants, middle classes, intellectuals—are identical, and that all the workers should mass themselves around the labouring class. This does not mean that the labouring class is essentially superior and should be especially privileged; but it is the most sensible way of arranging matters, because of the organization of labour, its social enlightenment, its achievements, the logical and historical personification which it is of anti-Capitalism, and the formidable weapons available to those who hold the means of production in their hands.

The working proletariat is, in actual fact, the active

THE TWO WORLDS

army. And in time of war it is not the part of the active army to command the reserve army, but to collaborate with it wherever the battle is fiercest.

Events also show—and one must not tire of proclaiming these truths—that one must embrace Internationalism in a practical way before one can emerge from chaos, because history, whether we want it to or not, speaks to us internationally. They show that nothing can be accomplished, even within frontiers, without disregarding frontiers. And finally, they show that Reformism must be rejected, as well as any combination with the plutocratic group which clings to power. The formula of Reformism no longer means anything. It really ceased to be of any value when it made of Socialism an equivocal medium in which the labouring class marked time.

There are two worlds: the socialist world and the capitalist world. Between the two there hovers the absurd mirage of a third world, democratic in name but feudal in fact.

We must either unite on the truth of this statement, or against it.

Youth must not allow itself to be deceived by these faked rejuvenations with which Fascism disguises itself, or by all its tinsel.

The greatest and most important reply to the exigencies of the times must certainly come from youth. It is not for youth to bring its driving force to bear on degrading traditions, nor to make a desperate attempt to turn the world from the Left to the Right. It is for youth to do something new, according to the dictates of nature and of science. The boy is father to the man, and the future belongs to him.

Let the former combatants, the survivors, the bleeding and maimed witnesses of the Great War, those who smashed one another for no reason at all over two thousand miles of front and have made the most appalling hecatomb of their generation—refuse to mount guard over governments which want to start again, and refuse to foster the germs of future war.

And may the feminine half of humanity also understand that order and peace are only to be found at the end of these few great truths.

Chapter Eleven

THE MAN AT THE WHEEL

Let us return once more to the figure of that man who is always standing between what has been done and what is to be done (indeed, his most common remark, when one speaks to him about the work, is: "It is nothing compared with what we are going to do").

"He is the target of our enemies, and they are quite right to make him so," says Knorin. "He is the name of our Party," says Bubnoff. "He is the best of the old iron cohort," says Manuilsky. "One respects the old Bolsheviks," says Mikoyan, "not because they are old, but because they never grow any older."

His history is a series of victories over a series of tremendous difficulties. Since 1917, not a single year of his career has passed without his having done something which would have made any other man famous. He is a man of iron. The name by which he is known describes it: the word Stalin means "steel" in Russian. He is as strong and yet as flexible as steel. His power lies in his formidable intelligence, the breadth of his knowledge, the amazing orderliness of his mind, his passion for precision, his inexorable spirit of progress, the rapidity, sureness and intensity of his decisions, and his constant care to choose the right men.

The dead do not survive except upon earth. Wherever there are Revolutionaries, there is Lenin. But one may also say that it is in Stalin more than anyone else that the thoughts and words of Lenin are to be found. He is the Lenin of to-day.

In many ways, as we have seen, he is extraordinarily like Vladimir Ilitch: he has the same knowledge of theory, the same practical common sense, the same firmness. In what way do they differ? Here are two opinions of Soviet workers: "Lenin was the leader: Stalin is the master." And also: "Lenin is a greater man, Stalin is a stronger. . . ." We will not, however, pursue these parallels too much as they might lead us to form a wrong idea of these two exceptionally great men, one of whom formed the other.

Let us say, if you like, that Lenin, especially because of circumstances, was more of an agitator. In the vast directing system which is now much better organized and more developed, Stalin must necessarily act far more through the medium of the Party, by the intermediary of organization, as it were. Stalin is not, nowadays, the man of great tempestuous meetings. However, he has never made use of that tumultuous force of eloquence which is the great asset of upstart tyrants and the only one, very often, of successful apostles: this is a point which should be considered carefully by historians who attempt to gauge him. It is by other paths that he came into and remains in contact with the working, peasant, and intellectual population of the U.S.S.R., and with the Revolutionaries of the world, who carry their spiritual country in their hearts—namely, many more than two hundred million people.

We have caught a glimpse of some of the secrets of his greatness. Among all the sources of his genius, which is the principal one? Bela Kun said, in a fine phrase: "He knows how not to go too quickly. *He knows how to weigh the moment.*" And Bela Kun considers that to be the chief characteristic of Stalin, the one which belongs to him in particular, much more than any other; to wait, to temporize, to resist alluring temptations and to be possessed of terrible patience. Is it not this power that has made Stalin, of all the Revolutionaries of history, the man who has most practically enriched the spirit of Revolution, and who has committed the fewest faults? He weighs the pros and cons and reflects a great deal before proposing anything (a great deal does not mean a long time). He is extremely circumspect and does not easily give his confidence. He said to one of his close associates, who distrusted a third party: "A reasonable amount of distrust is a good basis for collective work." He is as prudent as a lion.

This frank and brilliant man is, we have already seen, a simple man. He is only difficult to meet because he is always working. When one goes to see him in a room in the Kremlin, one never meets more than three or four people altogether at the foot of a staircase or in the anterooms. This inherent simplicity has nothing in common with the affected simplicity of a certain Scandinavian monarch who deigns to walk about the streets on foot, or with that of a man like Hitler having it trumpeted abroad by his propagandists that he neither smokes nor drinks. Stalin goes to bed regularly at four in the morning. He does not employ thirty-two secretaries, like Mr. Lloyd George; he has only one, Comrade Proskrobicheff. He does not sign what other people write. He is supplied with the material and does everything else himself. Everything passes through his hands. And that does not prevent him from replying or having replies sent to every letter he receives. When one meets him, he is cordial and unrestrained. His "frank cordiality," says Serafima Gopner. "His kindness, his delicacy," says Barbara Djaparidze, who fought beside him in Georgia. "His gaiety," said Orakhelashvili. He laughs like a child.

At the ceremony which concluded Gorky's jubilee, at the Grand Opera House at Moscow, during the intervals, some of the official personages met in the rooms which lie behind a former imperial or grand-ducal box. The noise was deafening and everyone was laughing uproariously. Among others there were Stalin, Ordjonekidze, Rykoff, Bubnoff, Molotoff, Vorochiloff, Kaganovitch and Piatinsky. They were recounting anecdotes of the Civil War, and recalling amusing incidents: "Do you remember when you fell off your horse?" . . . "Yes, the filthy brute, I don't know what was the matter with it. . . ." And there followed homeric laughter, a power of joy, a thunder of youth, which shook the old tsarist walls—a short, sweet respite from the grim labour of reconstruction.

Lenin, too, laughed at the top of his voice.

"I never met any man," says Gorky, "whose laugh was as infectious as that of Vladimir Ilitch. It was even strange that such an austere realist, a man who saw so clearly and felt so deeply the imminence of great social tragedies, a man immutable in his hatred of the capitalist world, could laugh like that, until he cried, until he choked." And Gorky concludes: "One must have great, solid mental health to laugh like that." *

People who laugh like children love children. Stalin has three, the eldest Jascheka and two little ones, namely Vasili who is fourteen, and Svyetlana who is eight. His wife, Nadejda Allilouieva, died last year; her terrestrial form is no longer anything but a fine, nobly plebeian face and a fine marble arm rising out of a great tomb in the Novo Devitchi cemetery. He has practically adopted Artiom

---

* I can hear Stalin's laughter from here if he ever heard the monumental ineptitude of the Vermot Almanack which says: "Stalin spends 250,000,000 francs a year for his personal needs."

Serguieff whose father was killed in an accident in 1921. He also takes a paternal interest in the two daughters of Djaparidze, shot by the English at Baku, and in many others. I can still see the delight of Arnold Kaplan and Boris Goldstein, little piano and violin prodigies, when they told me how Stalin received them after their triumph at the Conservatoire. He even gave each of them 3,000 roubles, saying to them: "Now that you are capitalists, will you recognize me in the street?"

Around Lenin's and Stalin's laughter, and, as it were, in the same category of phenomena, comes their irony. They both made constant use of it. Stalin very readily gives the expression of his thoughts an amusing or an exaggerated form.

Damian Biedny tells us a good story: "On the eve of the days of July 1917, Stalin and I were both occupied in editing *Pravda*. The telephone-bell rang. The Kronstadt sailors asked Stalin: "Shall we attend the demonstration with or without our rifles?" "What is he going to reply on the telephone?" I asked myself, curiously; "Rifles? That's your business, comrades! We writers always take our pencils with us." "Naturally," concludes Biedny, "all the sailors attended the demonstration with their 'pencils.'"

He can, however, be quiet when he wants to be. When Emil Ludwig exclaimed, after some remark of his: "You have no idea how right you are!" he replied softly: "Who knows, perhaps I may not be right." On the other hand, when the same writer asked him: "Do you think you can be compared with Peter the Great?" he replied, without any irony: "Historical comparisons are always hazardous, but that one is absurd." He does not seize every opportunity he is given to laugh aloud.

One of his main objects seems to be never to try to shine, and never to make himself conspicuous.

Stalin has written a great number of important books. Several of them have a classic value in Marxist literature. But if one asks him what he is, he replies: "I am only a disciple of Lenin, and my whole ambition is to be a faithful disciple." It is curious to observe how, in many of the accounts of work accomplished under his direction, Stalin systematically gives credit for all the progress made to Lenin, whereas the credit has been in very large measure his own, because, in any case, no one can carry out the principles of Leninism without himself being an inventor. In our own countries, the word "disciple" is one of praise —but these men only use it to belittle the particular part played by themselves and to put themselves back into the ranks of their fellows. This does not mean subjection, it merely means fraternization. One is reminded of the fine, clear-cut phrase of the philosopher Seneca: "Deo non pareo sed assentior"—"I do not obey God: I agree with Him."

If it still takes us some time to understand these people, it will not be because of their complexity, but because of their simplicity. It is quite obvious that it is something else than personal vanity and the pride that he has in his name that thrusts this man to the fore and keeps him in the breach. It is faith. In that great country in which scientists are really endeavouring to raise the dead, and are saving the living with the blood of the dead, in which musty and poisonous religions are blown into space by the winds of the open spaces, faith rises from the soil itself, like the forests and the crops. It is faith in the inherent justice of logic. It is faith in knowledge, which Lenin expressed so deeply, when he replied to someone who spoke to him about the cowardly attack of which he had been the vic-

THE MAN AT THE WHEEL

tim, and which shortened his days: "What can you expect? Everyone acts according to his knowledge." It is faith in the socialist order and in the masses in which it is incarnate, faith in work, in what Stetsky calls the stormy growth of productive forces: "Work," says Stalin, "is a question of dignity, heroism and glory." It is faith in the Workers' Code, the Communist Law, and its terrific integrity. "We believe in our Party," said Lenin; "in it we see the spirit, the honour and the confidence of our era." "Not everyone who wishes can belong to the Party," said Stalin; "it is not given to everyone to brave its labours and its torments."

If Stalin has faith in the masses, this is reciprocated. The new Russia worships Stalin, but it is a worship created by confidence, which has risen wholly from the bottom. The man, whose silhouette on the gigantic posters appears superimposed upon those of Karl Marx and of Lenin, is the man who looks after everything and everybody, who has done what has been done and who will do what is to be done. He has saved Russia in the past, and he will save it in the future.

We know well that, according to Stalin's own words: "The times have passed when great men were the chief makers of history." But, if one must deny the exclusive part played in great events, by the "hero," as laid down by Carlyle, one cannot dispute the relative part that he plays. Here again one must remember that things that are alike obey each other. The great man is the man who, foreseeing the course that things are taking, gets ahead of them instead of following them, and acts for or against them in advance. The hero does not create an unexplored country, but he discovers it. He knows how to stir up enthusiasm in crowds —and yet it is spontaneous—because he knows so well what causes it. Logic, properly applied, can get the best out of a man—and out of circumstances too. In all great circumstances a great man is needed, as a sort of centralizing machine. Lenin and Stalin did not invent history, but they organized it. They brought the future nearer.

We are created to bring the greatest possible amount of progress to the human mind, for we are certainly more the trustees of the human mind than of anything else in this world. The duty which we have loyally to carry out in our passage through the world is to avoid undertaking the impossible, but to go as far as our strength permits us to go in practical achievement. We must not try to make men believe that we can prevent them from dying. We must try to make them live a life of fullness and dignity. It is useless to fling ourselves heart and soul upon incurable evils, which are part of human nature; we should rather devote ourselves to curable evils which are part of the social order. We can only rise above the earth by earthly methods.

When one passes at night through the Red Square, through that vast scene which seems to be divided into two parts—that of to-day, that is to say of the nation of a large number of the Earth's inhabitants, and that which dates from before 1917 (which is antediluvian)—it seems as though the man who lies in the tomb, in the centre of that nocturnal, deserted square, is the only person in the world who is not asleep, and who watches over everything around him, in the towns and in the fields. He is the real leader—the one of whom the workers used laughingly to say that he was master and comrade at the same time; he is the paternal brother who is really watching over everyone. Although you do not know him, he knows you and is thinking of you. Whoever you may be, you have need of this benefactor. Whoever you may be, the finest part of your destiny is in the hands of that other man, who also watches over you, and who works for you—the man with a scholar's mind, a workman's face, and the dress of a private soldier.

THE END

INDEX

Abkhasian peasant tribute to the confidence placed in Stalin, 102
Action Française, 115
Aeroplanes, bombing, adequate defence against impossible, 248 *n*.
Afirkatza (Abkhasian hero), 20
"Against the Current," edited by Lenin and Zinovieff, 47
Agitator, secret, risks attaching to profession of, 12
Agrarian plan, fundamental objectives of Socialism on, 31
Agricultural machinery production in U.S.S.R. (1934), 201
    production, amount of roubles by which pre-war level was passed (1927), 155
        percentages Socialist and private (1927), 156
        increase in, under Five-Year Plan, 194
    work, mechanization of, 243
Agriculture, collectivization of, 152
Air-raids, Russia protected against, 248 *n*.
Alexander II, Tsar, 32
    murder of, 4
Alexander III, Tsar, feudal reaction under, 32
Alexander of Serbia (the late), cruel régime of, 263
Alexandroff, 39
Alexieff, treachery of, how punished, 66
Allied troops disembarking at Vladivostock, nations to which belonging, 112

Allied War Aims, imposture regarding exposed, 58
Allies, secret treaties among, signed before the conclusion of war, 58
    reason for creation of Poland as an independent State by, 80
    reason for seizure of Bessarabia, 80
    destruction wrought in Russia by, 112, 113
Alphabets, purpose of invention by Moscow scholars, 97
Alphonso XIII, ex-King of Spain, 265
Alsace-Lorraine, cession to France, an openly stated allied war aim, 58
American Gary Works, 202
Anarchists, 56, 85, 190
Anarcho-Syndicalists, 43
Anglo-Saxon Capitalism and Soviet Socialism, comparison of, 152
Arable land in "possession" of peasants, 122
Archbishop of Detectives, reports against Stalin made to, 27
Armenia, 2
    satisfactory condition under the Soviet Union, 102
Armistice, the, 110
Army, finance and foreign policy, same administration for under the Union, 97
    Corps, creation and subdivision of, 65
Artel (workmen's association), 4
    form of *kolkhoz*, 223

INDEX

Asia, principle of Leninist Marxism transgressed by Russian propagandists in, 104
   Central, introduction of Soviets into, 104
"Assemblers of the Russian Lands," the Tsars self-styled as, 98
Assembly of Five, object of, 53
   Stalin appointed a member of, 53
Assembly of Seven, object of, 53
   Stalin appointed a member of, 53
Austro-Hungary, Czechoslovakia extracted from, 108
Austro-Marxist doctrine of national cultural autonomy, 92
   error of, 92
Autonomy, national cultural, 91
Axelrod, 6, 38
Azerbaijan, 2
   satisfactory condition under the Soviet Union, 102

Bailoff prison, educational work of Koba (Stalin) at, 23
Baku, Social-Democratic organization of, brought into Bolshevik ranks by Stalin, 41
   advance of English on, 63
   prison, overcrowding of, 22
   Stalin's life in, 22
Baku Proletarian, edited by Stalin (1907), 41
Balkans, the, reign of White Terror in, 262
Banks, Soviet, nationalized, no control exercised on, 174
Barbusse, H., on the "Five-Year Plan" (quoted), 142
Batum (Abkhasia), Stalin's establishment of committee at, 19
Beauharnais Saint-Lawrence hydroelectric station, horse-power production, 196 *n*.
Bela Kun, leader of Hungarian Bolshevik Revolution, 46
   view regarding concession of Ural factories, 119
Belgian Congo, scandal of, 82

Belgium, composition of, 108
Bessarabia, reason for seizure of by the Allies, 80
   Russian, engrafted on to Rumania, 108
Biedny, Damian, 22
Black Companies, marauds of, 36
Black Hundred, 18
   ultra-conservative Tsarist organization, 18 *n*.
Black Sea, 2
   despatch to, of French Naval Squadron with division of infantry (1919), 81 *n*.
   Squadron, intervention in the Ukraine, 103
Bogdanoff, 42
Bolshevik, Stalin becomes a, 24
   Party, consolidation of, in its illegality, 45
      proper manifestation of, to workers and peasants, 93
      special privilege of, 161
   positions, retirement of feebler elements of the Party from, how expressed, 168
Bolsheviks, tenets of, 24
   and Mensheviks, split between, 24, 29
   Russian, pre-Revolution campaign of, 25
   fight against Anarchists and Revolutionary Socialists, 26
   weakening activities of (1909–1911), 42
   in Duma, persecution of, 49
   question of the value of human life as considered by, 83
   attitude towards human life defended, 84
   initial leniency towards enemies manifested by, 86, 87
   attitude in relation to problem of nationalities, 93
   completion of Revolution by, 121, 122
   total opposition to capitalism, 124, 125, 126

INDEX

Bolsheviks, repudiation of Tsarist debts by, 129
  and Menshevism, schism between, how brought about, 163
Bolshevism, uncompromisingness of, 47, 48
  rally of Trotsky to, 59
Boot manufacture in U.S.S.R. (1934), 202
Boret, V., *The Infernal Paradise* (quoted), 230 *n.*
Brandlerians, 201
Bratsky Ostrog, hydro-electric station, prospective horsepower production, 196 *n.*
Brazil, wholesale destruction of coffee in, 211, 231
Bread and flour, abolition of ration cards for, 222
Brest-Litovsk, Treaty of, 110, 178
  concluding peace between Germany and Russia, 57
  cause of split between Russia and the subsequently victorious powers at, 59
  immediate conclusion jointly supported by Lenin and Stalin, 60
  first signatories of, 80
  position taken by Soviet Russia at signing of, 80
British diplomacy, imperial knavery of, 266
Bubnoff, on pre-Revolution campaign of Russian Bolsheviks, 25
Budget deficit in France (1930), 210
  in United States (1930), 210
Budienny Cavalry Army, advance of, 75
Bukharin, 206
  leader of Opposition group on Right, 177
Bulak-Bulakhovitch, successes of, 71
Bulgaria, mass executions in, 262
Buran, icy blizzard of Siberia, 23
Bureaucracy, 239
  abuse of, 186

Cadets (Constitutional-Democrats), 86
Canals, completion and construction, 244
Capital, private, re-appearance and development of, 123
Capitalism, 250
  immense power of, 12
  imperialist, disregard of human life by, 82
    principle of, upon what based, 81
  social preservation, evil result of, 95
  destructive, incrustation on outlines of national frontiers, 95
  essential propaganda of, 95
  total opposition of Bolsheviks to, 124, 125, 126
  foreign Russian Revolution not dependent on, 173
  disastrous results of, enumerated, 230, 231, 232
  disguise in aims of, 252
  strong politically, 258
  fight against, 270, 271
  and Socialism, compromise with only temporary, 126
Capitalist advance, new, taking place side by side with Socialist advance, 123
  and Socialist Systems, difference between workers under, respectively, 143, 144
  countries, wrong statements about unemployment in, 203
  industrial production, year of apogee of (1929), 201
  power, decline and general slump of predicted by Stalin (1928), 152
Capitalists, overthrow and expropriation of, 236, 237
  first blow to power of, 54, 55

Caspian Sea, 2
Cattle-breeding, advance needed in, 239
Caucasia, Northern, Headquarters Staff powerless to fight counter-Revolution, 64
and the Ukraine, delivery from the White Guards, 76
Caucasus, the, 2
first celebration of May-day in, 18
Cavalry Army, establishment by Stalin, 77
Central Asiatic Republics, created by Stalin, 105
Central Committee, resolution passed by (August 3, 1920) regarding Stalin's fresh activities, 78
decision of regarding action of New Opposition, 180
Centre of Leningrad, terrorist organization, 181
Chaman (Siberia) hydro-electric station, prospective horse-power production, 196 *n*.
Chaoba, Stalin's headquarters at, 19
Cheliabinsk Factory (heavy metals), 202
Cherkesses, illiteracy of, 205
Chicherin, 125
Chichua, Theophil, admiration of Stalin expressed by, 26
Chief of Police of Tiflis, reports against Stalin made to, 27
Chinese Communist Party, 106, 107
successes of, 106
Democratic Party. *See* Kuomingtang
problem, the, 105
Pseudo-Revolution, 105
ill-effects of, 105, 106
Revolution, 107
Soviets, 107
Churchill, Winston, 112
Civil War in Russia, 111
deciding and critical moments of (autumn 1919), 111

Civil War in Russia, won by Russian Revolution, 76
urgent problem of, 61
renewal of under activities of Wrangel, 78
cost to Russia, 111
general desolation following, 111, 112
amount of money and number of lives spent by England in, 112, 113
Civil War, Russian, why an inaccurate term, 79
Clemenceau, Georges, 59, 112, 121
and Hindenberg, Hitler raised into power by, 261
"Clemenceau's Doctrine," adopted by Trotsky, 179
Coercion, absence of, creating immense moral influence of Communist Party over nations adhering to Soviet Union, 93 *n*.
Coffee, customs duty on, in France, excessive, 211
wholesale destruction in Brazil, 211, 212, 231
Collective work, conception of, 150, 151
Colonial question, the, Socialist interest in, 104
Colonization, imperialist and capitalist, 104
Colonizing system, evils of, 82
Colrat, ridiculous remark made to Chicherin by, 125
Commerce, percentages Socialist and private (1927), 155, 156
Commercial treaties, condition on which concluded by the State, 125
Commodities, mass destruction of, 232
Common law, moral system of, national religious tradition subjected to, 97
Commune form of *kolkhoz*, 223, 224

INDEX

Communism, apostles created by, 235
Communist doctrine, interpretation of, cause of wide divergence in, 160
  International, dictatorship in impossible, 147
    Socialists leaving ranks of, 168
    network attacked by Trotskyism, 189
Communist Manifesto, 238
Communist Party of the Soviet Union, world-wide value of, 104
  immense organizing powers of, 235
  Russian, immense moral influence over nations adhering to Soviet Union, 93 *n*.
    a State force, 158
    serious doctrine of, 158
    unity and homogeneousness of, preservation vital, 158
    honour of, paragraph in Stalin's oath referring to, 164
  schism in, arising after death of Lenin, 164
  retirement of feebler elements from, how expressed, 168
  patience towards Trotsky shown by, 178
Communists, aversion of Japanese to, 106
  aversion of Kuomingtang (Chinese Democratic Party) to, 106
  martyrology of, 235
  alleged grievance against, 236
Competition increased by Socialism, 144, 145
  Socialist principle of, 145
  value to Socialist cause, 144
Concessions, formula of Soviet State regarding, 121, 122
Congress held at Stockholm (1906), 38

Congress of the Soviet Party, Fourteenth, discussion on industrialization, 152
  Fifteenth, discussion on collectivization of agriculture, 152
Conservatives, 249, 250
Constitutional-Democrats, 38
  aims of leaders of, 38 *n*.
  Parties, Russian, 37, 38
Control, undue importance attached to word, 174
Cooper, Mr., tribute to energy of Soviet workers, 234
Co-operation, road leading to Socialism, 136
Co-operative stores, system of, always existing in Russia, 136
  pushed forward, 136
Cossack counter-Revolution, spread of, 63, 64
Cossacks, attacks of, on Tsaritzin repulsed by Red Troops, 68
  rallying to support of Denikin, 75, 76
  Popular Assembly of (the Rada), 102 *n*.
Cot, Pierre, 248 *n*.
Cotton-fields, immense planting of, 197
Council of People's Commissars instructions to General Dukhonin to suspend military operations, 56, 57
Country districts, co-operation in, encouragement by Socialist State, 124
Crimean War (1854-56), 3
Croatia, component of Jugoslavia, 108
Current History (American) on the Five-Year Plan, 193
Customs duty on coffee in France excessive, 211
Czech counter-Revolution in Ural district, 63
Czechoslovakia, extracted from Austro-Hungary, 108

Dachnaks, 102
  explanation concerning, 102 n.
Daduet, Léon, 115
Daily Telegraph, on the Five-Year Plan, 193
Daniloff, 28
Death penalty, Stalin's pronouncement on, 86, 87
Death-rate in Russia compared with that in other countries, 208
Declaration of the Peoples of Russia, enactments of, 208
Democracy, possible barrier against Socialism, 11
Denationalization, Russification synonymous with, 89
Denikin, 62, 94
  penetration of Southern Front by White Army under, 72
  Cossacks rallying to support of, 75, 76
  total defeat of armies of, 76
  fall of, 101
  Army of, equipped by England, 112
Descartes, definition of intelligence, 169
Devdariani, Seide, Menshevik leader, 25
Dictatorship in the Communist International and the U.S.S.R., why impossible, 147
  of the Proletariat, 177
  meaning of, 170, 171
Dimitroff, 236
Diogenes, 169
Djerjinsky, 62
  and Stalin, measures for raising fighting efficiency of Third Army proposed by, 70
Djugashvili, Joseph Vissarionovitch, 1 (See also Stalin).
  (Stalin), leader of Marxist circle at Tiflis Seminary, 7
  Iossip, Stalin's work under name of, 27
  Vissarion, father of Stalin, 1

Dnieproguès, immense town on banks of Dnieper, 195
  hydro-electric station of horse-power production, 196 n.
Dobrudja, the, engrafted on to Rumania, 108
Dollfuss, workers massacred by, 262
Dominique, Pierre, on immensity of rise of industry in Soviet Asia, 196
Don Cossacks, 66, 67
Donetz basin, 74
Donetz workers, struggle against the hordes of Kalidin, 103
Doumergue, President of the French Republic, recognition of enemies of the Soviet by, 113
  policy of, in France, 263, 264
Dro (The Times), edited by Stalin at Tiflis (1907), 41
Dukhonin, General, relieved of his duties as Commander-in-chief, 57
  refusal to obey instructions to suspend military operations transmitted by Council of People's Commissars, 57
Duma, revolutionary members of, 41
Dwellings of workers, reconstruction, 184

Economic Plan, idea of, exclusively Soviet, 140
  ruin in Russia, period of, 120
Economics, union with politics, 5
  controlled, 140
Education, development of, immense increase in (1927), 155
  public in the U.S.S.R., 204, 205
  countries which show a decline in, 205
Eighth Army, advance of, 74, 75

INDEX

Eisenstein, cinematograph film exhibiting wretched condition of peasant life ("General Line"), 153
Eleatic philosophers, 169
Electric energy, production in U.S.S.R. (1934), 202
Electrification, 243
Electrification Commission, 139
　Plan, 139
　of Russia, plan for, 137 (See also *Goelro*).
Energy, self-criticism incentive and source of, 145
Engels, 238
　joint founder with Marx of First International, 5
England, amount of money and number of lives spent by, in Civil War in Russia, 112
　Denikin's Army equipped by, 112
　percentage of pre-war economic production in (1933), 201
　increase of unemployment in (1928-33), 202
　hatred of freedom of mankind shown by, 266
　and France, assistance to Wrangel and the White Russians rendered by, 78
　and Ireland, ill-assorted connection of, 108
English advance on Baku, 63
　Communist Party, 191
Enukidze, Comrade, 18
　early worker in cause of Revolution in Caucasus, 9
　on accessibility of Stalin, 9, 10
Epictetus, 41
Europe, complete Sovietization of in the future, 109
　waste of food and crops throughout, 232
European Polish Forces, defeat of Red troops by, 79

Exploiters and exploited, block created by on two disputed frontiers, 95

Factories, reconstruction of under Five-Year Plan, 195
Famine in Russia (1921), 120
Far Eastern question, 104
Farms, *See* Kolkhoz, Sovkhoz.
Fascism, 252
　weapon of against Socialism, 255
　uselessness of, 257
　disadvantages of, 269
Faure, Paul, 248 *n*.
Federalist Party in Georgia, 3
Feudal system, Russian peasant class victims of, 32
Finance, foreign policy and the Army, same administration for under the Union, 97
Financial Times on the Five-Year Plan, 193
Financing of Five-Year Plan, 199, 200
Finland and Baltic Provinces seized from Russia by German Army, 80
First Cavalry Army, raid by, 79
First International, founders of, 5
Five-Year Plan (State Plan), 130 and 130 *n*.
　(1928-32), 40, 192 *et seq*.
　(1928-32), achievements of, enumerated, 194 *et seq*.
　financing of, 199-200
　sum in roubles represented by, 200
　elimination of unemployment in U.S.S.R. during, 202, 203
　success of, 212
　　tribute of great newspapers to, 215, 216
　(1932-37), inauguration of, 242
　what is to be expected from, 242
　results to end of 1934, 245 *n*.
Five-Year Plans, series of, beginning of, 140

Food, colossal waste of, 232
  supply of Southern Russia, organization by Stalin (1918), 63
Foreign commerce, nationalized, no control exercised upon, 173, 174
  loans not obtained by U.S.S.R., 199
  policy, finance and the Army, same administration for under the Union, 97
  trade a State monopoly, 123
Four Years Battle, 234
Fourth International, 165
France, cession of Alsace-Lorraine to, an openly stated Allied war aim, 58
  and England, assistance rendered to Wrangel and White Russians by, 78
  protection of enemies of Soviet Government by, 113
  official, recognizing Kolchak as Vice-Tsar, 113
  mobilization and training of White Guards in, 113
  opinion held of Stalin in, 149
  increase of unemployment in (1928-33), 202
  percentages of pre-war economic production in (1933), 201
  Budget deficit in (1930), 210
  customs duty on coffee in, excessive, 211
  scandal of middlemen in, 222, 223
  vintage production reduced in, 231
Franco-Russian alliance, largely responsible for World War, 43
French Colonies, treatment of natives in, 265
  taxation of natives in, 265
  and English troops invading Russia after termination of the Great War, 79
French Colonies, and Russian Diplomacy, plotting between, 43
  Communist Party, 191
  diplomacy overtures to Russia, 87 *n.*
  Government, Russian Government financed by, 38 *n.*
  supply of arms to Kolchak's Army, 112
  Liberals, behaviour towards Russia of the Revolution, 116
  Naval Squadron, despatch to Black Sea, with division of infantry (1919), 81 *n.*
  public, means of inculcating true knowledge of Russian Revolution among, 87 *n.*
  Republic, Presidents of, recognition enemies of Soviet by, 113
  Revolution (1789) curtailment of, 83
    view of Victor Hugo regarding (quoted), 83
    proclamation of equality by, 92

Gandhi, servile dreamer and enemy of progress, 266
Gazeta Polska on the Five-Year Plan, 193
Geneva Conference, failure of, 129
George, David Lloyd, 59, 112
Georgia, date of inclusion in Russian Empire, 2
  oppressive treatment of, 2, 3
  clash of different races in, 3
  Federalist Party in, 3
  liberation of, movement in promotion of, 3
  satisfactory conditions under the Soviet Union, 102
Georgian Mensheviks, Stalin's campaign against, 25
Georgians not Russians, 89

INDEX

German Armies, countries in which the fall of Soviet power was brought about by, 101
  Army of occupation, reinforcing Cossack counter-Revolution, 63, 64
    Baltic Provinces and Finland seized from Russia by, 80
  under Hitler, 209
  Communist Party, 190
  occupation of the Ukraine, 102
  Social Democratic Party, 191
  troops of the Baltikum, fighting in collaboration with the Allies, 81
Germany, Treaty of Rapallo signed with, 129
  percentage of pre-war economic production in (1933), 201
  increase of unemployment in (1928-33), 202, 203
  and Russia, peace between concluded by Treaty of Brest-Litovsk, 57
Gil Robles, heir of 1931 Spanish Revolution, 265
Goelro (electrification of Russia), idea of, 137
Gori (Georgia), birthplace of Stalin, 1
Gorky, 42, 206, 233
Great European Powers, immense loan of United States to, for reconstruction purposes, 129
  Powers, outrages inflicted on Russian people and industries by emissaries of, 114, 115
Great War (1914-18), cost to Russia, 111
Greek Orthodox Church, suppression of privileges, 94
Grinko, on financing of Five-Year Plan, 200
Guesde, Jules, 48

Haase, 48

Haisists, 191
Heavy industries, development of, 132, 135
  importance of, 133, 134
  achievement under Five-Year Plan, 194
Heredity, law of, error of, 174
Herriot, 230 *n.*
  attitude criticized, 214
Hetman Peliura, overthrow of the power of in the Ukraine, 103
Hindenberg and Clemenceau, Hitler raised into power by, 261
Hitler, A., 39, 103, 209, 255
  re-arming of Germany by, 262
Hoover Dam, Colorado, hydro-electric station, horse-power production, 196 *n.*
Hugo, Victor, on the subject of the French Revolution (*Les Misérables*, quoted), 83
Human life, disregard for by imperialist capitalism, 83
  value of in the light of Socialism, 82
    question as considered by the Bolshevists, 83
  race, problem of future of, ix
Hungarian Bolshevik Revolution, leader of (Bela Kun), 46

Ibañez, Blasco, 13
Idealist Conference of Zimmerwald (1915), 49
Ilitch, Vladimir, breach between Mensheviks and Bolsheviks widened by, 29, 30
Illiteracy, abolition of, 244
Imperialism, foreign, threatening the Soviet East, 105
India, British rule in, 266
Individual decisions, objections to, 150
Individualities, collective, kind of bonds by which attached to one another, 97

INDEX

Individuality, moral and intellectual, preservation and enrichment of, 96
Industrial and transport shortage, so-called increase in alleged, by New Opposition, 182
    concessions, condition upon which granted by the State, 125
    enterprises, State-owned, 122; number hired out, 122
    production, percentages respectively collectivist, private enterprise and co-operative (1927), 155, 156
Industrialization, proper meaning of, 132
    discussion on, 152
Industry, Socialist metamorphosis of villages through intervention of, 131
    nationalized, no control exercised on, 173, 174
    investments in, 185
    new branches of, started under Five-Year Plan, 195
    enormous new centres of, arising in Russian territory, 196
Initiative, genius for, 33
Intellect, subjection of sentiment to, 15
Intelligence, definition of (Descartes), 169
Intelligence Service, enormity committed by member of, 115
    treachery of, 115
International. *See* First International, Second International
Internationalism, in relation to Socialist principles, 90
Ireland, ill-assorted connection with England, 108
Irkutsk (Siberia), deportation of Stalin to, 22
Iskra (*The Spark*), newspaper established abroad by Lenin, 18
Isvolsky, 43

Italy, number of unemployed in, 203
    ruin of, under Mussolini, 260
Ivanovitch, Stalin present at Stockholm Congress (1907), under name of, 38

Japan, threatening the Soviet East. 105
    militarism of, 267
    and Washington pact, 267
Japanese, aversion to Communists, 106
    Army, total number of men in, 209
Jaroslavsky, 188
Jaurès, 43
Jewish Workers' League, 90
Jitomir, 62
Jordania, ill-timed recognition of, 113
Jugoslavia, composition of, 108
    a grouping not a federation of states, 108
Junker rising threatened in Petrograd, 57

Kaganovitch, on constancy of Stalin's political activities, 46
    quoted, 62
Kai Chek, campaign against Soviet China developing under leadership of, 106
Kalidin, struggle of Donetz workers against the hordes of, 103
Kalinin (quoted), 61
Kameneff, view retarding concession of Ural factories, 119
    hostility to revolutionary methods, 163
    an "Oppositionist," 171
    and Zinovieff, hostility to Lenin's plans for a rising, 52
    New Opposition led by, 179
Kandelaki, 21
Kartsevadze, Revolutionary Socialist, 23
Kaskovo, occupation of line by Red Army, 72

INDEX

Kautsky, 48
Kerensky, 53, 54 57
  rise of (1917), 49
  half-hearted policy respecting the Russian Proletarian Revolution, 53
Kernovo, occupation of line by Red Army, 72
Kharkoff, main attack on Southern Front towards, 76
Khashim, assistance rendered to Stalin by, 20
Kienthal Conference, 1916, 49
Kirghiz Republic, newly created, 105
Kiroff, Serge, assassination of, 114, 181
Knorin, 47
Koba, Comrade, return of Stalin from deportation under name of, 22
  work carried on by Stalin under name of, 27
Kolchak, 94
  fall of, 101
  Army of, supplied by French Government with arms, 112
  foreign soldiers taking part in offensive of, 112
  recognized as Vice-Tsar by official France, 113
Kolkhosians, 225
  ownership among, 223
Kolkhoz, co-operative farms, 220, 221
  pouds of grain given to the State by the, 221, 222
  two forms of, 223
  disaffection of, 225
  representing shell of Socialist organization, 227
Korin, direction of advance indicated to, 74, 75
Kramatorsk Factory (heavy machinery), 202
Krasnaya Gorka fort, defection of garrison, 71

Krasnaya Gorka fort, capture through agency of Stalin, 71
Krasnoff, General, mistaken leniency shown towards, 85, 86
  organization of White Cossacks by, 86
  Army of, desertion of Nossovitch to, 66
Kremlin, the description of, vi, vii
  patrimony of Russian families, installed within, 89
Kronstadt rising, 178
Krylenko, appointed Commander-in-chief of the Russians, 57
Kuibicheff, director of the State Plan, 130
Kulaks, rich peasants, strong position of, 153, 154
  oppressive conduct of, 177
  alleged danger of progress made by, 183, 184
  opposition from, 225
Kuleika (Siberia), Stalin's exile at (1913-17), 46
Kuomingtang (Chinese Democratic Party), 106
  aversion to Communists, 106
Kurnatovski, liaison agent between Stalin and Leninism, 16
Kusnietz, six new towns in main basin of, population of, 196

La Bruyère, 166
Land, industrialization of, 184
Language, maternal, products of, preserved and enriched, 96, 97
Larousse Encyclopaedic Dictionary, condemnation of Treaty of Brest-Litovsk, by, 58
League of Nations, U.S.S.R. admitted to, 247
Lebedeva, 35
Left, the, traitors of, more dangerous than those of the Right, 240
Lena (Siberia), shooting outrage at, 43

INDEX

Lenin, v, vi, viii, 40, 61, 64, 66, 171
   association with Populists, 4
   entrance into public life, 5
   successful opposition to Vorontsoff, 6
   accessibility of, 10
   various names adopted by, 16
   establishment abroad of newspaper *Iskra* (*The Spark*), 18
   Stalin becomes a supporter of, 24
   creative genius of, how applied, 30
   profound interest in the peasant problem, 31, 32
   peasant programme of (1900), 32
   simplicity and modesty of, 1, 34, 35
   method of delivery when speaking, 38
   attitude of, in situation of defeat and of victory contrasted, 40, 41
   campaign against the Otzovists (1907), 41
   opposition to promoters of the Edification of the Divine Principle, 42
   estimation of Stalin's writings, by, 45
   resources of both legality and illegality employed by, 44
   condemnation of Trotsky's methods by, 45
   "Social Democrat" founded by, 47
   against idea of Motherland, 48, 49
   arrival at Petrograd (April, 1917), 49, 50
   motion, regarding Imperialist character of the war carried by, at Zimmerwald Conference, 49
   originator of Socialist States within the State (1917), 51
   rising projected by, 52, 53
   letter of incitement to Russian Proletarian Revolution, 53

Lenin, genius manifested by, at opening stage of second Revolution, 56
   threatened treatment by Spiridovna, 56
   President of the Council for National Defence, 70
   letter to General Staff of Southern Front giving them their change of orders, 76
   resistance to idea of nationalization of Socialism, 92
   view regarding concession of Ural factories, 119, 120
   secret of greatness of, 126
   opportunism of, 127
   on value of co-operation, 136
   plan for the electrification of Russia, 136, 137
   on increase of competition through Socialism, 144
   death of (January 1924), 146
   oath to, pronounced by Stalin, 146
   fight against particularism, 162
   schism in Party arising after death of, 163, 164
   on feasibility of Socialistic reconstruction of Russia, 172
   common sense and clearness of vision of, 175
   question of democracy chief concern of, from an early date, 185
   condemnation of methods of Trotsky and the Mensheviks, 186
   on one great difficulty in Socialist reconstruction, 218
   and Stalin, opposition of Trotsky to, 30
      meeting between, described by Stalin, 33, 34, 35
      jointly, support immediate conclusion of Treaty of Brest-Litovsk, 60
      close co-operation between, 60

INDEX

Lenin and Stalin, Marxist formula of nationalities drawn up by, 91
Lenin and Trotsky, comparison between, 166, 167
Lenin, Alexander, execution of, 4
Leninism, adaptation of Marxism, 16
  defence of by Stalin, 164
  opposition of civilized European Socialism to, 171
  new kind of, adopted by New Opposition, 180, 181
  divergence from the principles and tactics of, 182
  and Marxism synonymous, 30
  and Stalin, liaison agent between, 16
Lettish Division, 75
Levelling principle, 237
Liberalism, middle-class, 250
Liberation of Labour (The) expansion of, 6
Liberty, individual, and reciprocal union, selection and exact classification of, 96
Lighter industries, advocates of, 132
  increase in production of, 198
Literature, development in the U.S.S.R., 206
Lithuanian workers, distinct Social-Democratic Party of, 90
Live-stock, question of, 239
London, Congress of Russian Social Democratic Party in (1907), 40
Lovestonians, 191
Ludwig, Emil, question put to Stalin as to why he became a Revolutionary, 15
Lugansky Locomotive Factory, 202
Lunacharsky, 42, 206
Lvoff, Prince, government of (1917), 49

MacDonald, James Ramsay, 255

Macedonia, component of Jugoslavia, 108
Machine-building and training of operatives carried out simultaneously, 135
Magnitogorsk Factory (metallurgy), 202
Mallet, 214
  report on the progress of the new Republic, 61
Mamontoff, 86
Mantascheff workers, discontent created among by Stalin, 19
Manufactured goods industries, 243
Manuilsky, 47, 92
  situation on Southern Front (autumn 1919), described by, 72
  significance of succession of Oppositions, 168
  error of the "law of heredity," 174
Marcus Aurelius, 41
Martoff, 38
Marx, Karl, vi, 14, 238
  joint founder with Engels of First International, 5
  originator of scientific Socialism, 5
  secret of greatness of, 127, 128
Marxism, aid rendered to Revolutionaries by, 13
  unconscious practice of, 15
  Leninism an adaptation of, 16
  whole principle of summarized, 14, 33
  principles of, applied to warfare, 81, 82
  what is meant by, 237, 238
  Leninist, principle of, transgressed by Russian propagandists in Asia, 104
  example of pure relativity, 127
  and Leninism synonymous, 30
  and the question of Nationalities, Stalin's studies on, 45
Marxist formula of nationalities, 91

Marxist theory and practice, organic suppleness of connection between, 31
Marxists, Russian, secret groups of, in Transcaucasia, 2
Masaryk, hatred of working classes, 263
Mass cultivation, as an inducement to Socialism, 218, 219
Masses, the, collaboration with, sole means of ensuring proper government, 151
  importance of trust in, 151, 152
May-day, first celebration in the Caucasus, 18, 19
Mechanical energy, place taken by the U.S.S.R. among the nations in (1927), 155
Menjinski, defence of the Bolsheviks' attitude towards human life (quoted), 84
Menshevik "schema," conduct of Russian Revolution (1905), entrusted to, 36
  Trotsky always a, 166, 168
Mensheviks, 56, 102
  tenets of, 24
  Georgian, Stalin's campaign against, 25
  and Bolsheviks, split between, 24, 29
  in majority at Stockholm Congress of Russian Social-Democratic Party (1906), 40
  weakening activities of (1909–1911), 42, 43
  Nationalist, 85
  and Bolsheviks, schism between, how brought about, 163
  methods of condemned by Lenin, 186
Menshevism, lapse towards, 159
Middle-class machine, temptation to make use of, 117
  methods, compromise with adopted by Stalin, 128
  power, elimination of, 99, 120
  régime, abolition of, 88, 94
Middle-class Russian Revolution only, believers in, 171
  writers, mistake regarding the "levelling principle," 237
  abolition decided upon, 118
  help of, not needed by workers, classes in capitalist countries in forming a new society, 174
Middlemen, scandal of in France, 222, 223
Military organization, Stalin's views as to importance of, 77
  power, strong, available for each State of the Union, 97
  School of Petrograd, pupils of, organized rising of, 86
Miliukoff, juridic study on Soviet Union (quoted), 93 n.
Millerand, President of French Republic, recognition of enemies of the Soviet by, 113
Minin, 62
Minsk, formation of Social-Democratic Party at Congress held at (1898), 6
Mir (rural commune), 4
Molstoff, 45
Money, again put into circulation, 123
Monopolies, all in possession of Soviet State, 199
Montenegro, component of Jugoslavia, 108
Moscow, secret and conspiratorial meeting at (1893), 5
  Revolutionary-Socialist rising at (1918), 63
  danger threatening, 73
  scholars, purpose of invention of alphabets by, 97
Moslem workers, within the former European-Asiatic empire of the Tsars, address to, 94
Motor-cars, fully equipped, scrapping and destruction of, 232

INDEX

Muravieff, abandonment of cause by, 63
Muscovites and Tatars, differences between cultivated and developed, 98
Mussavatists, 102
  explanation concerning, 102 *n*.
Mussolini, 39
  apostasies and crimes of, 260, 261
  and foreign policy, 261

Napoleon, saying of (quoted), 26
Narodniki (Populists), 4
  origin of, 3, 4. *See also* Populists
Nation, original meaning of word, 95
Nations, relationship between themselves, evils attendant upon, 95
  contemporary, aim of to live to the detriment of one another, 98, 99
National Constellation, the, 88 *et seq.*
  culture and national spirit, preservation and enrichment of, 96, 97
  defence, right and wrong significance of, 134
    percentage represented in total Soviet Budget, 208, 209
  development, maximum of, together with minimum of, combination under, 98, 99
  feelings and peace antagonistic, 95
  frontiers, incrustation of destructive capitalism on outlines of, 95
  revenue (1927), amount of, 155
Nationalism, exaggerated idea of, the result of oppression, 96
  perverted idea of, 99
  weapon of Fascism against Socialism, 255
Nationalities, Marxism in relation to, Stalin's studies upon, 45

Nationalities, different, existing in Russia, alliance of subsidiary basis of Soviet Republic, 88
  question of, Stalin's capacity for dealing with, 88
  Marxist formula of, 91, 92
  problem of, attitude of Bolsheviks in relation to, 93
  question of, Stalin's report on, at Conference of Bolshevik Party (April 1917), 92
  Stalin becomes authorized director of the policy of the Party on, 94
  policy of, far-reaching effects, 107, 108
  problem of, insoluble, Soviet solution applied to, 109
Nationalization of Socialism, erroneous, 92
Nepman, 126
New Economic Policy, 126, 127, 138, 139
  creation of, 121
  vital importance of, 124, 136, 165, 166, 177, 178, 182, 183, 184, 224
New York Times, on the Five-Year Plan, 193
Newspaper calumnies respecting the Five-Year Plan (quoted), 203
Newspapers, great tributes to the success of the Five-Year Plan, 215, 216
  Soviet, increase in circulation of, 205
Nicholas II, Tsar, abdication of, 49
Nihilists, foreign name for Populists, 4
Nijeradze, Kaisom, Stalin styles himself, 28
Nikolaieff, order given to, to kill Kiroff, 181
Ninua, Comrade, assistance rendered to Stalin by, 11
Nossovitch, desertion to Krasnoff's Army, 66

INDEX

Nossovitch, tribute to Stalin's ability as a commander, 66
Novorossisk, 74

Octobrists, 38
Oil industry, established at Uralsk, 198
Okhrana (Police Service), arrest of Stalin by, 21, 41
  secret agents of, reports made against Stalin by, 27
Operatives, training of, carried out simultaneously with machine building, 135
Opportunism, 190
Opposition, the, 157 *et seq.*
  components of, discussed, 157, 158
  phenomenon of, how evolved, 158, 159
  animosity between individuals not the cause of, 159
  essential and most pernicious characteristics of, 161
  functions of, differing from those of self-criticism, 161
  a grave tendential malady, 161
  lines of self-criticism not followed by, 161
  split brought about by, leading to definite schism, 161
  questions on which most active, 162
  gravitating around personality of Trotsky, 164
  group on Left (Trotskyites), 176, 177
  on Right (Bukharin's), 177
  New, leaders of, 179, theses of, 179
  "platform" of, 180, 181
  new, kind of Leninism adopted by, 181
  present continued existence of, 181
  accusations of deviations made by, inaccurate, 182, 183

Opposition, the, many of the charges brought by, without proof, 183
  dangerous measures proposed by, 183, 184
  enjoinment of promotion of undertakings already in force, 184, 185
  uselessness of, 188
  firm attitude of Stalin towards, 189
Oppositions, succession of, significance, 168
Oppositionists, 85
Oppression, creating exaggerated idea of nationalism, 95
Orakhelashveli, explanation of Stalin's success as an expositor, 10, 11
Order of the Red Flag, Stalin twice decorated with, 79
Ordjonekidze, Serge, assault upon, 23
  quoted, 25
  praise of Stalin by, 47
Otzovists, campaign directed against, by Lenin and Stalin (1907), 41

Palchinsky, 144
Pan-Russian Bolshevik Conference, Stalin elected member of Central Committee, 50
Parasitic war, the, 157 *et seq.*
Parkhomenko, pardon of, 82
Patriotism, frenzied, excitation of, 96
  placed not against but in Socialism, 96
Peace and national feelings, antagonistic, 95
Peasant class, Russian, victim of feudal system, 32
  industry, combination, advantages of, 154
  labour, restriction of, 120
  market, capture of an objective, 123, 124

INDEX

Peasant class, programme of Lenin (1900), 32
    question, the, 217 *et seq.*
Peasants, hostility and revolt of (1921), 120
    arable land in possession of, 122
    concession to, regarding excess crops of wheat, 123
    payment of tribute to State in kind, 122, 123
    character of, 124
    distrustful of Revolutionaries, 124
    re-education of, 133
    individual, working singly, wretched and precarious conditions of, 153, 154
    naturally not inclined to Socialism, 218
    methods in which help has been rendered to by the State, 220, 221
    pouds of grain given to the State by, 221
    and workers, proper manifestation of Bolshevik Party to, 93
    See also Kulaks
Peasantry, question of, contrasted views of Right and Left Opposition on, 176, 177
People's Commissar for Nationalities, Stalin elected (1917), 88
    Trotsky's old title of, 165
Pepperists, 191
Perm, 62
    surrender by Third Army, 69, 70
Petrograd, arrival of Lenin and Stalin at (April, 1917), 49, 50
    Junker rising threatened in, 57
    re-establishment of revolutionary resistance at, by Stalin (1919), 70, 71
    workers of, privations, 117
    front, Stalin at, 62
    Soviet, 51

Petrograd. *See also* Military School of Petrograd
Piatinski, 47
Piestoffski, S., on close co-operation between Lenin and Stalin, 60
Pilsudski, despotism of, 263
Pinon, R., despatch of French Naval Squadron to Black Sea with division of infantry (1919) (quoted), 81 *n.*
Plekhanoff, 6, 38, 48
Plenum of Central Committees and of Control Commission, efforts towards reconciliation with Trotsky and Zinovieff, 186, 187
Poincaré, 43, 59, 112, 115
    attack on the U.S.S.R. in *La Naçion*, 213
Poland, why created an independent State by the Allies, 79, 80
    present hostile attitude towards the Ukraine, 103
    percentage of Poles really inhabiting, 108
Police, revolutionary, attitude towards common law as well as political prisoners, 84
    force, chief of, report upon Stalin, 28
Policy, honest line of, 240
Polish army, rout of, 79
    Communist Party, 190
    Front, collapse of, 79
    workers, distinct Social-Democratic Party of, 90
Politica, the, on the Five-Year Plan, 193
Political prisoners in Russia, increasing numbers of (1905–1909), 36
    skirmishes, revolutions distinct from, 13
Politics, union of economics with, 5

INDEX

Politics, Stalin's opinion as to the only honest kind of, 16
Population, annual increase in U.S.S.R., 204
Populists (*narodniki*), origin of, 4
  violence of, 4
  rise and fall of, 4
  association of Lenin with, 4
  reactionary aims of, 5
Pouds of grain given to the State by peasants and *Kolkhoz*, 221
Pravda (*The Truth*), Stalin a founder of, 43
  suppression and reappearance of, 45
Preobrajensky, amendment regarding construction of Socialist State rejected, 52
  motion that Socialization of Russia should be dependent upon the establishment of Socialism in every other country, 170
Printing-press, secret of Stalin, adventures of, 19, 20
Printing-press, secret, 27
  of Stalin, ultimate fate of, 21
  presses, secret, 187
Prisoners, strike of, organized by Stalin, 22
  common law and political, attitude of revolutionary police towards, 84
Produce, disorder in distribution of, 251
Proletarian power, appearance as landowner, purchaser and vendor, 123
Propaganda, method selected by Stalin, 17
Prosveshtchenie (*Enlightenment*) Stalin's articles in, 90
Provisional Government, the, 110
Pskoff, 71
Purga, icy blizzard of Siberia, 23

Racial characteristics, preservation and enrichment of, 96
  liberation combined with social liberation, effect of, 93
  minorities, not unimportant, 97
Rada, the, Popular Assembly of Cossacks, 102 *n*.
  struggles of Ukrainian workers and peasants against, 103
Radek, Karl, 206
  statement regarding Trotsky's new "Dictatorship of the Proletariat," 171
Railway strikers at Tiflis, Stalin's advocacy of demands of, 19
Railways, increase in length of permanent way in territories administered by U.S.S.R. (1927), 155
  State-owned, recovery in traffic, 122
Ramishvili, Noah, Menshevik leader, 25
Rapallo, Treaty of, signed with Germany, 129
Ration cards for bread and flour, abolition of, 222
Reading and writing, increase in capability for, among inhabitants of Soviet Republics (1930–33), 195
Reciprocal union and individual liberty, selection and exact classification of, 96
Red Army, destitute state of, 112
  privations of, 120
  third foundation of Socialist State, 134
  total number of men in, 209
  of the Ukraine, 65
  Asia, reconstruction of, 197
  Flag, running up of, at Smolny Institute, 111
  Square, Moscow, v
  Terror, the, 86
Troops, repelling attacks of Cossacks on Tsaritzin, 68

INDEX

Red Army, general offensive launched by, after collapse of Polish Front, 79
  defeat by European Polish forces, 79
Reed, John, *Ten Days That Shook the World*, 55
Reform, ultimate danger of, 24
Reformers and Revolutionaries, difference between, 122
Reformism, 190
  lapse towards, 160
Relativity, pure Marxism an example of, 127
Religious tradition, national, subjected to moral system of common law, 97
Renaudel, 48, 49
  decision of regarding those taking part in Zimmerwald and Kienthal Conferences, 49
Repression, problem of, 85
Restaurants, number of millions of persons fed in, 199
Revolution, universal, forerunner of, 84
  See also French Revolution, Russian Revolution, Spanish Revolution
Revolutions, distinct from political skirmishes, 13
  short-sightedness of objectors to, 84
  occurring as result of Great War, 251
Revolutionaries, 249, 250
  aid rendered by Marxism to, 13
  pure, so-called, collaboration with worst enemies of Revolution, 65
  peasants distrustful of, 124
  and Reformers, difference between, 122
Revolutionary Army, triumphant success of, 76
  members of the Duma, 41
  Military Committee of the Republic, 77, 78

Revolutionary Army, professional, method of becoming a, 15
  terrible risks undergone by, 11, 12
  qualifications requisite for work of, 12, 13
Socialist prisoners, quarrels among, 23
-Socialist rising at Moscow (1918), 63
Socialists, 85, 86
Socialists of the Left, 66, 67
War Council, 64
Romanoffs, hated rule of, 6
Roosevelt, President, political economy of, 267
Rothschild workers, discontent created among by Stalin, 19
Rouble, the, stabilization of, 122
  value in English money, 111 *n*.
Rumania, countries engrafted on to, 108
Russia, abolition of serfdom in, 3
  establishment of *Zemtvos* in, 3
  increase of political prisoners in, (1905–09), 36
  and Germany, peace between concluded by Treaty of Brest-Litovsk, 57
  cause of split at Brest-Litovsk with the subsequently victorious Powers, 58, 59
  invaded by French and English troops after termination of the Great War, 79
  overtures on the part of French diplomacy to, 87 *n*.
  only one of the countries forming the Soviet Union, 89
  dictation of, in Socialist matters, dislike of, 90
  unity of each racial group combined with unity of collection of nations called, 91, 92
  first country entering paths of Socialism, 110
  cost of Great War (1914–18) to, 111

INDEX

Russia, cost of Civil War to, 111
    famine in (1921), 120
    period of economic ruin in, 120
    destruction wrought in, by the allies, 112, 113
    of the Revolution, behaviour of French Liberals towards, 116
    transformation from agricultural to industrial country, 131
    co-operative store system always existent in, 136
    electrification of, plan for, 137, 138
    immediate task of, 170
    socialization of, in relation to the World Revolution, 170
    Socialist reconstruction of, feasibility, 172
    death-rate in, compared with that of other countries, 208
    insufficiency of transport in, 212, 213
    protected against air-raids, 248 *n.*
    Northern, wheat-supply cut off, 64
    Southern, food-supply, organization by Stalin (1918), 63
    See also Tsarist Russia, White Russia
Russian and French Diplomacy, plotting between, 43
    Army, new Commander-in-chief of (Krylenko), 57
    Communist Party, Central Committee, Stalin elected General Secretary, 128
    Empire, transformation into a Socialist nation, 111
    Government financed by France, 38 *n.*
    Liberal Party, envisagement of, 42
    people and industries, outrages inflicted on, by emissaries of the Great Powers, 114, 115

Russian and French Diplomacy, propagandists in Asia, principle of Leninist Marxism transgressed by, 104
    restrictions and privileges, suppression of, 93
Russian Revolution, First (1905), 32, 35
    causes of failure of, 35, 36
    conduct of abandoned to Menshevik "schema," 36
    suppression of, 37
    abstention of Social-Democrats from, 171
    Second (Proletarian) (1917), 46
    Stalin's advocacy of, 52
    date of occurrence (October 25th, 1917), 53
    success of, 53
    decrees of, 54, 55
    alien enemies of, 66
    Civil War won by, 76
    counter-attacked by the Great Powers, 79
    completeness of, contrasted with curtailment of French Revolution, 83, 84
    perpetration of, means taken for, 85
    means of circulating true knowledge of, among the French public, 87 *n.*
    factors giving an impetus to, 93
    organization of, 111
    means of consolidation, 124
    completion by Bolsheviks, 121
    sole cause of success of, 124
    to be regarded only as provisional, 170
    international tasks of, abandoned, 171
    development and support in other countries, 173
    not dependent on outside help, 173
    building up of Socialism in Russian territory by, 174, 175

INDEX

Russian Revolution, First (1905), would-be destroyers of, 190
   middle class (1917), 49
   half-hearted policy of, 50, 51
   Middle-class only, believers in, 171
   Social-Democratic Party, Second Congress, 24, 124
   difficult period for (1909–11), 42
   Labour Party, resolution respecting question of Nationalities, 90
   Union of Lithuanian and Polish Parties and Jewish League with, 90
   territory, building up of Socialism in, 174, 175
Russification, synonymous with denationalization, 89
Rykoff, Comrade, 18

Sadoul, Jacques, comparison between Lenin and Trotsky, 167
St. Petersburg, Stalin's activity at (1911), 43
   See also Leningrad
Second International, aims of, 5
   foundation of, 5, 9
   view taken at regarding "Dictatorship of Proletariat," 171
von Seekt, German ally of Kai Chek, 106
Self-criticism, incentive and source of energy, 145
   lines of, not followed by the Opposition, 161
   functions of the Opposition differing from those of, 161
Seneca, 280
Sentiment, subjection to intellect, 15
Seraya Loshad fort, defection of, 71
Serbia, 108
Serfdom, abolition of, in Russia, 3, 32

Seventh Army, 70
   plot contrived by deserters from, 71
   treachery of former members of, 70
Shock troops, employment of, 77
Siberia, economic changes in regions hitherto comprised under, 105
Slepivo, occupation of line by Red Army, 72
Slovenia, component of Jugoslavia, 108
Smolensk, 62
Smolny, Lenin's office at, 60
   Institute, Leningrad, 114
     running up of Red Flag at, 111
Snowden, Philip (Viscount), 255
Social-Democrat, founded by Lenin and Zinovieff, date of, 47
Social-Democratic Congress, Fourth, at Stockholm (1906), Lithuanian and Polish Parties and Jewish League combining with Russian Party at, 90, 91
   Parties, distrust of Polish and Lithuanian workers, 90
   Party, formation at Congress held at Minsk (1898), 6
     Russian, Congress at Stockholm (1906), 38
     Congress in London (1907), 41
   Workers' Party, Russian, Stalin becomes member of, 9
Social-Democrats, abstention from 1905 Revolution, 171
   Russian, first programme of (1884), by whom launched, 6
   liberation combined with racial liberation, effect of, 93
Socialism, 250
   international network created by, 5

INDEX

Socialism, Marxian and Revolutionary, difference in aims of, 5
scientific explanation of, 4
democracy a possible barrier against, 11
task set out to be accomplished by, 15
fundamental objectives on agrarian plan, 31
half-hearted, demolition of, 54
value of human life in the light of, 83
geographic framework of, 88
nationalization of, erroneous, 92
patriotism placed not against, but in, 96
material for vast reserves of, 108
and capitalism, compromise between only temporary, 126
competition increased by, 144
principles of, manifestation of aversion to, among some of the leaders, 163
solid construction of, in Russia, immediate task, 170
civilized European, opposition to Leninism, 171
building up of, in Russian territory, 174, 175
peasants, naturally not inclined to, 218
watchword of, 225
basis of, 237
Soviet youth storm-troops of, 238
Nationalism as weapon of Fascism, against, 255
results of, in Russia, 271, 272
Socialist advance, new capitalist advance taking place side by side of, 123
cause, value of competition to, 255
creed, *Manifesto* of (1847), 30
Economic System, feasibility of, 154
industry, part played by under Five-Year Plan, 194, 195
Socialist advance, interest in the Colonial question, 104
movement in Georgia, 2, 3
nation, transformation of the Russian Empire into, 111
principles, Stalin the recognized interpreter of, 90
State, condition on which industrial concessions granted, or commercial treaties concluded by, 125
future of, upon what dependent, 124
foundations of, 134
stabilization of, important factor in rendering the proletarian victory general, 171
system, humanity of, 83
and capitalist systems difference between workers under respectively, 43
Socialistic reconstruction of Russia, feasibility of, 172
Socialists, leaving ranks of Communist International, 163
martyrology of, 235
Revolutionary, 56
Socialization of the world, ultimate task of, 169
Sosso, name by which Stalin was known in earlier years, 10
Southern Front, 72
Stalin at, 62
wide extent of, 73
situation on (autumn 1919), 72
Soviet Asia, immensity of rise of industry in, 196
Budget, percentage of represented by National Defence, 208
combination, aspirations surpassed, 98
East, threatened by foreign imperialism, 105
how justified, 105

INDEX

Soviet Economic Plans, realization of, in percentages, 142
- formula, advantage of, to every-one, 269
- Government, severity of, in its struggle with its enemies, explained (Stalin), 85, 86
- address to Moslem workers within the frontiers of the former European-Asiatic Empire of the Tsars, 94
- enemies of, protection by France, 113
- treacherous conduct of members of Intelligence Service towards, 115
- organizations, dislocation (1918), 63
- origin, Five-Year Plan, exclusively of, 138
- policy of nationalities, effect upon Transcaucasia, 101
- Republic, main and subsidiary basis of, 88
- Russia, position taken by, at signing of Treaty of Brest-Litovsk, 80
- Schools, primary, number of pupils in (1927), 155
- Socialism and Anglo-Saxon Capitalism, comparison of, 152
- solution, applied to insoluble problem of nationalities, 109
- State, creation of New Economic Policy by, 121
- formula of regarding concessions, 122
- in possession of all monopolies, 210
- resources of, 199
- Union, wealth and natural resources of collected into a common fund, 97
- minimum of combination together with maximum of national development under, 98

Soviet Union, nations under, advantages attaching to, 99
Soviet workers, achievements of, 233, 234
- writers, critics and journalists, enumerated, 206
- non-Russian, 206
- youth, storm-troops of Socialism, 238
Soviets, introduction into Central Asia, 103, 104
Sovkhoz, State farms, 220
Spain, increase of unemployment in, during 1934, 202
- Republicanism in, actions of, 265
Spanish Revolution (1931), 279
Spiridovna, threatening behaviour towards Lenin, 56
Stabilization, international, Stalin's refusal to accept idea of, 152
Stalin, 112, 171
- immense popularity of, v, vi
- home of described, vii
- dress of, vii, viii
- monthly salary of, vii, viii
- importance of, viii, ix
- birthplace of, 1
- original name of, 1
- parents of, 1
- early education of, 1, 2
- past and present appearance of, contrasted, 7, 8
- reason for expulsion from Tiflis seminary, 8, 9
- becomes member of Russian Social-Democratic Workers' Party, 9
- occupations followed by, in early years, 9
- accessibility of, 10
- directness of speech, a feature of his addresses, 10
- exposition of value and defect of middle-class democracy, 11
- success as an expositor explained, 11
- an opponent of violent language in oratory, 11

INDEX

Stalin, explanation as to why he became a Revolutionary, 15
opinion as to the only honest kind of politics, 16
hiding-places of, 17
method of propaganda chosen by, 17
intuition of how manifested, 18
public appearances of, 18, 19
creates discontent among Mantascheff and Rothschild workers, 19
headquarters at Chaoba, 19
establishment of committee at Batum, Abkhasia, 19
advocacy of demands of Tiflis railway strikers, 19
secret printing-press of, 19, 20
assistance rendered to, by Khashim, 20
strike of prisoners organized by, 22
arrest and imprisonment of, 22
deportation to Irkutsk (Siberia), 22
return from deportation under name of Koba, 22
educational work of among prisoners at Baku and Bailoff, 22, 23
attacked with and cured of tuberculosis, 23, 24
becomes a supporter of Lenin, 24
becomes a Bolshevik, 24
campaign against Georgian Mensheviks, 25
capture and escape of, six times repeated, 25
edits *The Struggle of the Proletariat*, 26
Some Remarks on the Difference of the Party, written by, 26
development of workers' movement under influence of, 26
report of chief of police force on, 28

Stalin, present at Stockholm Congress under name of Ivanovitch, 38
speech delivered by on "The Balance Sheet of the Five-Year Plan," 40
editor of *Dro* (*The Times*), at Tiflis (1907), 41
becomes editor of *Baku Proletarian* (1907), 41
Social-Democratic organizations of Baku brought into Bolshevik ranks by, 41
opposition to promoters of "The Edification of the Divine Principle," 42
campaign against the Otzovists (1907), 41
arrested (1910), 42
again arrested by the *Okhrana*, 41
activity at St. Petersburg (1911), 43
editor of *Zvezda* (*The Star*) and a founder of *Pravda* (*The Truth*), 43
estimation of writings of, by Lenin, 45
resources of both legality and illegality employed by, 44
consolidation of Bolshevik Party in its illegality by, 45
studies on "Marxism and the success of Nationalities," 45
exiled to Kuleika (Siberia) (1913-17), 46
arrival at Petrograd (April, 1917), 50
elected member of Central Committee of Pan-Russian Bolshevik Conference, 50
advocacy of Russian Proletarian Revolution, 52
support of Lenin's policy regarding construction of Socialist State, 52

INDEX

Stalin, appointed a member of the Assembly of Five and of the Assembly of Seven, 53
- journeys from one danger-point to another on the front during the Civil War, 61
- one of the chief organizers of victories of the Civil War, 62
- arrival at Tsaritzin, 63
- organization of food supply throughout Southern Russia by, 63
- military command taken over by, 64
- military and civil administration combined in hands of, 66
- disregards Trotsky's orders regarding re-establishment of Headquarters Staff, 67
- personal visit to whole front, 67, 68
- tribute to indomitable will of, 68
- re-establishment of revolutionary resistance at Petrograd (1919), 70, 71
- successful military operations of (1919), 71
- discards plan of operations along Southern Front laid down by Superior War Committee, 74, 75
- letter to Lenin suggesting alteration of plan of campaign on Southern Front, 79
- creation of Cavalry Army by, 77
- secret of success of, 76, 77
- conception of "another army"—a regular Army—put forward by, 78
- views regarding proper military organization, 77, 78
- Member of Revolutionary Military Committee of South-West Front, 79
- elected a member of the War Council of the Republic, 79

Stalin, twice decorated with Order of Red Flag, 79
- severity of, 82
- exceptions to, 82
- on the severity of the Soviet Government in the struggle with its enemies (quoted), 85, 86
- pronouncement on the death-penalty, 86
- capacity for dealing with question of nationalities, 88
- People's Commissar for Nationalities (1917–23), 88
- articles in review *Prosvesht-chenie (Enlightenment)*, 90
- recognized interpreter of Socialist principles, 90
- resistance of idea of nationalization of Socialism, 92
- report on national question at Conference of Bolshevik Party, 92
- becomes authorized director on the question of nationalities, 92, 93
- name of, indissolubly connected with creation of Union of Socialist Soviet Republics, 101
- tribute to confidence placed in from Abkhasian peasant, 102
- occupied with political affairs of the Ukraine, 103
- on the Socialist interest in the Colonial question, 104
- Central Asiatic Republics created by, 105
- assistance to the Chinese Communist Party, 107
- on privations of workers of Petrograd, 117
- action taken by, with regard to concession of Ural factories, 119, 120
- secret of greatness of, 126
- opportunism of, 127

Stalin, compromise with middle-class methods adopted by, 128
elected General Secretary of Central Committee of Russian Communist Party, 128
on the value of theory, 130
on transformation of Russia from agricultural to industrial country, 131
People's Commissar in Workers' and Peasants' Survey, 131
on importance of heavy industries, 133
on re-education of peasants, 134
on foundation of the Socialist State, 134
on Lenin's plan for the electrification of Russia, 137
criticism of Trotsky's plan for the economic renaissance of Russia, 137
value of competition to Socialist cause maintained by, 144
on the principle of Socialist competition, 144, 145
on the safety-valve of self-criticism, 145
oath to Lenin after his death, 146, 147
paragraph referring to the honour of the Party, 164
leader of the Party after the death of Lenin, 147
opinion held of, in France, 149
on objection to individual decisions, 150
trust in the masses enjoined by, 151
refusal to accept conception of international stabilization (Fourteenth Congress), 152
prediction of decline and general slump of Capitalist power (1928), 152
defence of Leninism, 164

Stalin, opposition to socialization of Russia as dependent on establishment of Socialism in every other country, 170
on effect of incorrect estimate of real revolutionary capacities of Russia, 171, 172
on the task of development and support of the Revolution in other countries, 172, 173
Questions of Leninism (quoted), 173
necessity of persuading workers' classes in capitalist countries to dispense with middle classes in establishing a new society, 174
common sense and clearness of vision of, 175
former adversaries of, becoming open enemies, 180
question of democracy chief concern of, from an early date, 185
firm attitude towards the New Opposition, 189
newspaper calumnies respecting the Five-Year Plan collected by, 193
on formation of Ural Kuznetsk combine, 198
influence on writers' movement, 205, 206
proposal for the abolition of ration cards adopted, 222
article entitled, "Dizzy with Success," 225
difficulties encountered by, with the *kolkhoz*, 226, 227
conversation with a comrade regarding delay in sowing, 228
on the "levelling principle," 237
on what is meant by Marxism, 237, 238
on the level of leadership, 240
report on the Five-Year Plan, 242

INDEX

Stalin, unbounded confidence placed in, 248
   present-day life of, summarized, 275 et seq.
   and Djerjinsky, measures for raising fighting efficiency of Third Army proposed by, 70
   and Lenin, opposition of Trotsky to, 30
      meeting between, described by Stalin, 33, 34, 35
      jointly support immediate conclusion of Treaty of Brest-Litovsk, 59
      close co-operation between, 60
      Marxist formula of nationalities drawn up by, 91
   and Leninism, liaison agent between, 16
   and Trotsky, qualities of, contrasted, 175, 176
   Automobile Works (Moscow), 202
Stassova, Helen, 235 *n.*
State Ministers, Russian, main functions of, 37
Plan (Five-Year Plan), 130 (and footnote, 130)
   rationing, 121
Stockholm, Congress held at (1906), 38
Strike of prisoners organized by Stalin, 22
"Struggle against War and Fascism" Movement, 270
Struggle of the Proletariat, Bolshevik newspaper edited by Stalin, 26
Sturona, Comrade, 18
Sudekum, 48
Superior War Committee, plan of operations along Southern Front discussed by Stalin, 74
Surge of the Don (*The*) White newspaper, 66

Surtax, levy of, proposed by New Opposition, 184
Su-Uk-Su cemetery, secret meetings held in, 19
Sverdloff, 171 *n.*
Switzerland, inhospitability of, 263

Tacitus (quoted), 2
Tajekistan, republic of, newly-created, 105
Tardieu, André, 255
Tartars and Muscovites, differences between cultivated and developed, 98
Technical experts, lack of, 135
Tendency, error in, a general deformation, 160
Thaelmann, 236
Theory, value of, 130
Third Army, demoralization of, 69
   surrender of Perm by, 69
   fighting efficiency, measures for raising, 70
   Corps front, Perm, Stalin at, 62
   International, attempt to supplant, 187
   Polish Army, almost complete annihilation of, 79
Tiflis railway strikers, Stalin's advocacy of demands of, 20
   Seminary, Stalin's place of education, 1
      Marxist circle at, 7
      reason for expulsion of Stalin from, 9
Todria, Comrade, 18
Transcaucasia, secret groups of Russian Marxists in, 2
   district of, countries comprised in, 2
   effect of Soviet policy of nationalism upon, 102
   liquidation of counter-Revolutionary government in, how made possible, 101
Transport, insufficiency of in Russia, 212, 213

INDEX

Transsylvania, Hungarian, engrafted on to Rumania, 108
Treaties, secret, among the Allies signed before conclusion of the War, 58
See also Brest-Litovsk, Treaty of; Versailles, Treaty of
Tretiakoff, 206
Trotsky, 43, 52, 171, 173, 174
an obstinate Menshevik, 30
opposition to Lenin and Stalin, 30
position of, as an agitator, 44
methods of; condemned by Lenin, 45
negotiations with regard to conclusion of Peace, 60
rally to Bolshevism, 59
disorders in the services directed by, 62 *n*.
order regarding re-establishment of Headquarters Staff disregarded by Stalin, 67
interference with affairs of Southern Front forbidden to, 73
short-sightedness of, 75 (and footnote, 75)
difference between Revolutionaries and Reformers (quoted), 122
plan for the economic renaissance of Russia, criticized by Stalin, 137
self-importance of, 159
hostile in some degree to revolutionary methods, 163
present humiliating position of, in exile, 164, 165
old title of People's Commissar, 165
attitude of, largely influenced by personal factor, 165
contradictory attitudes of, 166
schism of, main cause of, 166
too great attention paid to details by, 167

Trotsky, uncontrolled imagination of, 167
cause of defeat of, 169
on meaning of "Dictatorship of the Proletariat," 171
view that Russian Revolution must be considered only provisional, 170
Books by (*The New Current* and *The Blood of October*), giving rise to discussion, 178
patience exhibited by the Party towards, 178
adoption of "Clemenceau's doctrine" by, 179
methods of, condemned by Lenin, 186
exclusion from Central Committee, 187
expulsion from the Party, 188
discreditable associates of, 190
and Lenin, comparison between, 166, 167
and Stalin, qualities of contrasted, 175, 176
and Zinovieff, efforts towards reconciliation with, 187
Trotskyism, struggle against, 176
network of Communist International attacked by, 189
Tsankoff, forgery of (Zinovieff forgery), 116
Tsardom, danger to revolutionaries from forces of, 12
Tsarism, democratic, abolition of, 94
Tsarist debts, repudiation by Bolsheviks, 129
organization, ultra-conservative (Black Hundred), 18 *n*.
régime, foreshadowing of upheaval of, 43
abolition of, 88
main purpose of, 89, 90
Russia, mainstay of Western Imperialism, 104
Tsaritzin, 74
arrival of Stalin at, 63

INDEX

Tsaritzin, seizure of districts round, by White troops, 63
  means employed to check conspiracy at, 66
  attacks of Cossacks on, repulsed by Red troops, 67, 68
  front, Stalin at, 62
Tsars, self-styled "Assemblers of the Russian Lands," 98
Tsenkely, ill-timed recognition of, 113
Tuberculosis, Stalin attacked with and cured of, 23
Tula, danger threatening, 73
Turkestan, liquidation of counter-Revolutionary government in, how made possible, 101
Turkmenistan, republic of, newly created, 105

Ukraine, the, liquidation of counter-Revolutionary government in, how made possible, 101
  German occupation of, 103
  struggle of workers and peasants in, against the Rada, 102, 103
  overthrow of the Directorate and of the power of Hetman Peliura in, 103
  interview of the Entente (Black Sea Squadron) in, 103
  struggle against the White Poles in, 103
  present hostile attitude of Poland towards, 103
  struggle against Wrangel in, 103
  and Northern Caucasia, delivery from White Guards, 76
Ukrainians not Russians, 89
Ulianova, Maria, sister of Lenin, 4
Unemployment, elimination in the U.S.S.R. during the period of the Five-Year Plan, 202
  increase of, in European countries and the United States (1928–33), 202, 203

Unemployment, wrong statements about, in capitalist countries, 203
Union of the Russian People, ultra-Tsarist organization, 36
Union of Socialist Soviet Republics, creation of (1922), 101
  constitution of, summarized, 101
  dictatorship in, impossible, 147
  no supreme authority or individual sovereignty in, 148
  level of pre-War Tsarist economy reached by, 155
  place taken by among the nations in mechanical energy (1927), 155
  date of great rise of, 188
  increase of persons able to read and write in (1930–33), 195
  no foreign loans obtained by, 199
  no waste of national revenue under, 200
  not exempt from effects of economic depression, 199 n.
  enormous percentages of pre-War production (1933), 201
  agricultural machinery production in (1934), 201
  boot manufacture in (1934), 202
  production of electric energy in (1934), 202
  elimination of unemployment in, during the Five-Year Plan, 202
  population, annual increase, 204
  quality of work done and output compared with that in other countries, 204
  wages paid in, compared with those paid in other countries, 204
  public education in, 204, 205
  development of literature in, 205, 206
  newspaper attack on, by Poincaré, 213

INDEX

Union of Socialist Soviet Republics, admitted to League of Nations, 258, 259
Union of Soviet Writers, 207
United States, 191
  immense loan from, to European Powers for reconstruction purposes, 129
  percentage of pre-War economic production in (1933), 201
  number of unemployed in (March, 1933), 203
  Budget deficit in (1930), 210
  sowing of wheat in, reduced, 230
Unity of each racial group combined with unity of collection of nations called Russia, 91
Ural district, Czech counter-Revolution in, 63
  factories, concession offer regarding, by Urkwarth refused, 126
  industrial centres, 196
  Kuznetsk combine, foundation of, laid, 198
  Mountains, industrial centres beyond, 196
Uralsk, oil industry established at, 198
Urkwarth, offer regarding a concession of the Ural factories, 119
Usbekistan, Republic of, newly created, 105

Valois, Georges, report on treachery of Intelligence Service, 115
Vauthier, Lt.-Col., 248 *n*.
Vazek, on demonstrations organized by Stalin, 27
Vereshtchak, Simon, on prison life of Koba (Stalin), 22, 23
Vérité Russe, 114
Versailles, Treaty of, 245
Village life, changes in, enumerated, 228, 229

Villages, Socialist metamorphosis through intervention of industry, 131
Vintage production reduced in France, 231
Violent language in oratory, Stalin's opposition to, 11
Vladivostock, Allied troops disembarking at, nations to which belonging, 112
Vorochiloff, 248
Voronino, occupation of line by Red Army, 72
Vorontsoff, V. P., successfully opposed by Lenin, 6

Wages, amount of increase under Five-Year Plan, 195
  in the U.S.S.R. compared with those paid in other countries, 203, 204
Walloon-Flemish, conglomeration, Belgium a, 108
War, means of prevention of, 48
  Communism, explanation of, 120
  disappearance of, 121
  Council of the Republic, Stalin elected a member of, 79
Warfare, principles of Marxism applied to, 81, 82
Wells, H. G., on the electrification of Russia, 139
  admiration of Roosevelt's policy, 268
Western Front, Smolensk, Stalin at, 62
  Imperialism Tsarist Russia the mainstay of, 104
Wheat, policy in connection with, 120
  excess crops of, method of dealing with, 122, 123
  sowing of, in the United States reduced, 230
  supply of Northern Russia cut off, 64

INDEX

White Army of Yudenitch, 70
  penetration of Southern Front by, 72
  Cossacks, organization by Krasnoff, 86
  Guards, delivery of the Ukraine and Northern Caucasia from, 76
    treacherous work of, 85
    mobilization and training in France, 113
  Poles, struggle against, in the Ukraine, 103
  Russians, 56
  assistance rendered to, by France and England, 78
  troops, seizure of districts round Tsaritzin, by, 63
Wholesale prices, increase of, dangerous measure proposed by New Opposition, 183
Workers' classes, in capitalist countries to dispense with middle classes in establishing a new society, 174
  movement, 5
    development under influence of Stalin, 26
  of Petrograd, privation of, 117
  State, position of dangerous politically, 123
  and peasants, proper manifestation of Bolshevik Party to, 93
  and Peasants' State, 90
  and Peasants' Survey, People's Commissar in (Stalin), 131
Workmen, increase in number employed under Five-Year Plan, 194
Workmen's association (*artel*), 4
World Capitalism, dread of, arising, 172
  Revolution, no signs of (1921), 120
World Capitalism Revolution, dependence of socialization of Russia upon, 170
World War (The), 46
  Franco-Russian Alliance largely responsible for, 43
Wrangel, 62, 113
  assistance rendered to, by France and England, 78
  renewal of Civil War under activities of, 78
  struggle against in the Ukraine, 103

Young Communists, 187
Yudenitch, 62
  White Army of, 70
  advance upon Petrograd, 70

Zemstvos (autonomous municipalities), establishment of, in Russia, 3
Zimmerwald, Idealist Conference of, 52
Zinovieff, 173
  Social Democrat, founded by, 47
  view regarding concession of Ural factories, 116
  hostile to revolutionary methods, 163
  an "Oppositionist," 171
  exclusion from Central Committee, 187
  forgery, 116
  and Kameneff, hostility to Lenin's plans for a rising, 52, 53
  New Opposition led by, 179
  and Trotsky, efforts towards reconciliation with, 187
Zinovieff-Kameneff-Trotsky Opposition, decayed remnants of composing *Centre* of Leningrad, 181, 182
Zvezda (*The Star*), edited by Stalin, 42